The Angel Bible

The Angel Bible

The definitive guide to angel wisdom

Hazel Raven

A GODSFIELD BOOK

An Hachette UK Company
www.hachette.co.uk

First published in Great Britain in 2006
by Godsfield Press,
a division of Octopus Publishing Group Ltd
Endeavour House, 189 Shaftesbury Avenue
London WC2H 8JY
www.octopusbooks.co.uk

This edition published in 2009

ISBN: 978-1-84181-364-6

A CIP catalogue record for this book is available from the British Library

Printed and bound in China

10 9 8 7 6 5 4 3 2

Note

This book is intended to give general information only. The publisher, author and distributor expressly disclaim all liability to any person arising directly or indirectly from the use of, or any errors or omissions in, the information in this book. The adoption and application of the information in this book is at the reader's discretion and is their sole responsibility.

Contents

Part I

INTRODUCTION

What are Angels?

Angels are winged messengers: the word angel is derived from the ancient Greek *angelos*, meaning 'messenger'. Angels act as a bridge between Heaven and Earth, serving as a channel between God and the physical material world. Angels are deathless beings of pure consciousness, unlimited by the constrictions of time and space. They are eternally bound to the perpetual blissful energy radiating from the Divine. Each angel is a focus of God's love, channelling it without distortion.

Many believe that all angels were created by God in the same moment on the second day of creation, each one perfect, intelligent, immortal and in possession of free will. Most angels instantly chose to give up their free will and aligned themselves eternally with their creator. But a few angels wanted their own power and glory – these are the 'fallen angels'. The angels who gave up their free will serve God and protect humanity from 'fallen' angels.

People perceive angels in many different ways; the most profound encounters are as physical manifestations, which can take the form of winged beings. Angels are genderless beings of a vibration that is pure spirit; their male and female qualities are perfect and complete, so they are androgynous.

Do angels have wings? Most people are familiar with angels through religious art where they are depicted as perfect beings, with flowing robes, long hair, halos and wings, but angels are pure spirit and therefore have no gross physical form. So where did the notion that angels have wings come from?

Several religious sources list certain angels as having wings. Archangel Gabriel (Jibril in Islamic) who dictated the Koran to Mohammed was described as having '140 pairs of wings'. In the mystical Jewish texts 1 Enoch and 2 Enoch, there are also descriptions of angels with wings. Many cultures have depicted winged beings, while many myths, legends, statues and even cave paintings still exist of these miraculous creatures. Visionary accounts of heavenly messengers usually describe them as winged or appearing in a 'heavenly light'.

The light surrounding angels could be their astral body or aura. Mystics and healers often describe a subtle-energy field surrounding humans. The human aura is depicted as having several levels, but, on closer inspection, it is made up of billions of separate lines of energy, each radiating outwards and upwards from the central 'spiritual spine' and giving the appearance of feathers. The angelic energy field would appear to the human mystic as enormous, and the human mind may try to clothe the heavenly vision in human form.

This angel in stained glass depicts the Archangel Gabriel at the Annunciation of the Virgin Mary.

How to use this book The book is divided into two parts: Part I introduces the subject of angels and how you might invite them into your life, while Part II provides an extensive directory of angel lore. There are 11 chapters on angel hierarchies, colours, healing, crystals, the Kabala and much more. It also contains a range of practical exercises, meditations and affirmations.

Sources of Angel Lore

We cannot be sure where angelic tradition began on Earth, but the earliest writings of Sumeria, Egypt, Persia and India recognized winged beings or messengers of the gods. On a Sumerian stele (stone column) a winged being who inhabits the seven heavens is depicted pouring 'the water of life' into the king's cup.

The study of angels is known as angelology. Over the centuries many manuscripts have been written, and many exhaustive works on angelic hierarchies and scholarly traditions have been compiled, often copied or translated from earlier manuscripts.

As we look at sources of angel lore, we must understand that much of the material was written by mystics, prophets, lawgivers, poets and chroniclers. In early Christianity, for instance, there were numerous sources of angelic lore that once carried the same weight of authority as the current books of the Bible; however, this information slipped into oblivion when these texts were left out of the Old Testament.

The Bible mentions angels frequently, but with no detail or background provided, except in two or three instances. Gabriel and Michael are both mentioned by name in the Old Testament and Raphael appears in the Book of Tobit or Tobias. (Tobit is a book in the Old Testament of the Roman Catholic and Orthodox Bible, but it does not appear in the Hebrew Bible and is placed with the Apocrypha in Protestant versions.) Some angels in the Old Testament are described as 'men in white' because they are seen to be clothed in white linen garments. (White linen was a symbol of immortality to the ancients.)

St Peter receives angelic aid which allows him to make his miraculous escape from prison.

Other angel sources The three Books of Enoch (see page 66) are extracanonical writings rich in angelic lore. The Book of Enoch refers to 1 Enoch, which survives completely only in the Ethiopic language. Two further books survive: 2 Enoch or the Testament of Levi survives only in old Slavonic, while 3 Enoch survives in Hebrew. The three books of Enoch were omitted from the Bible, but they were still widely quoted centuries later by church authorities and they are often quoted in the New Testament.

Further fragments from 1 Enoch have been discovered, chiefly among the Dead Sea scrolls. Aramaic fragments are believed to contain the oldest list of angel names in existence.

Part of the Scroll of Isaiah*, one of the Dead Sea scrolls found in Qumran Cave I. This excerpt shows Isaiah 30:20 to 31:4.*

A celestial hierarchy Dionysius, the Pseudo-Areopagite, is the anonymous 5th century theologian and philosopher who wrote *Corpus Areopagiticum,* which had been falsely ascribed to the Dionysius in Acts 17:34 of the Bible. One of the books among the *Corpus Areopagiticum* was *The Celestial Hierarchy,* which quickly became established in mainstream Western culture as a classic work on the subject of angels. It was also adopted by St Thomas Aquinas as the foundation for his own angel lore in the *Summa Theologica,* which remains a cornerstone of Catholic belief.

Islam has always had a strong angel tradition. It lists a vast array of angels and seems to draw inspiration from the texts of the Zoroastrians, Babylonians, Assyrians and Chaldeans.

One of the richest sources of angelic lore is the Jewish mystical tradition known as the Kabala (see pages 70–71). There is no single book called the Kabala; rather it is a body of information. However, there are two important groups of original texts within the Kabala: the *Zohar,* the 'Book of Splendour'; and the *Sepher Yetzirah,* the 'Book of Formation'.

Angel friends Emanuel Swedenborg (1688–1772), who was a Swedish scientist, philosopher and mystic, believed that angels were perfected humans, much like the Buddhist bodhisattvas. He also believed angels were our soul-friends whose duty it was to help us evolve spiritually. Swedenborg claimed to have communication with angels on a daily basis, and he kept detailed accounts of these mental dialogues in his diaries. His angel books were published in Latin and contained his many years of research into the wondrous world of Heaven.

The New Age movement has brought about an angelic revival. Angelic contact is experienced daily by many spiritual seekers. In the past, Christian authorities have had a bit of a problem with angels; too much curiosity about angels was discouraged because of tricky theological questions caused by the bickering of early Christian sects. Jesus had no problem with angels, but St Paul warned against angelic contact. In spite of this, the Roman Catholic Church has always encouraged people to relate to their guardian angel.

Why Invite Angels Into Your Life?

Our fascination with angels grows daily. Ordinary people talk openly about how angels have helped them, stories of angelic intervention abound and inspirational artwork is everywhere. Interest in angels transcends language, cultures and boundaries.

Angels come in all forms, all shapes and sizes, and all colours. Some are complex and powerful beings, dealing in the secret mysteries that underpin the very foundation of the universe. Our five senses are simply inadequate to experience and describe these miraculous beings of God's eternal love and light.

Others bring comfort in moments of deep despair. These 'messenger' angels have the ability to show up just at the right time. Our guardian angel, although linked with the immense planetary angels, is always with us and will never leave our side. Some angels are inspirational, teaching us through cosmic virtues such as honesty, goodness, humility, purity, beauty and joy. Others seem to be the cheerleaders, gladdening our hearts and guiding us through joyous participation.

Why are so many ordinary people inviting angels into their daily lives? Perhaps angels are more evident because people are awakening from the spell of materialism, greed and separation from God cast by our greedy sense of our own importance. Or maybe God is sending more angels to Earth to help with the planet's spiritual evolution as we approach the 'end of days' prophesied in the Bible as well as by many ancient cultures. Countless seers and mystics have foretold the coming of this 'New Golden Age' when angels shall walk once more with men.

Mary is often portrayed as the Queen of the Angels, as here in the Coronation of the Virgin.

Each one of us has a guardian angel given to us before birth, to protect us on our path.

The Age of Aquarius In astrological terms, we are currently making the transition from the Age of Pisces – a time of paternal influence in which we handed responsibility for our behaviour, evolution and spiritual growth over to others – into the Age of Aquarius, in which we take on this responsibility personally.

Working with angels offers you the opportunity to develop wisdom, strengthen self-understanding and overcome obstacles by connecting with your inner light, which is a direct pathway to God. As you integrate your body, mind and spirit into one cohesive entity you raise not only your own vibrational rate, but also the vibrational rate of the whole of humanity and of the Earth itself. The term 'vibrational rate', 'vibrational

frequency' or 'state of consciousness' means the frequency of brain activity in the cerebral cortex. As we raise our vibrational rate, our goal is to achieve finer states of brain activity (spirituality), until in complete silence we experience unity with God.

Subtle energy has its own spiritual laws which are activated as our vibrational frequency is raised. The cerebral cortex produces thought by using energy in the form of photons – this action takes place on a quantum level. Some researchers have speculated that the two hemispheres of the brain become completely balanced in higher states of consciousness (vibrational frequency) and this brings on states of bliss.

Reconciling Heaven and Earth When we invite angels into our lives, we evolve spiritually by reuniting Heaven and Earth within. Angels await our call; they are longing to help us in everything we do in this life and beyond. There is no task they cannot help us with; in fact angels are completely dedicated to helping humanity spiritually as well as in practical ways.

Angels are obedient to cosmic law, which means that they give of themselves unstintingly, and they are duty-bound to direct the mystical love of God towards each one of us. They assist us in raising our own vibrational rate which ultimately helps to reunite us with our own God-consciousness, which, once we have experienced it, is so transformative that there is no going back.

Raising Your Vibrational Rate

The first and most important step in making a strong connection with the angelic realm is to purify yourself and your environment. The reason for this may not at first seem obvious to you, but angels exist at a higher vibrational frequency of which most humans are unaware. This is because angels live in the world of spirit (subtle energy) and humans exist in the physical world of the five senses. Angels are naturally attracted to people who have a harmonious higher state of consciousness.

Declutter your life To make room in your life for angels, you need to clear your home of all clutter. Clear away your unwanted possessions, give them to charity or recycle them. Clean and freshen your home on all levels. Open windows daily to let out stale energy – it will be cleansed and rendered harmless by natural daylight. Use sound to break up stagnant energy; a crystal singing bowl, bells, gongs, ting-shaws (small Tibetan cymbals), rattles or drums are useful for this. Clapping your hands together is also

Use drumming to clear stagnant energy and raise the vibrational energy of your space.

an effective way of breaking up stagnant energy – especially in the corners of a room. Use 'angelic' music to raise the vibration. Remember, the quickest way to open your Heart Chakra (see pages 122–123) is with beautiful music.

Check all areas of your home for any objects that are less than uplifting – clearing out your physical junk helps to clear your mind. Old furniture and especially second-hand jewellery needs extra cleansing; use incense and allow the smoke to carry away unwanted vibrations – remember to leave a window open as an exit route for stale energy.

Tibetan singing bowls have been used for centuries by Buddhist monks in meditation and religious ceremonies. They are now popular worldwide.

Discard clothing you have not worn in the last two years, especially clothes that no longer fit you or look drab. If you buy second-hand or vintage clothes, remember to have them cleaned thoroughly before wearing them.

Avoid people and places that drag your energy down. Once you can hold your higher angelic vibration you will be able to help others and raise their vibration just through your presence.

Sensing the Presence of Angels

As people become consciously aware of angels, the veil between our world and theirs becomes thinner. You do not need to be clairvoyant or psychic to experience angelic contact. It is also very important to remember that angels actually wish to communicate with you; they seek daily communion.

Angels are obedient divine beings who obey cosmic law. It is their duty to give freely of themselves, as an outpouring of their divine essence of love and light. Angelic assistance is always available; all you have to do is ask.

Most people never actually see an angel, but they are aware of their angel's presence. Angels can be perceived by any of the human senses. Here are some ways in which you may become aware of the presence of angels:

- The atmosphere of the room suddenly changes; you feel surrounded by a warm glow. The air tingles around you or you feel a rush of energy down your spine.

- A beautiful fragrance suddenly fills the room. This sweet perfume is described in different ways – as the aroma of summer flowers or sweet myrrh.

- You experience a particular taste sensation, often sweet – the taste of heavenly ambrosia. Alternatively, you hear an ethereal sound; angelic music is often associated with healing and renewal.

- You have feelings of love and an overwhelming sense of deep peace.

- Coloured lights appear from nowhere. Shafts of brilliant light or even spheres of colour dance in front of your eyes, especially when you are working with the healing angels or when drifting off to sleep.

Meditation can help us attain the stillness needed to become aware of energy changes around us.

- During angelic meditation sessions you experience a dazzlingly bright light in front of you, even when your eyes are closed.
- You feel the presence of angel wings brushing against you or enfolding you, or even angelic hands touching you on your shoulders.

- In meditation many people experience the 'angelic breeze', which is like a warm summer wind gently ruffling your hair. Some say that it is the angels uplifting the thousand-petal lotus flower (the symbol of the Crown Chakra, see pages 102–103).
- You may become aware of an increase in the number of coincidences that occur in your life. Or your problems seem to solve themselves – sometimes in the most unexpected ways.

Angelic Signs and Calling Cards

Sometimes angels manifest their presence in ways that anyone can see. You can ask for an angel to appear as proof of your angelic contact. Here are a few common angel signs.

Clouds You may see angels in cloud formations, especially over sacred sites or when you have asked for angelic assistance. Sometimes you will see clouds that resemble feathers.

Flowers Many people find that their flowers last longer on their angelic altar. One student of angel lore found that her

Angels often signal their presence in cloud formations and in clouds that look like feathers.

roses lasted months and, after an especially profound encounter, one of the roses changed colour.

Feathers White feathers may appear in the most unlikely of places. When you have found your white feather, carry it around with you to keep your angel close. Once, when I was teaching an angel seminar, I mentioned that white feathers are a common angel sign. After the talk a woman in the seminar said that despite what she had heard she was not convinced of the existence of angels. Just at that moment, one of the other students noticed a pure white feather stuck to the sleeve of her cardigan.

Words Often after you have asked for angelic help you will hear the word 'angel' mentioned in a song on the radio or on television, or someone will say the word to you in an unlikely context.

Crystals Angels can suddenly appear in your crystals. They appear in 'angelic' crystals such as Celestite, Seraphinite or Danburite, but frequently an angel form will manifest itself in your Clear Quartz crystal after you start reaching out to the angelic realm.

A white feather is the calling card of the angelic realm, and they seem to be everywhere.

Angelic gifts Many affordable angelic gifts are available today, such as little angel pins, glass angels, angel fridge magnets, angel sprinkles (to put inside greetings cards), angel stickers and angel worry stones. If you receive one unexpectedly from someone, you can be sure the angels have guided them to give it to you as 'proof of their presence'.

Invoking Angels

Drink soothing herbal teas to help relax the mind and body, which in turn will allow you to achieve heightened states of awareness.

Angels are God's celestial messengers. They are not our servants, but God's servants, so it is not appropriate to worship them. Even if they are awe-inspiring, remember that they are a reflection of the perfection of God and it is this energy that opens our hearts in adoration.

Angels do not have free will as humans do, but respond to the 'call' of God. Angels cannot interfere with our own free will. When we call upon angelic aid, we must do so from a place within ourselves of love, humility, trust and clarity. As long as your request is positive and does not interfere with anyone else's free will, and does not interfere with your life plan, then the angels will be able to answer your call.

In the past, mystics and saints spent many years meditating, praying and fasting before they experienced major spiritual experiences. Today, because so many people are using meditation practice on a daily basis and the veil between our world and the world of spirit is becoming ever thinner, we can move rapidly into the angelic realms.

It is easier to attune to the angelic consciousness if we prepare ourselves by connecting through our heart centre with our higher self. By using our higher consciousness as our guiding light, we can begin the necessary process of mental purification.

Connecting to the higher self Physical purification consisting of fasting and cleansing will improve our higher-self connection. Fasting should be undertaken for at least 24 hours (abstain from solid food but not liquids). Addictive foods and substances should also be avoided. Fasting relaxes the subtle-energy systems, and calms and focuses the mind.

Soothing herbal teas such as chamomile relax the body and mind, allowing heightened states of awareness to manifest. Purifying scented candlelit baths containing sea-salt, halite crystals, herbs, flower petals and aromatherapy oils also profoundly open our hearts to spiritual beauty.

Bathing is considered to be balancing and cleansing, and if done before meditation, it helps cleanse the body and mind.

Controlling our ego (lower mind) – which is attached to self-aggrandizement and selfish thoughts – by counting our blessings daily also opens the doorway to the angelic realm. Meditation makes the lower mind the obedient servant of the higher self.

Writing to Your Angels

When you have problems, you can write to your angels. Open your heart, do not hold back your thoughts, and allow your feelings to pour onto the paper. Let go and ask the angels to resolve the problems to your highest good and the good of all. Leave it up to the angels. Do not try to manipulate the situation. You may be pleasantly surprised at the speed with which the problem is resolved, often in an unexpected way. Angels work in ways in which you would not even dream.

A simple way to purify your thoughts is to write down all your concerns, listing everything that makes you angry or causes you to behave in an unangelic way. Do not hold anything back, just keep writing; tell your angels what makes you fearful, disillusioned or disappointed. Emotions have an effect on healing and health. When we relive negative

Candles are very useful when working with angels, but take great care; never leave a burning candle unattended.

Writing to your angels helps cleanse you of your angry emotions.

emotions, it causes a reaction that is perceived clairvoyantly as dark areas in the aura, which can develop into holes or tears if the negative event is relived many times. When you have finished do not read what you have written; burn the piece of paper. As you do so, feel the cleansing effect it has on your mind.

Purging anger It is also effective to write to someone who has upset you or caused you pain. Since you are going to burn the letter after you have written it, there is no point in holding anything back. As you write to the person, tell them exactly how you feel. Anger initially prepares the body to correct injustice, but must be released. When it is not discharged, it solidifies and hardens into hatred. We must honour our emotions, but we also need to elevate our consciousness, which is a deliberate act of personal empowerment.

Sometimes we may refuse to forgive in order to punish. A simple way of releasing anger towards someone is to acknowledge what you are truly feeling about that person's behaviour, then consciously choose not to punish yourself for carrying this emotion. You can say out loud, 'I now intend to release all my suffering over this situation'. Then visualize the person you need to forgive surrounded in angelic light.

Angel Affirmations

We can reinforce our angelic connection by asking angels to help us achieve our goals by motivating us to make our dreams come true. You may be surprised, however, at how dramatically different your wishes become once your consciousness merges with the angelic stream of love and light.

Before we call in the angels, we need to look at what an affirmation is. We make positive or negative affirmations all day long. Our body believes every word we say. How many times during the day have you found yourself making a negative statement about yourself?

From an early age we are taught to use what linguists call nominalization – a verb (a doing or process word) being made into a noun (a static thing). For example, if you say you cannot handle a relationship, you are talking about a relationship as if it was a static physical thing, rather than talking about relating – a dynamic, active process of communication. The problem arises because the art of relating, when it is referred to as a relationship, is perceived as static and no responsibility is being

Call on the angels to help you de-programme your consciousness.

taken for the active, continuing process of relating to another person. When someone systematically nominalizes, they restrict the choices they have because they are perceiving the world in a fixed way.

Never underestimate the power of words to affect you deeply. Advertisers, religious leaders, politicians and the media know this and bombard our sensory awareness with their messages.

Affirmations Combat this 'programming' by using angel affirmations:

- Call on the angels and use their power to help de-programme yourself. You will see a change in your health, your behaviour, and your whole attitude to life.

- Write out a positive affirmation for yourself. Make it as powerful and appropriate to you and your situation as possible.

- Keep all your statements positive. As you say the affirmation, imagine or feel as if it has already happened.

- Two good angelic affirmations are: 'I allow higher states of angelic awareness to manifest in my life' and 'In blissful unification my angels guide me daily'.

Allow the angels to guide you in forming your positive affirmation.

Creating an Angel Altar

An altar is an important link in establishing a powerful connection with the celestial realms. It is a tangible focus, a portal to serenity, somewhere you can still your mind and open your heart to the angels. It will quickly become your own sacred space, a sanctuary for your soul that is charged with harmonious energy, somewhere you can come to each day to seek renewal.

Creating an angelic altar offers valuable grounding to your spiritual transformation, providing an opportunity to explore your creativity, expressing yourself emotionally, artistically and spiritually. Angels are attracted to places of joy, harmony, love and peace.

Choose items for your altar that have been inspired by the angels through your meditation. Only include items that have meaning for you. These will help you become more mindful of the issues and challenges of the particular aspect of your life you are currently seeking to harmonize.

Once you have established a daily routine of attending your angelic altar – whether to clean, purify or reorganize it, or to change some of your sacred objects or light your candles – it will be much easier to include a set amount of time for meditative thought and prayer.

Be guided by your angels It can be a valuable exercise to meditate on what items to include in your altar before you start, allowing your angels to guide you. What matters most about your altar is the way it affects your inner being. It should make you feel centred, loving and open to the angelic qualities of love, beauty, harmony and peace.

Experiment with the layout; if an item irritates or upsets you, or is less than inspiring, remove it. You could place crystals, angelic art, photographs of loved ones, shells, bells, incense, candles, flowers, essential oils, religious icons, angel cards, affirmation cards, wind-chimes, feathers or a small notebook and pencil on your altar.

Remember to place a representation of anything you want to bring into your life, such as love, spiritual wisdom, compassion, peace or abundance. Make sure you never leave unattended lit candles on your altar; ensure that the room is well ventilated as candles consume oxygen, which can lead to headaches or drowsiness.

An altar provides a powerful focus for meditation, contemplation and the sacred aspects of our lives that we wish to develop.

Using Angel Cards

Angel cards are an excellent way to communicate with angels. Packs can be purchased from most New Age shops. They were originally designed to encourage individual creativity and enhance interaction in relationships. Angel cards provide positive key words that help you focus on a particular aspect of your inner life.

To enhance the experience of communicating with the angels, however, it is much more effective to make your own set of cards. It is not difficult and you do not have to be artistic. All you need is a pen and some stiff paper or card – preferably white on one side and coloured on the other.

You can stick some small shiny angel shapes onto the cards, which 'dedicates' them to the angels. On the white side of the card write a positive quality that you wish to bring into your life. This is called a *key word*.

There is no definitive list of positive qualities associated with angels, so you can make as many cards as you like. You can also add to your cards as your understanding develops.

How to choose an angel card

- Pick a card at the beginning of each day. Spend a moment focusing on your day ahead and see which angel card attracts your attention. Keep your card with you or place it where it will be clearly visible to you throughout the day.

- Choose a card just before you go to sleep, slip it under your pillow and let the angels inspire your dreams.

- Choose a card at the beginning of any new project, venture or cycle, and on your birthday or anniversary.
- At New Year choose 12 cards for the coming year – one for each month – and make a note of each card on your calendar.
- Choose an angel card for a friend who needs help. Focus on your friend's problem – healing, job interview or exams – and surround them in the angelic quality of the card.

Place an angel card under your pillow in order to invite the angels to inspire your dreams.

Key words to get you started

Abundance • Acceptance • Balance • Beauty • Believing • Blessing Commitment • Compassion • Confidence • Courage • Creativity • Delight Empathy • Enthusiasm • Faith • Forgiveness • Freedom • Friendship Generosity • Happiness • Harmony • Healing • Honesty • Hope Humour • Inspiration • Joy • Love • Patience • Peace • Purification Sensitivity • Simplicity • Truth • Wisdom

Angels in Everyday Life

The first rule of working with angels is to understand that they are here to help us in every sphere of our lives; however, angelic help can never be abused. If you wish to use angelic energy for selfish reasons or if you use the angels as a commodity to bolster your ego, be warned that nothing good will come of it, as nothing will happen. There are specific angels for various aspects of everyday life.

Angels of love These angels are directed by Archangel Chamuel (see page 246) and specialize in making your daily life more harmonious. No task is too small or too large for these angels and they will help in any situation that requires heartfelt communication.

Angels of healing As one of the principal angels of healing, Archangel Raphael (see page 240) has the capacity to guide all healers, orthodox and complementary. Invoke his assistance to guide the hands of physicians, surgeons and complementary medicine practitioners.

Ask the angels to be part of all your creative endeavours in the kitchen.

Invoke his presence in hospitals, hospices and clinics. Invoke his presence to heal the rifts between nations, on the battlefield and in areas where there have been natural or manmade disasters. Invoke his presence to guide research scientists as they search for new cures for diseases.

Travelling angels These angels, directed by Archangel Michael (see page 250), will offer protection from physical dangers. Visualize Archangel Michael around you when you travel.

Parking space angel As you set out on your journey ask the parking space angel to help you find a safe parking space.

Kitchen angel If you ask the angels to assist you in all your creative endeavours you may find they turn up in the most unexpected places. Ask the angel Isda to bless your food, making it more nutritious and delicious.

Angel of lost objects Losing your keys, jewellery or important documents is stressful. Immediately ask the angel Rochel to assist you in finding the lost object.

Ask Archangel Raphael, one of the principal angelic healers, to guide you in your healing work.

Exam angels Ask Archangel Jophiel (see page 108) and the angels of illumination to help you study and pass exams. They can also help you absorb new skills and offer illumination and wisdom to fuel your creativity.

Your Angelic Journal

Personal experience and essential wisdom can dissipate like a dream unless they are written down. Keeping an angelic journal is an effective way of recording your magical angelic journey; it is unique to you and can become a tangible force that attracts even more angelic energy into your life.

Choose any notebook that you find beautiful, one that you will treasure for the rest of your life. You could customize a plain notebook with angel pictures.

Writing an angelic dream journal opens your subconscious mind to angelic inspiration. Record dreams, thoughts, visions and meditations.

You could use your angelic journal for many things: to record loving or inspirational messages, poems or sayings; and to keep images of angels, loved ones or people you find inspirational. You could also use it to record your dreams, visions and meditations.

It is not always easy to make time to write down each meditation experience, but angelic encounters in meditation, though inspirational, can be disorientating. After each meditation, allow yourself time to assimilate what you have learned. Write down your experiences, however fragmented, vague or nebulous they may seem to you. Enter fully into the experience with all your senses.

The following steps will help you to integrate the impressions:

1 Thinking about your experience brings it into the mental body – the Solar Plexus Chakra (see pages 102–103).

2 Turning your experience into images brings it into the emotional body – the Heart Chakra (see pages 102–103).

3 Talking about your experience with another person anchors it in the physical body via the Throat Chakra (see pages 102–103).

4 Writing down your experiences for future reference (including drawing images) anchors it in the Sacral Chakra (see pages 102–103).

Each step takes time and takes you a step away from the actual experience, but a great deal of genuine clairvoyance ends up as illusion if not fully grounded in the physical realm. By recording your experiences in writing, you ground them in the here and now.

Do not be overly concerned if you cannot fully understand the experience right away; fragmentary information often occurs in subsequent meditations. Some experiences may make no sense to you for weeks, months or even years, so your journal becomes a special way of assimilating and accumulating understanding. Never be concerned with your spelling or writing style; allow yourself literary freedom.

Your Angelic Gratitude Book

Counting your blessings is a sure-fire way of raising your vibrational rate (see pages 18–19). Do you give out positive energy that others find charismatic and uplifting, or do people avoid you because you moan over every little problem?

Positive thoughts, emotions and words strengthen our energy field, raise our vibrational rate and attract angelic light. Negative thoughts, emotions and words weaken our energy field, while reliving negative events intensifies our emotions and makes holes in our aura (see pages 230–231) that attract parasitic or dark energy.

Many people who work with the angelic realm keep a daily record of all the positive things that happen in their life – this becomes their gratitude book. Make or buy a notebook especially for this purpose; you can customize a plain notebook with angelic images that you find uplifting.

In your gratitude book make a list of all the things you are grateful for in your life – such as your family, friends and loved ones. Record every moment of joy, a beautiful sunset, the perfume of flowers, or even something as simple as a compliment from a friend.

Gratitude attracts positive energy into your life and strengthens your energy field.

Angelic Talents

Angels give us magical gifts and have inspired composers, poets, artists, musicians, writers, teachers and healers. Often the recipient has no previous desire for the talent! The only thing recipients of these 'gifts' have in common is that they are conscious of an external heavenly source for their abilities.

There are many examples of musicians being inspired by angels. They hear the celestial music and capture the sounds to be played on human instruments and sung by human voices.

The gifted English religious poet Caedmon, who died sometime between 670 and 680 CE, was a humble labourer at Whitby Abbey when he was inspired in a dream not only to sing a hymn he had never heard before, but also to remember every detail of the hymn he had sung in his dream.

Ask the angels to help you develop new skills and guide the daily practice of existing talents.

Composer Joseph Haydn (1732–1809) relied on the angels to inspire him. He claimed that his great oratorio *The Creation* came from above. Composer George Frederick Handel (1685–1759) was also inspired from above; his famous *Messiah* – composed in only 24 days, during which time he hardly ate or slept – was due to a vision of God.

Temples of Light

Dreams are an excellent way of working with angels. During your sleep your spirit travels to the higher or lower astral realms. If you are plagued by nightmares, your spirit goes to the lower astral regions. Our thoughts, words and actions create our level of consciousness. By focusing on positive human virtues, we are able to raise our vibrational rate (see pages 18–19), which banishes nightmares and allows us to visit the spiritual homes of the archangels.

Each archangel has a temple 'anchored' in the etheric realm (our physical world where our bodies serve as vehicles for our souls), which lies within the influence of the Earth's planetary grid. This is the Earth's subtle-energy field, very much like the system of ley lines. Angelic temples are normally situated over the Earth's 'power' vortexes, where many ley lines cross, or over remote mountain ranges or small islands that are the remains of larger islands or land masses. They can also be situated over sacred sites on Earth, such as the Egyptian temple at Luxor or at Fátima in Portugal where the Virgin Mary appeared to three children during the First World War.

Mystics, initiates and 'spiritual masters' have used these temples since the dawn of human civilization. They were established by the 'Spiritual Hierarchy' (made up of ascended souls such as Ascended Masters, saints and Bodhisattvas who oversee the spiritual evolution of humanity) under the guidance of the archangels.

The spiritual path Each of these angelic temples has a different focus, function and purpose which will help you on

Angelic temples can be situated over sacred sites such as the Temple of Hatshepsut in Egypt.

your evolutionary path. This path is also sometimes known as Jacob's ladder, the Ladder of Light, the Tree of Life, ascension into cosmic consciousness or return to paradise.

The spiritual focus of each temple relates to a 'cosmic virtue' which each archangel enshrines. When spiritual seekers visit a temple during meditation or sleep they are 'nourished' and inspired by that particular cosmic virtue.

Each 'Temple of Light' has a different appearance. Some are like Greek temples with many gracefully carved stone columns, similar to the Parthenon, while other temples resemble stone pyramids or other sacred buildings that have existed throughout the history of mankind. Temples of Light are always exquisite; their marble or crystal floors hold a central altar where a flame burns of the colour that archangel has as its focus (see page 160 for the Angelic Temple Meditation).

Channelling Messages from the Angels

Angels are the invisible power of creation, and our guardian angel is our first link to this invisible world. Our guardian angel's task is to teach and guide us. They help us build on the knowledge we have already acquired by other means. They link information together and help us discover the underlying patterns and fundamental insights of God's creation. Angelic revelation can come in a dream or the waking moment immediately after a dream, but channelling is a more direct route to angelic inspiration.

It is important to establish a strong loving personal friendship with your guardian angel, based on trust and mutual respect. This helps you to build and identify with your own angelic consciousness. Once you have suitably raised your vibrational rate by uniting with your guardian angel it is easy to channel other angelic beings.

Connecting with your angels by channelling increases your spiritual awareness.

Your guardian angel's tone is always loving and supporting. All angels, without exception, respect our dignity and free will. Your Angels will never sound authoritarian or commanding or make choices for you. If the 'tone' of what you are channelling is ever less than respectful, or at any time you feel yourself taken over or controlled by any outside force, you should immediately stop your connection with this energy.

There is always a direct link between you and your guardian angel and you may be so familiar with its energy that you may not realize you have already been receiving its guidance. This is why your guardian angel is a good source to the world of channelling.

CHANNELLING

YOU WILL NEED

Pen and paper or computer

WHAT TO DO

1 Have pen and paper ready or sit at your computer. Formulate your questions by writing them down.

2 Make yourself relaxed and comfortable. Centre, ground and focus yourself.

3 Calm your mind, open your heart and summon your guardian angel.

4 Ask your guardian angel to open a harmonious channel for you.

5 Write down what is given to you (without changing or censoring it in any way).

6 Note that you will carry more light in your personal energy field at the end of a session – spiritual information is always encoded in light.

Part II

THE ANGEL DIRECTORY

AMOS · PROPHETA
SVPER · TRIBVS · SCELERI
SET SVPER · QVATVOR
COVERTA · EV · PROEO
VENDIDERIT · PROARG
STV · ET · PAVPERE · PR
CIANE · III
DAVID
· P ·

ANGEL HIERARCHIES

The Seven Heavens

Although angels exist in every dimension, they are traditionally thought to inhabit seven heavens, a belief that is integral to the monotheistic religious traditions – Islam, Christianity and Judaism. The seventh heaven is where God dwells. But the tradition of seven heavens goes back some 7,000 years to Sumeria. On an ancient Sumerian stele, a winged being – an inhabitant of the seven heavens – is depicted pouring 'the water of life' into the king's cup. The Sumerian civilization of Mesopotamia gave birth to the Assyrian, Babylonian and Chaldean civilizations, which in turn influenced all Near Eastern religions and angelology.

The seven heavens are the spiritual realms. Many of the names of the seven heavens are found in the Old Testament and are derivatives of the word 'heaven'.

The first heaven Called *Vilon* (from the Latin *velum* meaning veil), the first heaven is also sometimes called *Shamajim* or *Shamayim*, a common word in the Bible for heaven. This is the lowest heaven and is associated with planetary angels and angels that rule the stars and natural phenomena such as the atmosphere, wind and water. The first heaven is ruled by Archangel Gabriel and is said to be the paradise where Adam and Eve first dwelt, and where the Tree of Life and Tree of Knowledge grow.

The second heaven Considered by some to be the holding place of sinners awaiting the Day of Judgement, the second heaven is called *Raqia* (meaning 'expanse' in Genesis 1:6, 1:14, 1:17). Zodiac angels rule over this sphere and fallen angels are held prisoner in this

heaven. *Raqia* is the dwelling place of John the Baptist in Islamic tradition and this heaven is ruled over by Archangel Raphael and Zachariel.

The third heaven *Shechakim* or *Shehaqim* (meaning the 'skies' in Psalms 18:11), is a strange heaven, as hell is found in its northern region. A river of flame flows through this icy land and it is here that the angels punish the wicked. The angel Anahel rules over this domain with Jagniel, Rabacyle and Dalquiel, the three

When Jesus was baptized, he saw the heavens open and the Holy Spirit come down to him.

Sarim (Hebrew for 'princes'), an angelic order of 'singing angels'. In the southern half lies a paradise; this celestial garden has a gate of gold (the famous 'pearly gates') through which all perfected souls pass at death. Two rivers flow through it: the river of milk and honey and the river of oil and wine.

The fourth heaven *Zebhul* (the 'lofty place' in Isaiah 63:15) is ruled over by Archangel Michael. It is where the 'heavenly Jerusalem' is located – the Altar and Temple of God. The 'City of Christ' from St Paul's apocalyptic vision is a city of gold with 12 walls encircling it, and 12 walls within these, punctured by 12 gates of great beauty. The city is encircled by four rivers – of honey, milk, wine and oil.

The fifth heaven *Machon* (the 'dwelling' in Deuteronomy 26:15), ruled by Archangel Sandalphon, is where vast choirs of angels sing God's praises by night and God's chosen people sing his praises by day. Some of the fallen angels are also held here.

Angels declare their presence through the manifested beauty of light.

The sixth heaven *Makon* (the 'habitation' in Psalms 89:14, 97:2), ruled by Zachiel, is where the Akashic records are stored. These record all the happenings on Earth, including the deeds of every individual who has ever lived on Earth as well as their punishment or reward (karma).

The seventh heaven *Araboth* (the 'clouds' in Psalms 68:5) is ruled over by Cassiel, the angel of solitude and tears, and one of the angels that rules over Saturn. It is the abode of God, the Throne and the absolute Holy of Holies. The highest orders of angels, Seraphim, Cherubim and Thrones, dwell here and it is the home of the blessed spirits and unborn souls.

Nine Ranks of Angelic Beings

In Heaven there are many ranks (or choirs) of angelic beings, and various sources have compiled their own hierarchies of angels. The Old Testament refers to princes, sons of God, holy ones, watchers, Angels, Archangels, Seraphim and Cherubim. St Paul writes in the New Testament of principalities, thrones, might and dominations and powers, while Pope St Gregory I (*c.*540–604 CE) stated that there were nine ranks of angels in Heaven – the five from St Paul's list, as well as Angels, Archangels, Cherubim and Seraphim.

The 5th-century scholar Dionysius, the Pseudo-Areopagite (see page 13), had already described these. From Heaven to Earth there are three levels or spheres of angelic influence. The first and closest to God are the Seraphim, Cherubim and Thrones; the second includes the Dominations, Virtues and Powers; and in the lowest rank are the Principalities, Archangels and Angels. The *Celestial Hierarchy* of Dionysius, with its three ranks of three, was inspired by the work of neo-Platonic philosopher Plotinus (*c.*205–270 CE).

No one, it seems, can agree on the ordering of the celestial hierarchies. Authorities from other Christian sources and other religions list different celestial hierarchies and even vary the order in which they are listed. The Pharisees (who were active from 536 BCE to 70 CE), upon whose thought traditional Judaism is based, believed in angels, as did the celebrated Greek philosophers Aristotle and Socrates. Aristotle called them intelligences, while Socrates had his *daimon*, an attendant spirit who guided him throughout his life.

This 14th-century Italian fresco, The Concert of Angels, *at Santa Maria delle Grazie in Saronno, is a wonderful portrayal of a heavenly choir.*

The great philosopher and Catholic theologian St Thomas Aquinas (1255–1274) used the *Celestial Hierarchy* (see opposite page) as his model when he wrote the *Summa Theologica,* in which he discusses God, creation, angels and human nature. Thomas Aquinas believed that angels were pure spirits created by God to sustain the universe, and that if we ignore angels we disrupt the very fabric of the universe. He also believed that each individual has a guardian angel but that they come under the category of the ninth order of angels.

Sphere One

This first sphere contains the three highest orders of angels, which are closest to God. Within this sphere are the Seraphim, Cherubim and Thrones.

Seraphim The Seraphim are the highest order of angels in the Dionysian hierarchy (see page 52) and also in Jewish law. Seraphim means 'the inflamer' from the Hebrew root word *saraph* ('burning'), and they are the angels of 'divine' fire, love and light. Seraphim have the power to purify us with the lightning flash and the flame – they hold the unveiled light of God and are the great illuminators. Next to God they are the most light-filled beings in creation. Seraphim have six wings, surround the throne of God and continually sing the *Trisagion*, a hymn of praise to God that translates as 'Holy, Holy, Holy'.

Ruled by: Archangel Seraphiel, sometimes called the 'Prince of Peace', and by the Archangel Metatron who presides over Kether (crown) on the Kabalistic Tree of Life (see page 76). Also listed are Jehoel, Michael and Lucifer before he fell from grace.

Cherubim Cherubim are the next closest beings to God after the Seraphim. The concept of Cherubim is Assyrian or Akkadian in origin; the Akkadian word *karibu* means 'one who prays' or 'one who intercedes'. They appear in Assyrian, Chaldean and Babylonian art and writings, which is where the biblical prophets Isaiah and Ezekiel may have encountered them. This influence may have coloured the accounts given of Cherubim in Genesis and other Old Testament books.

This six-winged Seraphim in mosaic decorates the Genesis Cupola of the great medieval basilica of San Marco in Venice.

The Cherubim hold the energy of the Sun, the Moon and the stars. The mighty Cherubim are not the cupid-like beings often portrayed in art, but instead are vast cosmic beings.

Ruled by: Zophiel, Ophaniel, Rikhiel, Cherubiel, Raphael and Gabriel.

Thrones The Thrones are always in the presence of God. In the Old Testament, Ezekiel describes them as a whirlwind, a great cloud of fire, their wings joined to one another like great fiery wheels full of eyes. They are the wheels of the Merkavah, the chariot throne of God. They carry the energy of God in the form of divine justice – they allow the will of God to be made known to the ministering angels. The Virgin Mary is said to be a Throne.

Ruled by: Tzaphkiel, Zadkiel, Raziel, Jophiel and Oriphiel.

Sphere Two

This second sphere contains the next three highest orders of angels – the Dominions, Virtues and Powers.

Dominions This order of angels – sometimes called the Dominations, Lords or Lordships – oversees the lower angelic hierarchy and acts as a channel for God's love through the energy of mercy, wielding power without oppression. The Dominions manifest God's majesty and rule over the level where the spiritual and physical realms begin to merge. Their emblems of authority are a sceptre or orb carried in the left hand and a staff of gold held in the right hand.

Ruled by: Zadkiel, Muriel, Yahariel and Hashmal.

Virtues The Virtues can suspend the laws of nature to work miracles here on Earth. This order bestows grace and valour to mortals who need inspiration and courage. Sometimes the Virtues are referred to as the 'shining' or 'brilliant' ones and are said to inspire the saints. Jesus was accompanied by two Virtues when he made his ascension into Heaven. The Virtues of Heaven, on seeing Jesus rise, surrounded him to form his escort. The Virtues were also the midwives to Eve when she gave birth to Cain.

Ruled by: Uriel, Cassiel and Gabriel.

Powers Powers are also known as authorities, potentates and dynamis – 'Karmic Lords' who protect our souls and are the keepers of the Akashic records (see pages 260–261). They have the task of keeping demons under control. In this capacity Powers prevent demons from overthrowing the world. They are often

seen as the angels of death and rebirth, because they guard the pathways to Heaven and guide lost souls back onto the path to Heaven.

Ruled by: Chamuel, Sammael, Camael, Ertosi and Verchiel.

Divine inspiration inspired by the Light of God was a common theme in paintings over the centuries, and provides us with images of angels.

Sphere Three

The third sphere contains the last three orders – the Principalities, Archangels and Angels (including guardian angels).

Principalities Principalities are the guardians of nations and oversee the work of the angels below them. Principalities watch over countries, towns, cities, villages and sacred sites. Archangel Michael is said to be the Principality of Israel, but other countries such as Spain also have him as their guardian, too. Principalities also guide religions and religious leaders to the path of truth. They work with guardian angels to inspire us.
Ruled by: Haniel, Anael, Cerviel and Requel.

Archangels Archangels are also known as ruling angels. In the New Testament the term 'archangel' occurs only twice: in 1 Thessalonians and in Jude. In Revelations 8:2, John refers to the 'seven angels who stand before God', which is traditionally interpreted to mean the seven archangels. The Book of Enoch names the seven as Uriel, Raguel, Gabriel, Michael, Seraqael, Haniel and Raphael. Other lists give different variants.

Enoch saw the seven angels before the throne of God as alike (they were also composite rather than single beings and represent countless others). They were all equal in height, had brilliant faces and identical robes. They were seven yet one – the unity of angels. They controlled and harmonized everything in God's creation. They controlled the movement of the stars, the seasons and the waters on the Earth, as well as plant and animal life. The archangels also kept the record of all the incarnations of every human being.

A 16th-century version of the Archangel Gabriel at the Annunciation of the Virgin Mary. Gabriel is often depicted carrying a lily (a symbol of purity).

St John saw seven torches (archangels) before the throne of God burning as one. The seven torches are represented by the seven-branched candelabra (menorah in the Jewish tradition) – seven lamps all giving out one light, the light of God. The sevenfold presence is an ancient tradition adapted by Christianity where the central light was replaced by a cross, with three altar candles burning on either side.

Archangels operate on many different levels at once since they are messengers bearing divine decrees. They direct the will of God; ignoring one of his divine messengers is perilous.

Angels There are millions of angels helping in many different tasks. They guard all physical things and people. Everything in creation is looked after by an angel. Angels bring cosmic harmony and beauty to our lives. They include the angels of love, joy, courage, peace, hope, faith, freedom and harmony. There are many references to angels in both the Old Testament and the New Testament, but they are not usually identified with a particular name.

Guardian Angels

Our guardian angel's task is to protect, guide and strengthen us against the forces of evil. Although these angels are the lowliest of the heavenly powers, they are still linked to the immense 'planetary' angels. Our guardian angel is therefore our first route to God.

We all have our own guardian angel who will never leave us. Our guardian angel is appointed to us when we first incarnate; they journey with us through all our incarnations, evolving as we evolve through a shared destiny.

A guardian's task is to channel as much angelic light towards us as possible to inspire us in the ways of righteousness and support us against the forces of negativity. They bring comfort in our hour of need and assist us throughout life. Some Christians believe everyone is born with a guardian angel, but if the person is baptized then their guardian's task is to bring them to God. Their guardian angel does this by praying constantly to God for their soul's enlightenment. This is why guardian angels are sometimes called the 'angels of prayer'.

Most people's first conscious contact with the angelic realm is through their guardian angel. This initial experience of an angelic presence is often tangible in moments of acute spiritual or physical danger, in moments of grief, despair or illness, or of joyful inspiration.

Our guardian angel can never override our free will or help us if we choose to ignore the offered assistance. Free will is a most sacred gift, which allows us to choose moment by moment whether we align our consciousness with good or evil. Some people feel their guardian angel is actually their higher self or, as in Buddhist

This 17th-century painting, Hagar and Ishmael Rescued by the Angel, *shows the pair being guided out of the wilderness towards water by an angel sent from God.*

teachings, it is our Buddha-nature, the divine spark within each individual.

Guiding angels We all have a guiding angel who works with us as well as our guardian angel. Your guiding angel will change as you evolve spiritually or need to learn different spiritual lessons. Some people have several guiding angels working with them.

Elemental Kingdom

The children of the angels are the magical nature spirits who create abundance and balance on the Earth when they are honoured and appreciated. They often appear as coloured lights or swirling mists. Nature spirits help us understand the rhythms of nature, and our place within the world. The elementals work closely with the angels of sacred sites to

Tree spirits connect us to the multi-dimensional web of life, which all living things inhabit.

help us understand what our ancestors knew instinctively – the importance of the correlations between the phases of the Moon, the tides and the seasons.

Our planet Earth is a living being that is also evolving through the lives of the creatures she nourishes. The planetary angels, devas and other nature spirits help the Earth through all her stages of growth from the very beginning.

Fairies Fairies, elves, gnomes and goblins are earth spirits and rule over the flowers, plants, trees, soil, sand and crystals. Earth is the least dynamic and most static of the four basic elements. Earth spirits teach us how to nourish ourselves and live in abundance as co-creators in balance and harmony. This means living responsibly with regard to all life on the planet. By focusing on the powerful energy that flows around us, we bring stability and abundance to every area of our lives. Tree and plant spirits, as our ancestors knew, have the power to heal all our ills if we choose to work with them. Simply find a tree that feels harmonious and welcoming and ask to work with its spirit essence.

Mermaids Undines and mermaids are water spirits who rule over the water and tend to the creatures that dwell within this realm. Water spirits teach us to cleanse and balance our emotions. They teach us to go with the flow by following the path of least resistance. Water can take on any shape, it is often difficult to contain and is sometimes enormously powerful. The water spirits have a great deal to teach us about adapting to different situations without losing our basic receptivity.

The medium of water is receptive and carries the messages of the areas it has passed through. Water has many hidden messages and will become increasingly crucial to humanity in the years to come.

Salamanders Salamanders are fire spirits who guard the secrets of transformational fire energy. They are found in large numbers around volcanoes. Fire spirits teach us about the dynamic energy of our life-force, the spark of divine fire that resides in every one of us. This force calls us daily towards the light and awakens us from our slumber. Fire purifies, burns and

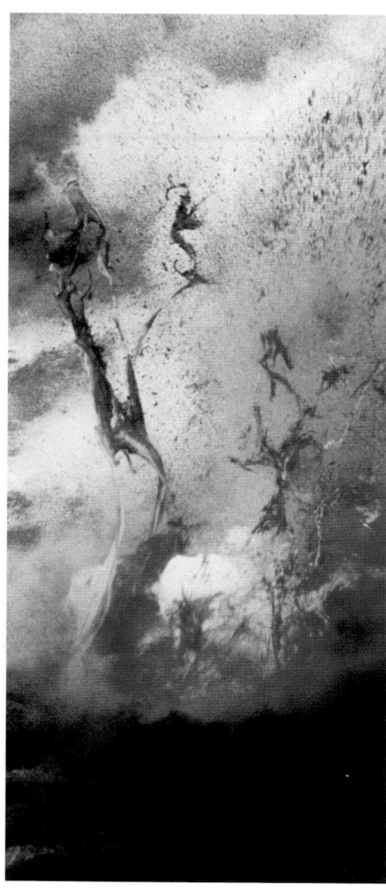

Transformational fire spirits ignite our divine fire to awaken our spirit.

destroys the old so that the new may emerge. Creative fire teaches us spiritual fortitude. The lightning flash, the ultimate fire, brings unprecedented spiritual growth and soul illumination.

Sylphs Spirits of the air, sylphs carry our prayers to the angels. Air is light, flexible and free. It is also invisible and cannot be seen except by the effects it creates. Most life forms need air to live. Working with the sylphs increases our mental prowess, intuition, communication, creative imagination and the sudden flash of inspiration. Birds, which are the creatures of the air, gladden our heart with their songs; they sing to us of the hidden beauties within creation.

Devas Devas are more evolved than the elementals and they often work with humans, especially as guardians of sacred sites and ancient groves. They can also be found dwelling in beautiful Clear Quartz crystals. If you are fortunate enough to find a Devic Temple crystal, it will become a great source of information. These crystals have a vibratory signature

that allows us to access information for bringing Heaven and Earth together. They teach us to raise not only our own frequency but that of others and of the Earth. The devas who dwell in quartz crystals can teach you about healing, both personal and planetary.

A creature of the air, the magnificent eagle is the symbol of the new age of enlightenment.

Angels of Enoch

There is a branch of extracanonical writings that is rich in angelic lore: the three Books of Enoch (see page 12), attributed to the great-grandfather of Noah. The Book of Enoch or 1 Enoch survives completely only in the Ethiopic language; 2 Enoch survives only in Old Slavonic and the final 3 Enoch survives in Hebrew. The final Enoch book is made up of 'The Dream Visions', 'The Book of Heavenly Luminaries' and 'The Parables' or 'The Similitudes' and fragments of 'The Book of Noah'. The three Enoch books were written down between 200 BCE and 100 CE by various authors with differing religious standpoints. The texts were omitted from the Bible, but they have been widely quoted over the centuries by church authorities.

Enoch was a key figure in both Christian and Jewish angelic lore. His vivid and detailed descriptions of Heaven and his intricate angel theology may have provided inspiration to other writers – St John's vision in the 'Book of Revelation' is a prime example.

Enoch's mystical text, the Book of Enoch, opens with a dream-vision in which he is asked to intercede with God on behalf of the fallen angels, those who left their heavenly home. Enoch lists all the 'fallen angels' by name and their part in the 'fall'.

He sees fiery Cherubim (1 Enoch: 17) 'who were like flaming fire, and when they wished they appeared as men'. He was shown the places of the luminaries and was taken by Archangel Michael into the higher heaven and shown the workings of the universe and the whole of creation. In another section he describes the place of final punishment

for the fallen angels.

There are fragments of other journeys that Enoch makes with the angels to the 'Tree of Wisdom' and 'Garden of Righteousness'.

In 1 Enoch 70: 'The Final Translation of Enoch', we see Enoch transformed into Archangel Metatron. As Metatron, he is the most important angel in the Merkavah texts. His name means 'throne-sharer' or lesser Yahweh (God).

Enoch was transformed into the Archangel Metatron through the purification of God's fire, to become the most important archangel.

ANGELS AND THE KABALA

History of the Kabala

One of the richest sources of angelic lore is derived from the Jewish mystical tradition known as the Kabala. Jewish folklore claims that before God created the world we live in, he taught the Kabala to the angels. Adam was the first man to receive these teachings, which were given to him in book form by the Archangel Raziel just as he and Eve were cast out of the Garden of Eden.

The teachings of the Kabala were supposed to enable Adam and Eve – or at least their descendants – to return once again to paradise (paradise comes from the Hebrew word *pardes* meaning 'orchard'). It is claimed that the Book of Raziel or *Sepher Raziel* was therefore the first book ever written and was an extensive compendium of ancient Hebrew magical lore.

The Kabala teachings were lost, but were then given to the prophet Abraham, only to be lost once again when the Jewish people lived in Egypt. (One tradition states that Abraham actually hid the book in a cave.) After the Jewish exodus from Egypt, Moses was given the teachings when he went up the mountain to meet Jehovah.

Kabala is a Hebrew word meaning 'to receive inner wisdom' and is passed on as an oral tradition. There is no single book called the Kabala; rather it is a body of information. Two original texts exist within the Kabala – the *Zohar,* the 'Book of Splendour', and the *Sepher Yetzirah,* the 'Book of Formation'; the latter is accredited in legend to Melchizedek, a priest king of Salem (later Jerusalem), which was given as a revelation to Abraham, the father of the Jewish nation.

The structure of existence as described by Kabalists shows the descending logical stages through which God brought the original divine scheme into being. Various spellings can be found for the Kabala and these correspond with different historical periods and traditions. The expression 'Tree of Life' was popularized in the Middle Ages.

Most spiritual traditions have a 'creation' story in which a creative power from another realm creates the universe. The Jewish mystical tradition of the Kabala is no different: God, the Divine Presence, omnipotent, indefinable and without form, manifests the world from nothing. When God created the world, and made what was formless into form, the first idea created light. God then separated the light from the darkness (male/female or yin/yang), and thereby defined polarity.

Versions of the 'Tree of Life' as an expression of cosmology are found all over the world. This one is by Gustav Klimt (1862–1918).

The Creative Power of Sound

The 22 letters of the Hebrew alphabet consist entirely of consonants and are considered sacred. These consonants have a vibration or energy signature, which means they are alive with creative cosmic power. This cosmic power is latent and can only be activated by the human voice when it provides the vowel sounds; Kabalists emphasize that prayer is not effective unless it is spoken aloud.

Sound is generated as a vibratory motion of particles and objects. The vibrations that produce sound exhibit an energy, a sonic vibrational pattern, that is found throughout nature, not only within ourselves and our world, but far beyond into the realms of the cosmos. The vibrational patterns of sound possess the key to understanding the patterns of being and the organization of matter in the physical universe.

On the cosmic scale, sound is a universal unseen power, able to bring about profound changes on many levels – physical, emotional and spiritual. Sound is among the most transformative energies on the planet. Sound can restore balance and harmony to our lives. Conversely, sound also has the ability to adversely affect us and bring our already strained vibrational rates (see pages 18–19) to new levels of imbalance.

The ancients knew what modern physicists now understand – that all is in a state of constant vibration. They share the belief that the world was created through sound. In Genesis, the first book of the Old Testament, one of the first statements is: 'And the Lord said "Let there be light".' John wrote in the New Testament: 'In the beginning was the Word, the Word was with God, and the

Word was God.' From the Vedas of the Hindu tradition comes an almost identical statement: 'In the beginning was Brahman with whom was the Word. And the Word is Brahman.'

The ancient Egyptians believed that the god Thoth created the world by his voice alone. In Popul Vah, the sacred text of Mayan tradition, the first real people are given life by the sole power of the 'word'. The Hopi story of creation tells that all animals were created by Spider Woman singing the Songs of Creation over them.

Each letter of the Hebrew alphabet has a numeric value: the first three letters of the alphabet, Aleph, Beth and Gimel, have values 1, 2 and 3, respectively, and so on through the entire 22-letter alphabet.

Kabalists believe that calculating the numeric value of a word defines its archetypal eternal essence. Therefore, any two words or phrases that have the same numerical value will also have the same essence. The art of finding words with the same numeric value is called gematria and is usually conducted on biblical names and names of angels.

Aleph

Mem

Shin

These are called the 'mother' letters in Hebrew and correspond to the elements air, water and fire. The sounds are common to all languages.

The Absolute

The Kabala is an esoteric mystical teaching that elaborates fundamental principles of mystical creation and metaphysics. The principles of the Kabala are used to illustrate ideas concerning the nature of the Absolute, the fundamental cosmic laws and the hierarchies of creation. The Kabala is a profound mystery teaching, pertinent to modern theories concerning creation events and to the understanding of the nature of the higher dimensional realities that sustain all things.

Beyond the spheres just above Kether at the top of the Tree of Life is the Divine, which some people call the 'Mind of God'. It is unknowable, perfect, pristine and absolute. Nothing can exist without the power of God, yet it is a 'no-thing' and it is 'everything' containing all possibilities.

Kabalists use various terms and distinctions to depict that which is beyond human comprehension. These images and terms are subtle attempts to point us in the direction of the incomprehensible that is pre-existent to the creation of the universe.

It is depicted as triune in nature, as *Ain*, *Ain Soph* and *Ain Soph Aur* (see illustration on opposite page).

Ain: Void (nothing or absolute nothingness, inconceivable and unspeakable).

Ain Soph: Limitless All (endless and boundless, all possibilities or God Immanent).

Ain Soph Aur: Infinite Light or Limitless Light (the third aspect of the Absolute).

It is said that the Divine generates a sequence of veils of negative existence. To illustrate these three realms of negative existence, we could depict Ain as being blank, Ain Soph as completely black and Ain Soph Aur as white. These three realms of negative existence or non-being are eternal in respect of sustaining all things, in all dimensions (space) and for all time. They are the quantum universe, beyond but responsible for space, time and reality.

These are the stages that the Divine must go through to bring about manifestation or point of light. This point of light is omnipotent and omnipresent: it is limitless and without dimension, containing all possibilities.

A metaphor for the Absolute – the Mind of God, which is unknowable.

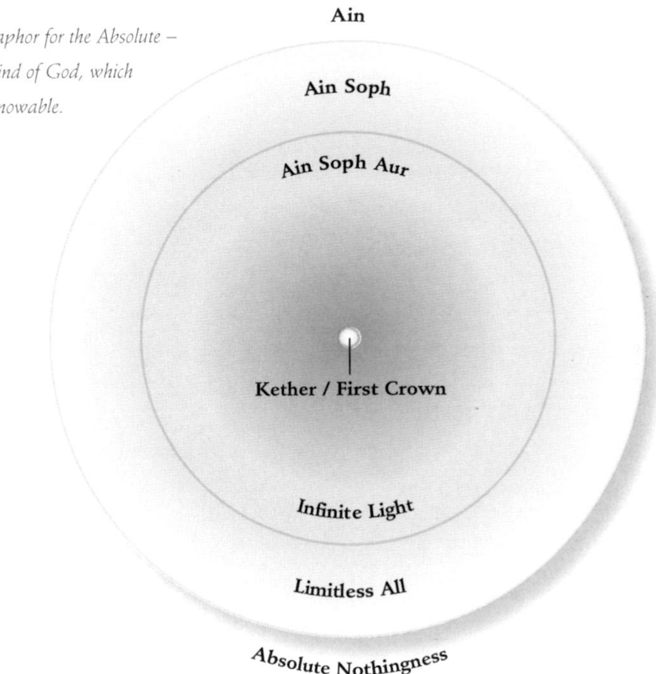

The Archangels and the Ten Sephiroth

The divine energy descends from above and gives birth to the ten sephiroth. You can imagine them as emanations or spheres. Each sephirah (the singular form of sephiroth which means 'vessel') represents an energy signature. The Tree of Life is a visual representation or map of the return pathway of ascension to God-consciousness. By ascending from bottom to top in reverse order (ten back to one) through the sephiroth we can return to God. With the help of the sephiroth, humanity ascends to God by attaining the meaning of each sephirah, one at a time.

The Tree of Life can be used as a template for a multitude of belief systems. It allows us to arrange and order our lives

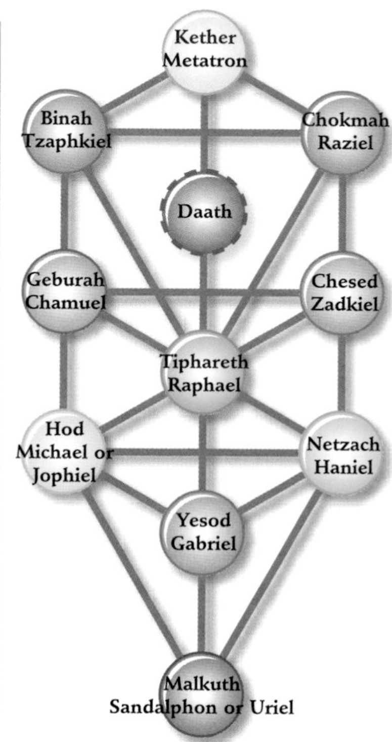

The Kabalistic Tree of Life is a magical map that leads to enlightenment or union with God.

in sympathy with the manner in which we see and understand the world.

Making your way through the sephiroth is difficult, because each sephirah is said to be divided into four sections that correspond to the Four Worlds. Also within the sephiroth is the sacred, unknowable and unspeakable name of God: YHVH (Yahweh), or the Tetragrammaton. The Tetragrammaton is so sacred that other names pertaining to God such as Jehovah, Elohim or Adonai are substituted in the text. The letters YHVH correspond to the Four Worlds.

The sephiroth and their archangels

Kether (Crown)	–	*Archangel Metatron (Divine)*
Chokmah (Wisdom)	–	*Archangel Raziel (Cosmic Father)*
Binah (Understanding)	–	*Archangel Tzaphkiel (Cosmic Mother)*
Chesed (Mercy)	–	*Archangel Zadkiel (Tzadkiel)*
Geburah (Severity)	–	*Archangel Chamuel (Khamael)*
Tiphareth (Beauty)	–	*Archangel Raphael*
Netzach (Victory)	–	*Archangel Haniel*
Hod (Glory, Majesty)	–	*Archangel Michael or Archangel Jophiel*
Yesod (Foundation)	–	*Archangel Gabriel*
Malkuth (Kingdom)	–	*Archangel Sandalphon or Archangel Uriel (Auriel)*
**Daath (Knowledge)*	–	*Holy Spirit (Shekinah) or knowledge*

**Some Kabalists consider Daath to be a place of mysterious powers and miracles. Daath and Kether are the same sephirah from two different aspects.*

The Three Triads

Within the structure of the Tree of Life are the three triads (triangles), formed from the first nine sephiroth with the tenth forming the base. Each triad has the male (positive) and female (negative) principle (attribute of the Divine) with a milder principle between them creating a balance between the two.

Each principle functions according to its characteristics or nature. In general, the male principles (sometimes called forces) are characterized as being positive, active or dynamic and the female principles are said to be passive. The principle residing between each male and female principle is thought to harmonize the opposites.

The first triad In the first triad, Chokmah (the male principle) is opposed by Binah (the female principle). These principles are thought of as the Father and Mother respectively. Chokmah, also called the active Wisdom of God, acts upon Binah, the passive Understanding of God. Kether is the harmonizing principle that keeps a balance between the two.

The second triad In the second triad (in which the father, mother and child are represented) the sephiroth are Chesed, Geburah and Tiphareth. Chesed (male) is the kind, merciful father protecting and guiding the child, while Geburah (female) is the strict, authoritarian mother. The balancing principle is Tiphareth, which is often compared to the sun.

The functions of Tiphareth (which combines the characteristics of Chesed and Geburah) are frequently compared to those of nature. Tiphareth is both the warming sun that gently shines and also the fierce heat that kills.

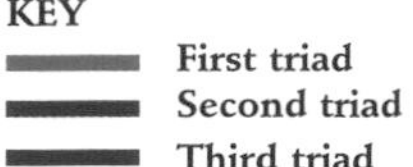

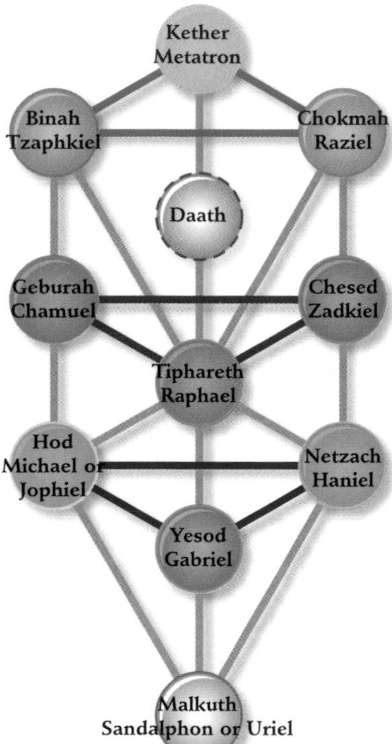

The three triads within the Tree of Life structure are shown superimposed over the Tree in green, purple and orange.

The third triad The third triad represents the child's emergence into adulthood. Its sephiroth (Netzach, Hod and Yesod) symbolize the struggle between the dualistic forces of instinct and intellect. Netzach (male) represents the endurance and the victory of God. It stands for the all-enduring drive of nature, allowing humanity to act naturally instead of by contrivance.

The opposing sephirah Hod (female) contains the qualities of intuition, imagination and inspiration. Yesod (the child) is now fully grown and is the harmonizing sephirah between Netzach and Hod. It is in the sphere of the Moon. Yesod is the potential magic power within oneself. Yesod is thought to be the link between Tiphareth (the Sun) and Malkuth (the Earth). Malkuth as the base sephirah represents the Earth.

The Three Pillars

There are many patterns on the Tree of Life. The three pillars or columns provide an important one (see illustration right). The Divine descends from above using these three pillars as structure: this is how the formless takes form. Kabalists use the middle pillar as a direct route to God.

The Pillar of Severity The left-hand column is *Boaz* or the Pillar of Severity and is water, passive and female. Boaz is made up of Binah at the top, Geburah in the centre and Hod at the base. This is the pillar of form and the three sephiroth on this side are concerned with restriction or constraint.

The Pillar of Mercy The right-hand column is *Jachin* or the Pillar of Mercy and is fire, active and male. Jachin is made up of Chokmah at the top, Chesed in the

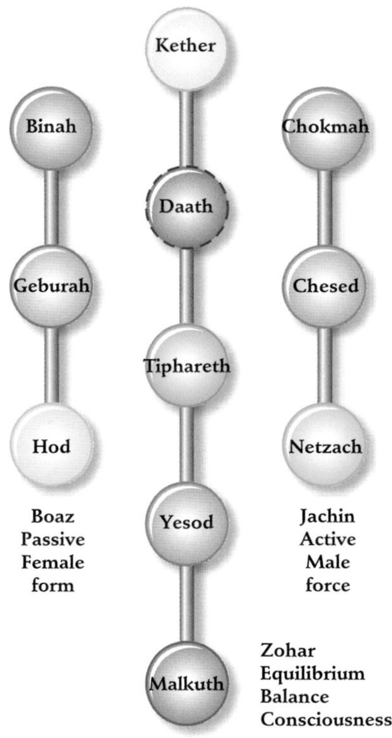

centre and Netzach at the base. This is the pillar of force and the three sephiroth on this side are concerned with movement and expansion.

The Pillar of Equilibrium The middle column is *Zohar* or the Pillar of Equilibrium and is air and balance. Zohar is made up of Kether at the top, Tiphareth and Yesod in the centre and Malkuth at the base. This is also known as the Pillar of Consciousness and it contains the hidden sephirah Daath (see pages 86–87 for more information).

BALANCING VISUALIZATION

This visualization corresponds to your spiritual spine bringing balance. Sit comfortably in a quiet space.

WHAT TO DO

1 Start by becoming aware of your breathing and relax. Focus your awareness just above the Crown Chakra. Visualize a sphere of brilliant white light.

2 See a beam of light descending from the sphere above your head. See it filling your Throat Chakra as a lavender-blue sphere.

3 See a beam of light descending from the sphere of light at your Throat Chakra to your Solar Plexus Chakra. Visualize it filling your solar plexus with golden light.

4 See a beam of light descending to your Sacral Chakra. Visualize it filling your Sacral Chakra with silvery-violet light.

5 See a beam of light descending to your feet, where it forms a black sphere. As you visualize each sphere of light in turn, see the connecting tube of light.

6 To close the session, bring yourself back to everyday waking reality.

The Three Parts of the Soul

Kabalists believe that the soul has three parts, each coming from a different sephirah. However, each part is not necessarily active in all people. The *Zohar* calls these three elements the *nefesh, ruach* and *neshamah*.

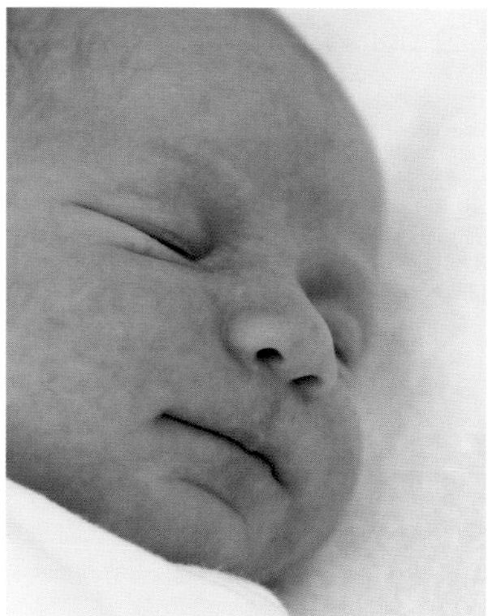

The nefesh is found in all humans and enters the physical body at birth. It is the source of one's physical and psychological nature. The next two parts of the soul are not implanted at birth, but are slowly created over time; their development depends on the actions and beliefs of the individual. They are said to only fully exist in people who have been awakened spiritually.

Nefesh comes from Malkuth and sustains the body, giving it life and allowing it to participate in the material world. Ruach originates from Tiphareth and is the spirit. It is the aspect that allows us to transcend the lowly human condition by developing our intellect and reason. It is the aspect of your soul that

At birth nefesh *enters the physical body so that we can take part in the material world.*

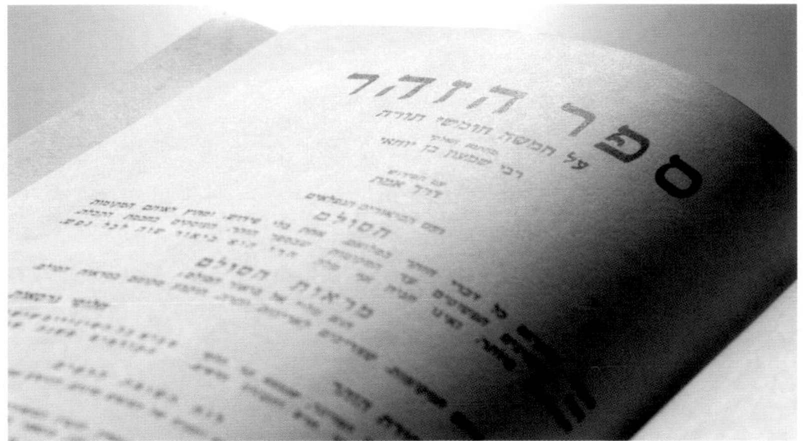

Zohar or the Book of Splendour is one of the central texts of the Kabala.

stirs you into the deep contemplation of God and helps you distinguish between good and evil actions.

Neshamah is an emanation of Binah, the Cosmic Mother. It is the super-soul, pure spirit that can never die or be corrupted: it is the eternal aspect of God. This part of the soul is provided both to Jew and non-Jew alike at birth. It allows one to have some awareness of the existence and presence of God and allows us to have an afterlife.

Further aspects of the soul A later text added to the *Zohar,* entitled the *Raaya Meheimna* and by an unknown author, suggests there are two more parts of the human soul, the *chayyah* and *yehidah*. Chayyah gives awareness of the divine life-force, while Yehidah is the highest part of the soul which allows full union with God.

Some Kabalistic works suggest there could also be a few additional, non-permanent states to the soul that people can develop on certain occasions. One of them is *ruach ha kodesh,* a part of the soul used for prophecy.

The Lightning Flash

The Lightning Flash can be used for meditation or visualization by following the energetic pathway upwards or downwards and seeing each sephirah 'light up'. This focuses your intent since energy always follows thought (intent). Focusing spiritual energy on each sephirah and the lightning pathway, enhances our communication with God.

As each sephirah represents a different state of consciousness, by moving along the paths we can see what changes are occurring in our conscious awareness. The Lightning Flash is another Kabalistic tool to help us understand God. Kabalists try to describe the indescribable by using examples and approximation. The following is a pronunciation guide for the names of the sephirah, which you may find particularly useful when meditating on the Tree of Life using the Lightning Flash.

- Kether (pronounced 'ketta')
- Chokmah (pronounced 'hochma' with a 'ch' as in 'loch')
- Binah (pronounced 'beena')
- Daath (pronounced 'daarth' as in Darth Vader from the movie *Star Wars*)
- Chesed (pronounced 'chesed' with a 'ch' as in 'loch')
- Geburah (pronounced 'geboor')
- Tiphareth (pronounced 'tifaret')
- Netzach (pronounced with a soft 'ch')
- Hod
- Yesod
- Malkuth (pronounced 'maalkut')

There are many pathways created by the fixed sephiroth on the Tree of Life. The Lightning Flash is an important pathway for the divine energy (emanation) of God to descend through. This descending pathway is called involution.

The divine light comes through Kether into Malkuth as a lightning flash which flows constantly from left to right and back again. The energy flows from Kether into Chokmah and Binah and then into the 'non-sephirah' Daath. Duly charged with cosmic power, it then moves to the sephirah of Chesed and on to Geburah, flowing finally through Tiphareth, Netzach, Hod and Yesod and then is earthed in Malkuth.

The reverse of the Lightning Flash is the evolution pathway or serpent path, which is similar to the awakening and upward movement of *Kundalini* energy, found in the Root Chakra. The evolution movement of energy starts in Malkuth and moves through Yesod, Hod, Netzach, Tiphareth, Geburah, Chesed, Daath, Binah and Chokmah and finishes at Kether.

As you visualize the Lightning Flash and move your awareness through each sephiroth, you can sound each name in mantra-fashion. This utterance of the sound brings spiritual energy to cleanse and refine each sphere of consciousness and opens the pathway to God.

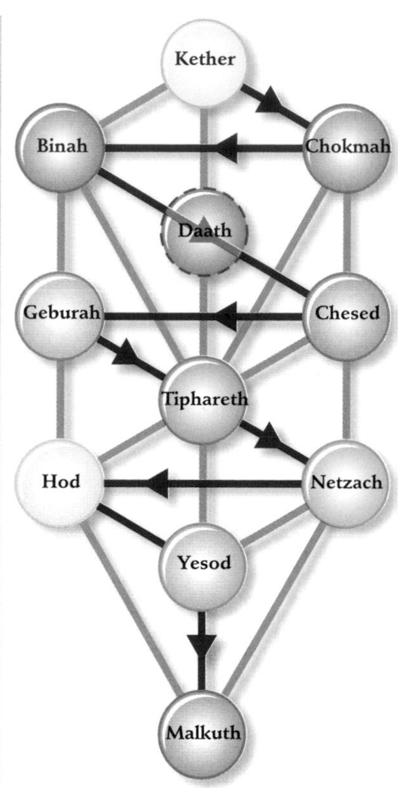

This descending path through the Tree of Life is called the Lightning Flash or involution. It is often used as an aid to meditation.

Daath

The lower seven sephiroth are separated from the top three, the 'Divine Trinity', by the 'non-sephirah' Daath, the place of knowledge, known as the void, abyss, veil or empty room. It is a non-place, as it is transpersonal and without form.

The existence of a void between the three supernal sephiroth of Kether, Chokmah and Binah and the seven lower sephiroth is a well-developed idea within the Kabala. When you look at the progress of the Lightning Flash down the Tree of Life, you will see that it follows a path connecting the sephiroth except when it makes the jump from Binah to Chesed, thus reinforcing the idea of a void or gulf that must be traversed. There is no easy sideways path to this sphere: the only easy access to it is from above or below on the middle pillar of balance.

Daath means knowledge, all knowledge, and the best way of approaching the

The symbol of Daath is an empty room. It hides a great secret; light a candle in your mind to help you pass through Daath safely.

void, the great unknown, is through acquiring knowledge. But, as you will find, knowledge is not enough; you need to balance the knowledge you acquire with Binah (understanding) and Chokmah (wisdom).

This non-sephirah contains the knowledge of the past, present and future. It is the womb of silence and is traditionally the home of the Holy Spirit (*ruah ha kodesh*). To access the 'Holy of Holies' you will travel through Tiphareth, which is ruled over by Archangel Raphael. He will help you to develop balance and compassion in your life so you can acquire knowledge of the self.

DAATH VISUALIZATION

This visualization allows us to bring light into our darkness. Very often when we are in the 'dark' (ignorance) it is perceived by the 'little ego' as the unknown. Sit or lie comfortably in a quiet space where you will not be disturbed. You might like to study the section on angelic alignment (see pages 218–219) before you begin.

WHAT TO DO

1 Sit down comfortably.

2 Close your eyes, relax and take slow breaths, becoming aware of your breathing.

3 Imagine yourself in a dark room.

4 Allow your eyes time to adjust to the darkness and your mind time to adjust to the silence. When you are ready and feel comfortable in the darkness, light a candle in your mind. Use your mind as the spark of light to ignite the flame.

5 Keep a written record of all your Kabalistic experiences, dreams, visualizations and meditations in your journal.

The Caduceus

The Caduceus or Wand of Hermes (messenger and scribe of the Greek gods) is a symbol of wisdom, healing and fertility. It was actually an olive branch with two shoots decorated with garlands of flowers or ribbons that became stylized as two snakes. According to ancient legend, the god Apollo gave the Caduceus to Hermes.

Aesculapius, the Greek god of healing, is also portrayed carrying a rod entwined by snakes; he was killed by a thunderbolt from Zeus who was worried that such a brilliant physician would make men immortal. Thoth, the Egyptian god, also carries a caduceus and it has appeared in Babylonian culture as well.

The green snake starts at Malkuth and curls to the left, touches Yesod, curls to the right touching Netzach, then back to the centre to Tiphareth, and finishes at Geburah. The green snake represents ecstacy and nature, where God is found in action and the natural world of trees, plants and flowers.

The orange snake also starts at Malkuth and curls to the right, touches Yesod, curls to the left touching Hod, then back to the centre to Tiphareth, and finishes at Chesed. The orange snake represents analysis and comprehension, which is the Hermetic Gnosis way to God-consciousness through the intellect.

The circle between the two wings is over Kether. The left wing covers Binah and the right wing Chokmah. Once the Caduceus is laid over the Tree of Life we see a new and sophisticated movement, more representative of the yin and yang balance, which is in sympathy with our current Age of Aquarius, where opposite but complementary exist in each other.

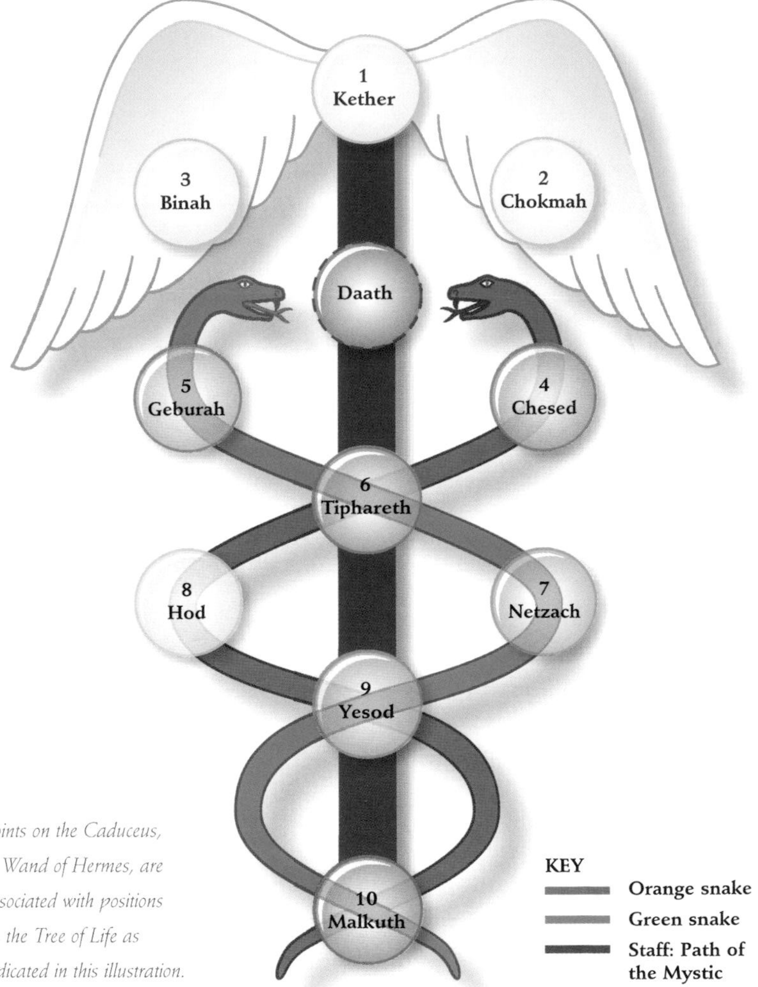

Points on the Caduceus, or Wand of Hermes, are associated with positions on the Tree of Life as indicated in this illustration.

The Ladder of Light

In the Old Testament (Genesis 28:10–22), the patriarch Jacob dreamed of angels ascending and descending to Earth on a fiery ladder. In the vision, God stood beside Jacob and promised to be with him always. The ladder of angels symbolized the bond between Heaven and Earth.

In the Kabala, the Ladder of Light brings the teachings of the Lurianic Kabala into a single image. Rabbi Isaac Luria (1534–1572) was one of the greatest Kabalists and his work was based exclusively on the Old Testament and the *Zohar* (see page 70). Rabbi Luria brought the numerous tangled strands together to form a cosmology that was more comprehensive and comprehensible. His most profound insight was into the nature of God as creator. In his view, God was like the 'big bang' (the 20th-century scientific theory of creation) and more importantly is still evolving, via the process of his creation. At the moment of creation, 'holy sparks' flew off in all directions – some fell into this world, others returned to their source. This cataclysm started evolution. His teachings, the *Shattering of the Vessels*, formed the core belief system of subsequent Kabalists and formed Kabalistic theosophy.

The part of God that is the creator aspect is called Adam Kadmon, the archetypal man. The 'holy sparks' long to return to their state of unity with God, so Kabalists believe. The fundamental building blocks of the Tree of Life are the ten sephiroth – the Ladder of Light is an extension of the Tree of Life, offering insight not only into the world around us (other dimensions) but also into our inner world (inner dimensions).

This 15th-century French painting entitled Jacob's Ladder *clearly illustrates Jacob's dream of angels climbing up to heaven.*

The Four Worlds

The Ladder of Light takes us upwards through four imperfect worlds. These Four Worlds are, to the Kabalist, an exploration of the complex relationship of interpretations of the Kabala. This exploration can give us profound insights into our psychological make-up and each individual person interprets the Kabala in their own way.

The letters YHVH correspond to the Four Worlds. In classical Kabala, the Four Worlds describe the structure of the cosmos from the Godhead down through the angelic realms to this physical world.

These Four Worlds together can be considered as a linear hierarchy, each containing its own full Tree, in which Malkuth in one world becomes Kether of the world below, and Kether of one world becomes Malkuth of the world above. Malkuth is seen as the complementary fulfilment of Kether: the first is Divine Immanence, the latter Divine Transcendence.

Atziluth, which means 'emanation or nearness to God', is the spiritual world of archetypes from which come all manifestation of forms. This is the world closest to the creator, Adam Kadmon. It is the absolute divine reality, the Deity, perfect and immutable, representing the male and female polarities of God.

Briah is the mental world of creation where archetypal ideas become patterns. It is also called the Throne. The archangel Metatron, who constitutes pure spirit and is in charge of a myriad of angels, inhabits this world. All the other archangels who rule over each of the ten sephiroth also dwell in this world as they ultimately bring the imaginative consciousness of God into form in the lower worlds.

Yetzirah is the psychological world of form, where the patterns are expressed. This world of formation is full of angels. These angels are still pure spirit wrapped in luminous garments. They are divided into ten ranks, according to the ten sephiroth, and each angel is set over a different part of the universe and derives its name from the element or heavenly body it guards.

Assiah means 'the world of making' and is the physical world where materialism is manifested. Although the details differ among the various Kabalistic schools, the basic consensus is that theuniverse of Assiah constitutes the sub-spiritual or lower world. Each of these Four Worlds relates to a particular type of consciousness.

KEY

God
Atziluth
Briah
Yetzirah
Assiah

This Ladder of Light incorporates the teachings of Lurianic Kabala into a single glyph. Instead of one Tree there are five Trees which overlap.

Path-working with the Angels

The technique known as path-working is an important aspect of the Western Kabala mystery tradition. Using the Tree of Life structure for this path-working allows us to create rich sources of imagery to change our consciousness and awareness and shift frequencies as we move between the sephiroth. This, in turn, allows us to gain direct personal experience, knowledge, understanding, wisdom, unity and ultimately God-consciousness or enlightenment.

There are many correspondences created as the divine energy descends from above and gives birth to the ten sephiroth. Once the ten sephiroth spheres are in place, 22 interlocking paths join them together. Each of the 22 interlocking paths is assigned a letter from the Hebrew alphabet, as well as one of the 22 Tarot face cards.

The sephiroth are also assigned the following: an archangel, a planet, a colour, herbs, trees, plants, flowers, crystals and specialist angels.

The ten sephiroth plus the 22 interlocking paths equal the 32 paths of wisdom in the archetypal world.

Path-working or visualization helps us to see ourselves from different perspectives.

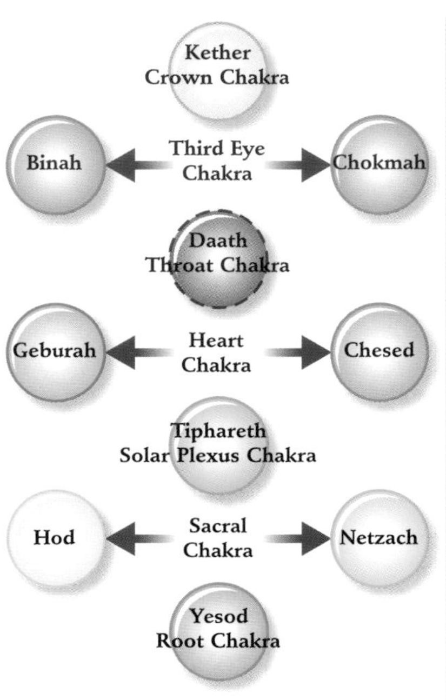

The diagram above represents the ten sephiroth (including the non-sephirah Daath) as they relate to the seven 'master' chakras.

Between the ten spheres and 32 paths are the 50 gates of inner light. The spheres, paths and gates of light form the Tree of Life pattern which can be applied to many different belief systems including the chakra system (see page 102).

When the ten sephiroth, the non-sephirah (Daath) and interlocking paths are placed over the main chakras, it is done in the following manner:

Kether = Crown Chakra
Binah and Chokmah = Third Eye Chakra
Daath = Throat Chakra
Geburah and Chesed = Heart Chakra
Tiphareth = Solar Plexus Chakra
Hod and Netzach = Sacral Chakra
Yesod = Root Chakra
Malkuth = Earth Star Chakra

The chakra and sephirah correspondences work out very well. By combining two sephiroth (the three pairs of opposites) at the female polarity chakras the Third Eye, Heart and Sacral Chakras, we come to a greater understanding of the female energy (yin) which also contains the child element of the trinity or balance.

The Cross of Light Ritual

Purpose *To bring purification, blessings and balance*

This ritual creates a powerful inner cross of light. The meditation is performed standing up as most priests and rabbis perform all their rituals and prayers standing. You might like to study the angel meditations (see pages 148–171) before you begin performing this ritual.

Stand with your feet firmly planted on the Earth to ground the energy and to allow a stronger flow of heavenly light to be established, which you first absorb and then send outwards to purify, bless and protect the world.

The Cross of Light Ritual creates an inner cross of light and power.

Translation of words

Atoh – *means Thou Art*
Malkuth – *means the Kingdom*
Ve Geburah – *means the Power*
Ve Gedulah – *means the Glory*
Le Olahm – *means Forever*

HOW TO PERFORM THE RITUAL

WHAT TO DO

1 Stand facing east, relaxed but with good posture, hands by your sides and eyes closed.

2 Visualize yourself growing taller and taller, until the Earth is a tiny dot beneath your feet and your head is in the highest heaven.

3 Perceive a sphere of pure brilliant white light high above you. Reach up to the light with your right hand.

4 While chanting 'Atoh', guide this light down to the point above and between your eyes (the Third Eye Chakra).

5 While chanting 'Malkuth', draw the light downward through your body to beneath your feet (Earth Star Chakra), filling yourself with pure brilliant white light.

6 Imagine the same point of pure brilliant white light far to your right. With your right hand, reach out and guide the light to your right shoulder, chanting 'Ve Geburah'.

7 Continue to draw the light across your body to your left shoulder, touching it, then extend the light far to the left with your left hand chanting 'Ve Gedulah'.

8 Open your arms outwards to form a cross; see yourself as a cross of brilliant white light.

9 Bring both hands together level with your heart (the prayer position) chanting 'Le Olahm'.

10 Clasp your hands in prayer, and breathe deeply to absorb all this light and energy.

11 Chant 'Amen'. As you breathe out, radiate the light and energy outwards, bathing your world in divine love.

12 Reworking the signing of the cross used by Catholics, you could use the English words and the ritual would be just as effective.

The Lesser Banishing Ritual of the Pentagram

Purpose *To purify and bring immediate angelic protection*

This ritual follows on from the Cross of Light ritual (see pages 96–97) to bring angelic protection and promote meditation. It also promotes clarity of thought and a still mind that is free of unwanted outside influences.

HOW TO PERFORM THE RITUAL

YOU WILL NEED

One Clear Quartz single-terminated crystal (see opposite picture for an example of single terminated).

WHAT TO DO

1 Stand facing east, perform Cross of Light ritual (see pages 96–97).

2 Still facing east, and using a Clear Quartz single-terminated crystal, trace a large pentagram in the air in front of your body with the point of the pentagram upwards. Begin at your left hip, up to just above your forehead, centred on your body, then down to your right hip, up and to your left shoulder, across to the right shoulder and down to the starting point in front of your left hip.

3 Visualize the pentagram as green light with a gold aura. Point your crystal into the centre and say 'YHVH' (Yod-heh-vahv-heh – the tetragrammaton translated into Latin as Jehovah).

4 Turn to face south. Repeat step 2 while facing south, but visualize the pentagram as yellow light with an indigo-blue aura and say 'Adonia' (another name for God translated as 'Lord').

5 Turn to face west. Repeat step 2, but visualize the pentagram as orange light with a white aura and say 'Eheieh' (another name for God translated as 'I am that I am').

6 Turn to face north. Repeat step 2, visualizing the pentagram as red light with a violet aura, and say 'Agla' (a composite of Atoh, Geburah, Le Olahm and Amen).

7 Return to face east, pointing your crystal into the same spot as in step 2. Vizualize the four flaming pentagrams around you connected by a line of blue fire.

Stand facing east holding a Clear Quartz single-terminated crystal.

8 Extend your arms out to your sides, forming a cross. Say: 'Before me Raphael, behind me Gabriel, on my right hand Michael, on my left hand Uriel, for about me flame the Pentagrams, and in the column stands the six-pointed star.'

9 Repeat step 1 of the Cross of Light ritual, by facing east, relaxed but with good posture, with hands by your sides and eyes closed.

10 To close the session, bring yourself back to everyday waking reality.

ANGEL COLOURS

Angels of the Rays

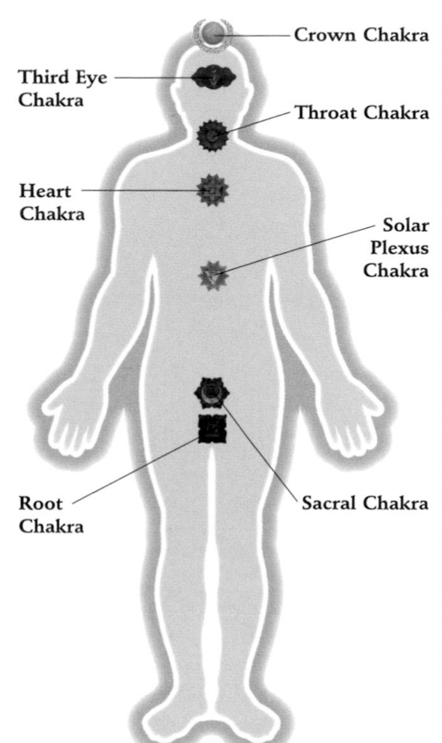

In some writings on sacred angelic lore, the seven archangels represent the seven rays of spiritual enlightenment and the seven colours of the rainbow. The seven rays are also correlated to the seven master chakras. Once you are attuned to the 'Angels of the Rays' and have developed sensitivity to the chakra centres you will have balanced your own energy levels, gained spiritual insight and be able to offer healing to others.

Chakras Centres of subtle energy, the chakras are vitally important for your physical and emotional well-being as well as your spiritual growth. Each chakra is associated with specific organs and endocrine glands. Chakras process subtle energy and convert it into chemical, hormonal and cellular changes in the body. Each chakra vibrates at a different frequency, colour and on a different musical note, and has either male or female polarity. The Crown, Throat, Solar Plexus and Root Chakras are male (positive); the Third Eye, Heart and Sacral Chakras are female (negative).

The seven master chakras are on the centre line of the body with the first five embedded within the spinal column. The Root Chakra opens downwards and the Crown Chakra opens upwards. The other five open from the front to the back of the body.

Light and colour Colour is a universal language that bypasses the logical mind and speaks directly to the soul. Each of the seven major visible colours has therapeutic qualities that can be linked through their resonance to the seven master chakras.

Ancient knowledge Light therapy, chromotherapy (colour therapy) and hydrochromatic therapy (colour tinctures) are ancient forms of natural healing. The coloured rays affect our physical bodies, emotions, moods, mental faculties and spiritual nature. We all have an intimate relationship with colour. Sometimes we give ourselves a subconscious colour treatment by choosing jewellery or clothes of a certain colour, or by surrounding ourselves with specific colour vibrations in our homes, offices and gardens.

Mostly our reactions are unconscious, and it is only when we start to use the magical signatures of colour in an informed and enlightened way that we can harness this wonderful vital force to improve the quality of our lives and our overall sense of harmony, balance and total well-being.

White light is composed of all the colours. Passing a beam of white light through a prism creates the seven colours of the rainbow spectrum.

Ruby Ray

Archangel Uriel

Colour *Ruby-red* • **Focus** *Spiritual devotion through selfless service to others* • **Chakra** *Root* (muladhara) – *element of earth – balance expressed as grounded, stable and reliable*

Ruby Ray is the sixth ray of spiritual light and the first ray of the visible rainbow spectrum. It influences the Root Chakra on the physical level (third dimension) and is the transmuting (transforming) ray of the Solar Plexus Chakra (fourth dimension). The Ruby Ray is perceived as deep red, moving through to deep purple with flecks of gold, just like the best-quality fine ruby crystals.

Uriel's name means 'Fire of God' or 'Light of God'. One of the most powerful archangels, Uriel is the 'Angel of the Presence' and is able to reflect the unimaginable light that is God. He is associated with electricity, lightning, thunder and sudden action and is often depicted holding a scroll (which contains information on your life-path) or carrying a staff.

The Light of God, transmitted by Uriel, gives us illumination. This illumination is vital for those who feel they have lost their way, so the Ruby Ray should be used whenever we feel lost, abandoned, fearful, forsaken, rejected, suicidal or dissipated.

Physical associations Parts of the body: genitals and reproductive organs; regulates adrenalin release into the bloodstream; blood; circulation; muscles;

feet; legs, knees, hips. Detoxifies the body by removing inertia. Warming. Increases physical energy and stops debilitation. Strengthens the ability to listen to the wisdom of the body. Do not use for red angry conditions such as high blood pressure, swellings, inflammation, agitation, hyperactivity, fever, ulcers.

Red, the first ray of the visible rainbow spectrum, can be used to summon Archangel Uriel to help release deep-seated energy blocks.

Emotional and mental associations Activates, vitalizes, signifies and arouses lust, desire and amour. Releases energy blocks deep within the system. Brings action, life-force, courage, stamina and endurance. Gives a new boost to processes that have been sluggish or stagnant. Survival issues reduced, restores the will to live. Dynamic, removes fear. Releases self-obsessive behaviour patterns.

Spiritual associations Teaches mastery of the material world, helps human beings connect with divine order to bring harmony and world peace. Brings spirituality into our everyday lives.

Orange Ray

Archangel Gabriel

Colour *Orange* • **Focus** *Creativity – also used for dissolving fear*
Chakra *Sacral* (svadhisthana) – *element of water – balance expressed as vitality, creativity and originality*

The second ray of the visible rainbow spectrum, the Orange Ray influences the Sacral Chakra on the physical level (third dimension). The Orange Ray is perceived as vermillion, moving from orange to orange-gold, like the best-quality hessonite garnets.

Archangel Gabriel, the messenger, is one of the four great archangels. He is one of only two angels (along with Archangel Michael) to be mentioned by name in the New Testament. The angel of the Annunciation, Gabriel announced the forthcoming birth of Jesus to Mary, his mother, and was also present at Jesus' death as the angel who watched over the tomb and gave the good news of his resurrection to the disciples (although he was not specifically mentioned by name). In Islam, Archangel Gabriel (Jibril) awakened Mohammed, the Prophet of God, and dictated the Koran to him. It is said that the Archangel Gabriel inspired Joan of Arc. Gabriel's colour is white when used as the transmuting (transforming) fourth-dimensional ray of the Root Chakra.

Physical associations Parts of the body: lower back, lower intestines, abdomen and the kidneys. Governs the adrenal function. Aids digestion.

Orange can be used to summon Archangel Gabriel to release stress and to enhance creativity.

Ameliorates bronchitis and asthma. Useful during the menopause. Balances hormones and aids fertility. Very motivating, balances body energy levels, increases vitality, works more gently than red by building up energy step by step. Unlocks deadlocked processes. Eases constipation.

Emotional and mental associations Ameliorates grief, eases bereavement and loss. Enhances creativity, optimism and a view of life that is positive. Helps ease fears and phobias. Releases the fear of experiencing pleasure.

Spiritual associations Stimulates joyfulness, which is spiritually uplifting.

Yellow Ray

Archangel Jophiel

Colour *Yellow* • **Focus** *Wisdom*

Chakra *Solar Plexus* (manipuraka) – *element of fire – balance expressed as logical thought processes, self-confidence and goal manifestation*

The third ray of the visible rainbow spectrum, the Yellow Ray influences the Solar Plexus Chakra on the physical level (third dimension) and is the transmuting ray for the Crown Chakra (fourth dimension). It is the second spiritual ray and is perceived as orange-yellow moving through to pale gold, like the best-quality crystals of Citrine.

Jophiel is the Archangel of Wisdom and works with the angels from the Halls of Wisdom. His ray is often called the sunshine ray. His name means 'Beauty of God'.

Archangel Jophiel's ray helps you develop a fresh approach to life, bringing back enchantment and pleasure. Jophiel builds connections to align you to your higher self through the multitude of dimensions; he can be thought of as a cosmic ladder. He can instantly help you recover soul fragments that may have been scattered by shock, fright or severe illness.

Jophiel's gifts include the wisdom flame, intuition, perception, joy, bliss and soul illumination. Invoke Jophiel when your creativity needs a boost to prevent feelings of low self-esteem, inertia or mental fog. He helps you absorb new information. His wisdom flame can be invoked to help you in any situation that needs clear mental perception, discrimination or inspiration.

Physical associations Parts of the body: pancreas, solar plexus, liver, gall-bladder, spleen, middle stomach, nervous system, digestive system and skin.

Fortifies, brightens, tones, stimulates, and reinforces energy. Strengthens weak body processes. Breaks down cellulite and removes toxins. Renews your *joie de vivre*. Colour therapists use it to heal arthritis, joint stiffness and immobility.

Emotional and mental associations Mental agility and learning enhancement. Wisdom and intellectual stimulant. Concentration aid. Brings stable uplift, freedom, laughter and joy. Increases self-control. Raises self-esteem and brings feelings of total well-being. Stimulates conversation and can also enhance communication. Prevents shyness, gives courage. Prevents mental confusion.

Spiritual associations Brings soul illumination; strengthens the connection with the higher self, guides and angels. Assists in recovering soul fragments that have become detached through illness or depression.

Yellow is used to summon the Archangel Jophiel in order to bring clarity and wisdom.

Green Ray

Archangel Raphael

Colour *Emerald green* • **Focus** *Healing and harmony*
Chakra *Heart* (anahata) – *element of air – balance expressed as unconditional love for ourselves and others*

The fourth of the visible rainbow spectrum, the Green Ray influences the Heart Chakra on the physical level (third dimension), and is the transmuting ray for the Third Eye Chakra (fourth dimension). It is the fifth spiritual ray and is perceived as a shimmering emerald green, like the best-quality faceted emerald crystals.

Archangel Raphael is the healing aspect of the Lord. He is known as the physician of the angelic realm, the divine healer for healing ourselves and for helping to find the inner guidance, love, compassion, balance and inspiration to heal others.

Raphael is one of the seven ruling angels or princes. He is one of only three angels recognized by the Christian Church, along with Michael and Gabriel. He is also known as the chief of the guardian angels, and patron of travellers. He is often depicted carrying a caduceus or as a pilgrim carrying a staff in one hand and a bowl of healing balm in the other. As over-lighting angel of healing, Archangel Raphael has the capacity to guide us in all our healing work – whether orthodox or complementary.

Physical associations Green is the colour of nature and sits exactly in the

Green can be used to summon Archangel Raphael to bring healing and balance.

nature and the Devic kingdoms and is the ray of great healers and healing. The Green Ray is used to heal tension headaches and migraines, gastric ulcers, digestive upsets, and all stress including extremely agitated emotional states. It helps ease heart, lung and thymus problems.

middle of the colour spectrum. It equalizes, calms and relaxes. Encourages personal growth by bringing harmony. Keeps mental and physical energy dynamically balanced. Releases painful tensed-up processes. It is attuned to

Emotional and mental associations Eases claustrophobia and feelings of restriction. Stabilizes the nervous system, soothes emotions, reduces mental confusion. Soothes all the senses. Aids development of healthy relationships with others.

Spiritual associations Develops divine vision, intuition and also insight through balance and harmony. Enhances creative visualization and manifestation techniques.

Blue Ray

Archangel Michael

Colour *Sapphire blue* • **Focus** *Communication*

Chakra *Throat* (visuddha) – *element of ether – balance expressed as easy communication with ourselves and others on all levels*

The fifth ray of the visible rainbow spectrum, the Blue Ray influences the Throat Chakra on the physical level (third dimension), and is the transmuting ray for the Throat Chakra (fourth dimension). It is the first spiritual ray.

Mighty Archangel Michael is the protector of humanity, the supreme incorruptible commander-in-chief of all the archangels, and he leads the heavenly forces – his 'legions of light' – against evil. His main colour is sun-yellow; in fact, the fiery power of the solar plexus is his domain, but because he carries a sword made of a sapphire, blue flame he is often associated with the empowerment and development of the Throat and Third Eye Chakras. The Blue Ray represents the power and will of God, as well as the powers of faith, protection and truth. As the warrior of God, he is often portrayed slaying a dragon.

Physical associations Parts of the body: throat, thyroid and parathyroid, upper lungs, jaw, base of the skull and body weight.

Soothes, restrains, inhibits and calms hot conditions. Reduces fevers and regulates hyperactivity, inflammatory and derailing processes; brings clarity and serenity. Eases ear and throat infections.

Eases stiff necks and stiff-neck attitudes. Natural pain-reliever. Lowers high blood pressure and heart rate. Calms the central nervous system, which reduces stress. Good for the sickroom and for those who are terminally ill.

Emotional and mental associations Combats fear of speaking the truth. Calms the mind, which helps you think more clearly. Brings peace and detachment from worldly concerns.

Spiritual associations Inspires you to become a seeker of higher truth and hidden knowledge. The Blue Ray represents the power and will of God, and carries the power of faith and protection. It helps us develop the surrendering of our little will (ego) to the higher will of God, so it can be used for developing devotion.

Blue can be used to summon Archangel Michael for protection and enhanced communication skills.

Indigo Ray

Archangel Raziel

Colour *Indigo* • Focus *Intuition and insight*

Chakra *Third Eye* (ajna) – *element of* avyakta *(primordial cloud of undifferentiated light) – balance expressed as intuition, clairvoyance, clairaudience, clairsentience*

Indigo is the sixth ray of the physical visible rainbow spectrum and the fourth-dimension transmuting ray of the Throat Chakra. It is a key to the development of latent psychic abilities and aids conscious connection to the 'spirit'.

Raziel is the archangel of the secret mysteries, whose name means 'the secret of God'. He gives divine information by allowing us to glimpse the enigma that is God. This experience takes our consciousness beyond the confines of time, so any glimpses of this level of existence will show past, present and future as the eternal now. According to sacred lore, Archangel Raziel stands daily on Mount Horeb, proclaiming the secrets of men to all mankind.

Raziel's knowledge is total, absolute, unequivocal and perfect. When we receive these amazing 'insights' we need no confirmation of our 'understanding' from others. Our Crown Chakra is opened, the flames of enlightenment descend, and we can transcend normal reality. These encounters with Raziel can seem extreme to our friends, family, work colleagues and even society in general, but once you have sure and certain knowledge of the workings of the Divine nothing will ever be the same again!

Indigo can be used to summon Archangel Raziel for enhancing intuition.

Physical associations Parts of the body: pituitary gland, skeleton, lower brain, eyes and sinuses.

Strongest painkiller of the rainbow spectrum. Releases negativity from the skeletal structure. Kills bacteria in food, water and air. Clears pollution on all levels. Ameliorates chronic sinus complaints. Eases insomnia, bronchitis, asthma and lung conditions. Relieves migraine and tension headaches. Ameliorates overactive thyroid conditions. Breaks up tumours and growths. Helps ease kidney complaints, controls diarrhoea. Lowers high blood pressure. Ameliorates back problems, especially sciatica, lumbago and any spinal complaint. Indigo can be addictive since it offers relief from everyday problems and difficult experiences.

Emotional and mental associations Sedates the conscious mind which acts as tranquillizer to the emotions. Creates internal communication. Helps you focus on personal issues – self-awareness, self-understanding and self-knowledge. It is used to treat obsession and all forms of emotional instability.

Spiritual associations Astral antiseptic, clears negative thought forms. Allows subtle impressions to be registered, aids telepathic abilities, intuition, clairvoyance, clairaudience, clairsentience. Increases spiritual knowledge. Indigo is the domain of mystery and psychic understanding; it is the ray of artists and also the acting profession.

Violet Ray

Archangel Zadkiel

Colour *Violet* • **Focus** *Self-transformation, spiritual growth, cosmic alchemy*
Chakra *Crown* (sahasrara) – *element of cosmic energy – balance expressed as cosmic consciousness, cosmic awareness, discernment and understanding*

Highest vibration in the rainbow, Violet is the seventh ray and has the shortest wavelength. It is also the fastest: as such, it symbolizes a transition point between the visible and the invisible to the normal human vision – therefore it has always represented divine alchemy and transmutation of energy from the gross physical into the Divine.

Archangel Zadkiel is the angel of mercy or benevolence. He is also known as 'the holy one', who teaches trust in God and the benevolence of God. He brings comfort in our hour of need. He is regent of Jupiter and of Thursday. He is often portrayed holding a dagger since he was the angel who stopped Abraham from sacrificing his son Isaac on Mount Moriah. He is leader of the angelic order of Dominions and one of the seven great angelic beings who stands before the throne of God. In the book *Ozar Midrashim* 11,316, by J. D. Eisenstein he is called *Kaddisha* and listed as one of the guardians of the gates of the east wind.

Physical associations Parts of the body: pineal gland, top of the head, crown, brain, scalp.

Ameliorates internal inflammation. Eases heart palpitations. Aids the correct function of the immune system. Ameliorates bruises, swellings and black eyes. Eases eye problems and eye strain. Soothes irritations, relieves pain, speeds up the healing process.

Emotional and mental associations Calms emotional turbulence, aids emotional recovery. Ameliorates addictions and addictive traits within the personality. Removes emotional obstacles.

Spiritual associations Inspires, frees the imagination, aids meditation, enhances psychic abilities and develops the intuition. Brings spiritual dedication and meaningful dreams. Used for past-life regression. Helps develop the Crown Chakra, aids soul connection and development and opens the gateway to higher mind. Gives psychic protection. Enables you to 'see' visions. Cleanses and purifies anything it touches, making it an all-encompassing mind and body healer.

The Violet Ray can summon Archangel Zadkiel for spiritual transformation.

Colour Meditation with Angels of the Seven Rays

Purpose *A rainbow tonic to determine which colour ray you are most in need of to bring balance*

If you have a need for a particular colour, work with the archangel who directs that ray. You may use the colour breath to fill the whole body or just part of the body. This applies to pain or any area of the body that particularly needs healing. You could just invoke the Angel of the Ray of the colour to which you are intuitively drawn.

Rainbows are symbols of hope, fortune and angelic joy in our world.

HOW TO PRACTISE THE MEDITATION

WHAT TO DO

1 Make yourself comfortable in a chair. Allow your eyes to close.

2 Begin breathing deeply, consciously relaxing every part of your body.

3 Once relaxed, invoke Archangel Zadkiel to fill the air around you with the colour violet.

4 Breathe in for the count of three, visualizing yourself inhaling the colour violet as you do. Visualize this strongly. Actually see yourself pulling the colour in through your nose out of the air, and watch it going into your body.

5 Hold your colour breath for the count of three, then exhale for the count of three. Repeat twice more. This will complete the first three-breath colour cycle.

6 Now invoke Archangel Raziel to fill the air around you with the colour indigo.

7 Breathe in for the count of three, visualizing yourself inhaling the colour indigo as you do. Again, see yourself pulling the colour in through your nose out of the air, and watch it going into your body.

8 Hold your colour breath for the count of three, then exhale for the count of three. Repeat twice more. This will complete the second three-breath colour cycle.

9 Continue with this process of three-breath cycles, invoking each Angel of the Ray and the appropriate colour.

10 When you have finished the process, you can either concentrate on breathing in clear white light, or just relax and allow your body to come back very slowly.

White Ray

Archangel Metatron

Colour *White light (brilliance)* • **Focus** *Spiritual evolution, enlightenment, light body activation and ascension* • **Chakra** *Soul Star*

The Soul Star Chakra is known as the 'seat of the soul' and is situated about a hand's length above your head. Sometimes referred to as the eighth chakra, it is the first of the non-physical chakras or transcendental chakras above your head. The Soul Star Chakra contains information relating to your soul; once this transcendental chakra is activated by Archangel Metatron, key information is then downloaded into your lower chakra system which initiates the process known as 'light body activation', 'ascension into cosmic consciousness' or enlightenment.

White light is the supreme ray. It contains and reflects all colours, even colours our human sight cannot perceive.

Invoking Archangel Metatron and using his white ray of brilliance brings unprecedented spiritual growth. His vortex of light is so luminous and vast that we often perceive him as a pillar of fire more dazzling than the Sun. He is the light Moses saw as the Burning Bush before being given the ten commandments. He is the light St Paul encountered on the road to Damascus. In fact, he is the light often seen by those who have had 'near-death experiences'.

Physical associations Parts of the body: all areas. Restores vibrancy, used as a 'cure-all'. It is the most versatile and harmonizing of all the rays.

Emotional and mental associations Cleanses and balances the emotions. Brings inner peace and tranquillity. It allows us to 'wipe the slate clean'. Dissolves emotional debris. Refines the emotions.

Spiritual associations Multi-dimensional. Brings spiritual growth to those who use it. Prepares the 'physical' third-dimensional chakras as corresponding states of awareness for spiritual enlightenment.

Brilliant white light is the supreme ray of the Archangel Metatron.

Pink Ray

Archangel Chamuel

Colour *Pink* • **Focus** *Relationships* • **Chakra** *Heart* (anahata) – *element of air – developing the higher emotions*

The balanced Pink Ray is the union of Heaven and Earth made manifest within the human heart. It is the product of the marriage of the physical Red Ray with the White Ray of spiritual awakening and fullness.

Archangel Chamuel helps renew and improve your loving, caring relationships with others by helping to develop the Heart Chakra. This is accomplished through the beautiful Pink Ray that represents our ability to love and nurture others, to be able to give and receive love, unconditionally free from all self-interest. It is a love that transcends and transforms the self and moves us through compassion towards the divine state of emotional maturity. Many people are afraid of opening their Heart Chakra. Those who have been able to overcome this fear have charismatic warmth that others find reassuring, soothing and uplifting.

Archangel Chamuel assists us in all of our relationships, and especially through life-changing relationship situations such as conflict, divorce, bereavement or even job loss. Archangel Chamuel helps us to appreciate the existing loving relationships we already have in our lives. His message is: 'It is only the love energy within any given purpose that gives lasting value and benefit to all creation.'

Physical associations Parts of the body: heart, shoulders, lungs, arms, hands and skin.

Heals any part of your body you have rejected or judge unlovely or unlovable. Eases physical tension and psychosomatic illness. Also useful where disease has been diagnosed and fear is blocking physical recovery.

Emotional and mental associations The Pink Ray is concerned with building confidence and self-esteem. It quickly dissolves the negative emotions of self-condemnation, low self-worth, self-loathing and selfishness. It ignites 'inner' happiness by showing you your unique talents and abilities and helps you nurture these attributes and value yourself. Stops depression, compulsive behaviour and destructive tendencies.

Spiritual associations Opens the Heart Chakra to develop healing gifts. Attracts soulmates, those with whom you can share your innermost thoughts and feelings. Prepares you to receive the Christ-consciousness, the Holy Spirit.

The delicate Pink Ray of Archangel Chamuel ignites happiness and prepares you to receive the Christ-consciousness.

Turquoise Ray

Archangel Haniel

Colour *Turquoise* • **Focus** *Self-expression through higher feelings and emotions – soul expression* • **Chakra** *Thymus – also known as the witness point or Higher Heart Chakra*

Turquoise is a balanced blend of green and blue. It helps to develop our unique individuality. It is the New Age colour of the Age of Aquarius that encourages us to seek spiritual knowledge.

Haniel is the archangel of divine communication through clear perception. He is a warrior angel; his authority assists you to fulfil your soul's mission, which is to praise, honour, love and reunite with God by using and trusting in your own great God-connectedness; this will inspire others, too. Invoke Archangel Haniel's Turquoise Ray to give you strength and perseverance when you feel weak. He will guide you through visions, personal revelations and angelic coincidences. Haniel is the protector of your soul. He provides you with the virtue of determination and supplies you with the energy required for you to fulfil your Dharma (which means gaining enlightenment by releasing illusion).

Turquoise invokes the essence of *shunyata*, the infinite blue emptiness radiating in all directions, absolutely clear, pristine and glorious. Through this blue sky stretching out to infinity, we can gain an understanding of the expansiveness and true soul freedom which could be ours if only we did not allow our horizons to become narrow and limited.

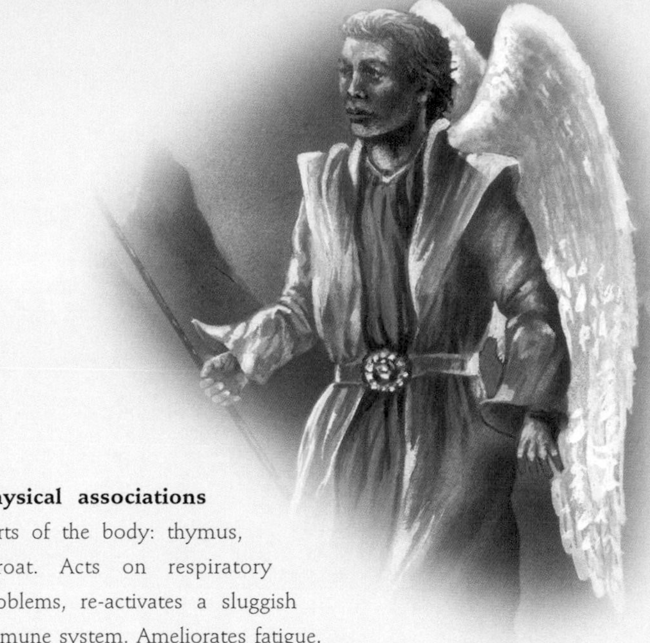

Physical associations
Parts of the body: thymus, throat. Acts on respiratory problems, re-activates a sluggish immune system. Ameliorates fatigue, weight problems, allergies, diabetes, heart disease, high blood pressure, sore throat, stiff neck, asthma, tension headaches, nervous complaints and dizziness.

Emotional and mental associations
Brings emotional freedom, confidence and inner strength. Calms the nerves and is a natural tranquillizer. Ameliorates emotional turmoil by balancing the emotions. Centring, eases panic attacks. Promotes heartfelt communication.

Throughout the history of mankind, turquoise stones have been used as amulets of protection.

Spiritual associations Widens our spiritual horizons and overcomes life's obstacles (even dark forces of negativity). Provides the spiritual armour necessary for soul salvation and soul freedom. Purifies the Throat Chakra. Enhances channelling and communication with spirit guides and angels. Heightens intuition and provides spiritual solace.

Lilac Ray

Archangel Tzaphkiel

Colour *Lilac* • **Focus** *Activating the Angelic Chakra – accessing angelic guidance*
Chakra *Angelic – also known as the Fifth Eye Chakra*

There are two very important chakras situated above the Third Eye Chakra. One is the Fourth Eye Chakra. Its Sanskrit name is *Soma,* which means water. It balances the fire of the Solar Plexus Chakra, bringing balance and harmony when it has been activated (see page 140 for the Sun and Moon in Harmony meditation). The Fifth Eye Chakra, which is situated at the top of the forehead, is called *Lalata* in Sanskrit. In the New Age movement it is often referred to as the Angelic Chakra. When awakened and fully activated it allows you not only to become master of your own destiny but also to have profound angelic contact on a daily basis.

The Angelic Chakra has a natural resonance with the very pale shade of lilac. It is the Violet Ray of spiritual transformation perfectly imbued with the white ray of spiritual purity.

Archangel Tzaphkiel is the angel of deep contemplation of God, representing the divine feminine watery aspect of creation. Tzaphkiel nurtures all things and give glimpses of other realities. She bestows blessings that are designed through faith to increase understanding by imparting wisdom which increases spiritual growth. Archangel Tzaphkiel casts out all that is superficial to spiritual development. She increases insight, mysticism and discernment by helping to

The delicate Lilac Ray of Archangel Tzaphkiel allows us to access angelic guidance.

fully develop the feminine side of your nature, but she will do this only if you ask to be reborn into a new level of consciousness which allows your heart to open fully and your soul's purity to be made manifest.

Physical associations Balances and harmonizes any area of the physical body. Clears blockages and eases tension headaches.

Emotional and mental associations Reduces restlessness, irritation and worry. Used for deep emotional healing work, bringing peace to a troubled mind. Lilac releases the thoughts, impressions and imprints of others. Aids objectivity and concentration. Supportive; helps to release addictions and addictive traits within the personality.

Spiritual associations Helps with inner and outer journeys, altered states of reality, deep meditation. Gateway to the unknown. Links to the angelic realm. Dissolves spiritual disease and old patterns of karma.

The Transmuting Rays of the Fourth Dimension

Archangel Melchizedek helps you to develop your 'Light Body' or 'Merkavah Body of Light' as part of seeking enlightenment. People on Earth who seek to raise their vibration through spiritual practices are said to be embarking on the 'Ascension Process'.

The Angels of the Rays, the seven archangels, direct the vital life-force of God to develop the physical or third-dimensional chakra system.

In this section we begin to develop our chakra centres and shift our awareness to become spiritually aware (which is the fourth dimension). Rather than existing as physical beings that have the occasional spiritual experience, it helps us to identify with our true nature. As we evolve spiritually, our physical body and our third-dimensional chakra system and frequency also evolve and we become 'lightworkers'.

A lightworker is someone who is aware that they have a spiritual higher purpose. They are not materialistic and are aware of the spiritual realms of the angels and seek to heal

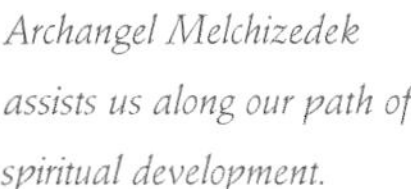

Archangel Melchizedek assists us along our path of spiritual development.

themselves, others and the environment using subtle healing energy. Lightworkers are aware of the interconnectedness of all life, and that self-healing and self-awareness are the path not only to spiritual liberation for themselves, but also to all sentient life.

This spiritual evolution into a lightworker causes a thinning of the 'veil' between dimensions. But, to become fully aware of the higher dimensions and activate our 'Merkavah Body of Light', we use the transmuting rays of the fourth-dimensional chakra system. This section explains the meditation that calls down the transmuting rays of the fourth dimension to anchor the fourth-dimensional chakra rays into your physical third-dimensional body.

Melchizedek is the angel who assists you and oversees the process. The colours are different because they are the transmuting rays of the chakras used for spiritual development.

Transmuting rays, colours and properties

Chakra	*Third (3rd)*	*Transmuting ray (4th)*	*Properties of ray*
Root	*Red*	*White*	*Purification, Resurrection*
Sacral	*Orange*	*Violet*	*Freedom, Forgiveness*
Solar Plexus	*Yellow*	*Ruby*	*Devotion, Peace*
Heart	*Green*	*Pink*	*Adoration, Divine Love*
Throat	*Blue*	*Indigo*	*Mystery, Miracles*
Third Eye	*Indigo*	*Emerald-green*	*Divine Vision*
Crown	*Violet*	*White-gold*	*Illumination, Wisdom*

Meditation to Anchor the Fourth-dimensional Chakra Rays

Purpose *Brings down the transmuting rays of the fourth dimension and anchors them into your physical third-dimensional body and chakra system*

Archangel Melchizedek transmits to humanity the 'Key to the Kingdom' encoded in light frequencies which penetrate the human body. To become aware of the higher dimensions, you can use this meditation to call down the transmuting rays of the fourth-dimensional chakra system.

HOW TO PRACTISE THE MEDITATION

WHAT TO DO

1 Make yourself comfortable in a chair. Allow your eyes to close. Begin breathing deeply, consciously relaxing every part of your body.

2 Once relaxed, invoke Archangel Melchizedek, the guardian of the White-gold Ray, to guide, protect and oversee the process. Ask him to send down the fourth-dimensional transmuting rays in order, starting at the Root Chakra and working upwards to the Crown Chakra.

3 Starting with the White Ray, allow it to fill the Root Chakra. Allow the energy to flow at its own pace; do not try to control the energy, allow it to find its own place of balance. Once all energy movement has ceased, you are ready to receive the next ray.

4 Next, allow the Violet Ray of the Sacral Chakra to descend and fill this energy centre. As before, allow the process to develop and find its own balance. Once all energy movement has ceased, you are ready to receive the next ray.

5 Continue in this way with: the Ruby Ray of the Solar Plexus Chakra; the Pink Ray of the Heart Chakra; the Indigo Ray of the Throat Chakra; the Emerald-green Ray of the Third Eye Chakra; and finally the White-gold Ray of the Crown Chakra. As each ray descends you will feel it developing the chakra centre to which it relates.

6 When you have finished the process, concentrate on breathing in the white-gold light of Melchizedek to cleanse, harmonize and integrate all your subtle-energy channels, your own personal labyrinth. The practice of circulating the white-gold light of Melchizedek increases our internal light or spiritual illumination, leading to enhanced sensitivity and an awareness of all that is mystical in nature.

The Transmuting Rays of the Fifth Dimension Meditation

Purpose *To develop greater spiritual gifts and understanding of the refined subtle-energy vibrations that are available to spiritual seekers*

Once you have anchored and developed your fourth-dimensional chakra system, you are ready to undertake this meditation, which brings down the transmuting rays of the fifth dimension and anchors them into your physical third-dimensional body and chakra system.

The fifth dimension is just beyond the fourth and has a more refined vibration than the fourth dimension. Each higher dimension's energy frequency is more and more subtle and refined. As we become aware of these higher dimensions, we acquire greater understanding of the nature of the universe, develop greater spiritual gifts and perhaps draw a step closer to the ascension path, which draws us closer to God.

HOW TO PRACTISE THE MEDITATION

WHAT TO DO

1 Make yourself comfortable in a chair. Close your eyes.

2 Invoke Archangel Metatron, guardian of the White Ray of brilliance, to guide and protect you. Ask him to send down the fifth-dimensional transmuting rays in order, starting at the Root Chakra and working up to the Crown Chakra. As each ray descends, you will feel it growing in the chakra to which it relates.

3 When you have finished the process, focus on breathing in the white diamond light of Archangel Metatron to cleanse, harmonize and integrate all your subtle-energy channels. Feel yourself surrounded by a host of angels as information is fully integrated into your chakra centres.

Fifth-dimension transmuting rays

Chakra	*Third (3rd)*	*Transmuting ray (5th)*	*Properties of ray*
Root	*Red*	*Platinum*	*Divine Alignment*
Sacral	*Orange*	*Magenta*	*Creativity*
Solar Plexus	*Yellow*	*Gold*	*Connection*
Heart	*Green*	*White*	*Christ-consciousness*
Throat	*Blue*	*Violet*	*Channel Energy*
Third Eye	*Indigo*	*White-gold*	*Balancing Brain*
Crown	*Violet*	*Clear*	*Illumination, Wisdom*

Colours from the Natural Environment

Archangel Sandalphon

Colour *Nature's colours* • **Focus** *Environmental awareness – personal and global responsibility*
Chakra *Earth Star – situated beneath your feet – the depth varies from person to person depending on how well grounded you are in your spiritual practice*

Nature has furnished us with all the colours displayed in the multitude of trees, plants, flowers and crystals. When we use nature's colours to heal ourself and the environment, we naturally tune into the energy of Archangel Sandalphon because he is guardian of the Earth and responsible for the welfare of human kind. Sandalphon is in charge of Earth healing and distance healing.

According to S. L. Mathers in the book *Greater Keys of Solomon*, Sandalphon is the 'left-hand feminine cherub of the ark'. He is considered a very 'tall' angel and Archangel Metatron's twin reflection of the Divine. As twins they are the Alpha and Omega, the beginning and the end: their presence also reminds us of the esoteric expression 'as above so below'.

Physical associations Increases prana life-force and aids physical vitality. Helps to integrate healing energy within the physical body, which is vital if stability and balance are to be maintained. Often healing energy is not fully accepted and assimilated, which means that it dissipates and has no lasting benefit.

Archangel Sandalphon uses Mother Nature's colours to heal us and our world.

Strengthens the immune system. Helps children to express their imaginative creativity.

Emotional and mental associations Increases prana which aids mental clarity and acumen. Instils and nurtures emotional maturity. Allows us to 'see' to the heart of the problem and take personal responsibility for our own actions and emotions. It also eases stress and psychological over-dependence on people, food, alcohol, tobacco and other addictive substances.

Spiritual associations Brings grounding to your spiritual practice. Shamans and others who work with natural magic use this energy. It is valuable for unifying the whole self by releasing the energy of alienation and fragmentation.

Meditation on Nature's Use of Colour

Purpose *To connect you via Archangel Sandalphon to the Earth – this cleanses your connection to the Earth and renews your physical body by increasing prana energy – it also helps you to develop a grounded spirituality, environmental awareness and a sense of personal and global responsibility*

Working with Archangel Sandalphon includes having respect for and being involved with all life on Earth. It is the shamanic path to enlightenment. Archangel Sandalphon awakens you from the trance state you may have been living in. Most people have a reality coloured by illusion, memory, conditioning, experience and the conscious mind.

The Earth Star Chakra, when fully activated, looks clairvoyantly like Rainbow Haematite, black with dazzling rainbows.

HOW TO PRACTISE THE MEDITATION

WHAT TO DO

1 Clear and dedicate a space for this meditation (see pages 18–19).

2 Sit in a comfortable steady posture; if you cannot sit cross-legged on the floor, sit on a straight-backed chair with your feet flat on the floor.

3 Invoke Archangel Sandalphon to bless, protect and oversee the meditation.

4 Visualize or feel roots growing out of the Root Chakra at the base of your spine if you are sitting on the floor or from the soles of both of your feet if you are sitting in a chair.

5 Allow your roots to connect you to your Earth Star Chakra; see it begin to glow and pulse with life-force.

Stonehenge is an Earth magic site where our ancestors celebrated the changing seasons.

6 Allow your roots to go down deeper into the Earth. Keep sending them down, deeper and deeper, until your roots reach the crystal at the very centre of the Earth. This etheric crystal is made from carbon and is a dazzling diamond containing all the colours you can imagine.

7 Draw this diamond energy upwards through your root system, feeling it rising higher and higher, until it touches your Earth Star Chakra. There it causes your Earth Star Chakra to blaze with all the colours that are imaginable.

8 Allow the energy to flow into your physical body, feel it nurturing every cell, every molecule, until your whole being is filled with rainbow light.

9 Allow yourself plenty of time to come back slowly to normal everyday awareness.

Metallic Rays

Silver Ray This ray is feminine (yin) in nature, soothing and comforting. It relates to the lunar energies of Archangel Auriel and angels of the Moon. The Silver Ray allows us to see ourselves in a different light. It illuminates and reflects energy: it is fluid, soft, yielding and a natural tranquillizer. The Silver Ray helps to balance the fluid functions of the body as well as the female hormones. This ray also governs the feminine right side of the brain. It helps you use your intuition and analyse your feelings and instincts.

Gold Ray Powerful and masculine (yang) in nature, the Gold Ray relates to the energy of the Sun and solar angels. The Sun has some positive physiological effects on humans, making us feel happy and positive when we are exposed to it. This ray clears parasitic energies and stops unwanted outside energy from influencing us, allowing us to remain

Amber (fossilized tree resin) set in ornate silver-work is worn to draw down the effects of the Silver Ray, which balances, illuminates and reflects energy.

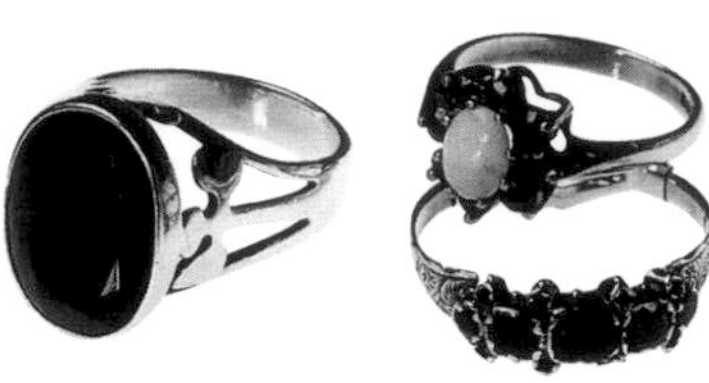

beyond corruption. It also helps with masculine, left-brain situations, where logic and systematic thought processes are required, and helps us take appropriate action.

Crystals set in silver and gold – silver reflects the feminine principle and gold reflects the masculine in nature.

Copper Ray Very feminine in nature, but in a different way from silver, the Copper Ray is the dynamic, vigorous, primal aspect of the feminine psyche. It carries the energies of renewal, creativity, birth and the female womb. The Copper Ray allows us to bring our dreams and desires to reality, especially if we tune into the energy of the great Earth Mother or Grandmother Energy. It holds ancient memories and creative power beyond our limited human understanding. It helps us to make life-changing decisions that make our dreams a reality.

Platinum Ray Masculine in nature, but in a different way from gold, the Platinum Ray brings healing to the male aspect of our personality. It helps overcome anger and aggression and releases pent-up fiery emotions. It transmutes competitive aggression into peaceful cooperation. The Platinum Ray is very piercing, penetrating, focused and pristine. It can reflect aggressive negative energy back to its source and exposes the untrue. It is very cleansing to the human energy system and the environment, giving us the skills required to flourish in the storm of chaos.

Meditation on the Sun and Moon in Harmony

Purpose *To harmonize the male and female aspects – balancing the right- and left-brain hemispheres to activate the Fourth Eye Chakra*

This meditation can appear complicated as you have to focus first on the Sacral Chakra, then move the energy you have created (life-force) up your spiritual spine (subtle-energy channel which runs from your perineum up to the top of your head) into the Fourth Eye Chakra, which is situated on your forehead just above your Third Eye Chakra. Here you visualize a full silver Moon disk over your left eye and a golden Sun disk over your right eye.

Silver Ray relates to the lunar energies of Archangel Auriel and angels of the Moon while Golden Ray relates to the energy of Archangel Camael and other solar angels.

The Moon is our closest celestial neighbour and influences the tides in the waters of the Earth.

HOW TO PRACTISE THE MEDITATION

WHAT TO DO

1 Invoke Archangels Camael and Auriel for blessings and protection. Sit in a comfortable steady meditation posture.

2 Focus your attention on your Sacral Chakra (your pelvis) and with each breath inwards imagine or feel your Sacral Chakra filling with life-force energy. As you inhale, breathe deeply, drawing the breath into the belly by expanding and pushing out the muscles; as you exhale, pull in the lower abdomen.

3 Once you have built up this energy (it should look/feel like an inflated orange balloon), use the power of your intent (will) to allow the energy to spiral upwards to your Third Eye Chakra.

4 Keep your focused intent on your Third Eye Chakra and become aware of the Fourth Eye Chakra. Visualize or see a silver lunar disk over your physical left eye and a golden solar disk over your physical right eye.

5 Allow these two disks to harmonize and balance. As they do, they transform into one central disk the colour of white-gold in position on your Fourth Eye Chakra.

6 Stay with this harmonious energy for as long as you like.

7 To finish the meditation, allow the harmonious energy you have created to flow though all your subtle-energy channels and aura (to cleanse and purify). Allow yourself some time to return to everyday awareness.

Meditation on Creativity and Soul Harmony

Purpose *To harmonize creativity with the soul's purpose for reincarnation*

Often we do not find our true path in life because we have been influenced when young into pursuing the wrong career. Once you find your true creative talent, your life flows smoothly and with ease. During times of stress, depression or despair, people call out to the angels for help. The angelic assistance offered may be to suggest a radical life change. Maybe you have the soul of an artist, designer, writer or poet. Maybe you wish to travel or live in a different country. Or maybe you need to live closer to the land and grow your own food. Everything is possible; do not let your fear kill your soul. Allow your dreams to manifest and watch miracles happen in your life.

HOW TO PRACTISE THE MEDITATION

YOU WILL NEED

Pen or pencil and paper

WHAT TO DO

1 Call on Archangel Uriel for blessings, protection and to oversee the process. Ask for illumination on your path through life and tell him you seek your soul's mission for incarnating in this lifetime.

2 Sit in a comfortable steady meditation posture with pen and paper close to hand in order to write down the information you receive. Focus on your breathing to relax.

3 Massage your Solar Plexus Chakra, both front and back, using clockwise circular movements, until you feel a strong tingling sensation.

4 Move your awareness to your Crown Chakra at the top of your head and visualize or feel a beautiful sphere of golden light entering your Crown. This sphere of light is sent to you by Archangel Uriel.

5 Move the golden sphere to your Solar Plexus Chakra. Allow yourself to absorb the golden sphere.

6 When you feel ready, write down exactly as it is given to you what your true path in life is. It is very important not to change or modify what you are given; just allow the words to flow onto the paper.

7 Give thanks to Archangel Uriel for your heavenly new life! Allow some time to return to everyday awareness.

Certain trees have specific planetary associations and are used for healing. Oak is used for strength.

Meditation on the Violet Flame of Transformation

Purpose *To transform lower energies into positive life-affirming energy*

This meditation draws on angelic help of Archangel Zadkiel, guardian of the Violet Flame of Transformation. Zadkiel's Violet Flame has the highest vibrational frequency which, when summoned, brings soul freedom and joy by releasing you from your limiting behaviour, concepts and karmic miasms (see page 270), including past-life memories that may have been carried over to this lifetime.

This flame purifies the chakra centres, giving relief from addictions and addictive traits. It works as an amplifier of healing and spiritual energies. When directed by Archangel Zadkiel it will break down blocked or stagnant energies caused by anger, hatred, resentment, bitterness, jealousy, intolerance, blame, fear and guilt. It gives protection from over-indulgence, miasms which have lodged in the emotional body.

The colour violet is the doorway to the unseen realms and purifier of the chakra centres.

HOW TO PRACTISE THE MEDITATION

WHAT TO DO

1 Sit in a meditation posture. Focus on your breathing, allowing your body to relax.

2 Once relaxed, call on Archangel Zadkiel, saying: 'Archangel Zadkiel, direct the energy of the Violet Flame of Transformation into all areas of my body and aura until I am purified of all negativity and I stand in my mighty I AM presence.'

3 Relax and let yourself be enveloped in the potent energy of the Violet Flame. Enjoy the magnificent experience as you feel your body and aura gently bathed and purified as the Violet Flame transmutes all that is negative and cleanses all areas of your mind, body and aura. Feel it instantly purifying all the chakra centres, giving relief from addictions and addictive personality traits.

4 Feel it breaking down and transforming blocks, stagnant or stuck energies. Allow it to calm your mind and activate the divine spark within you, thereby aiding spiritual growth and transmuting negative karma.

5 When you see the Violet Flame diminishing, the meditation is over. Allow yourself sufficient time to come back to everyday waking consciousness.

Violet candles aid spiritual development and give protection from lower astral entities.

Meditation on the Pink Flame Heart-star

Purpose *To summon Archangel Chamuel and the angels of love to develop your Heart Chakra*

This meditation to develop your Heart Chakra is vital in making a solid and true contact with your angels, and allows you to communicate with them at a higher level of awareness. Archangel Chamuel has loving relationships as his focus. Meditation naturally creates a channel for the angelic forces to flow, allowing our consciousness to merge effortlessly with theirs. Soothing music and a pink candle will enhance this meditation.

The traditional symbol for the Heart Chakra is a 12-petalled lotus flower with an inner centre containing two intersecting triangles called *trikonas* in Sanskrit; they make up a perfect six-pointed star. The Heart-star symbolizes spirit descending into matter and matter ascending towards spirit. This is the 'star' you are going to activate within your heart during this meditation.

Rose Quartz heart, a symbol of eternal love.

The traditional Hindu sound for the Heart Chakra is the *bija* mantra 'YAM' (pronounced ee-am). Use it to activate the Heart-star during the meditation.

HOW TO PRACTISE THE MEDITATION

YOU WILL NEED

A pink candle
Soothing angelic music

WHAT TO DO

1 Light your candle and put on the music you have chosen.

2 Sit in a comfortable steady meditation posture. Focus on your breathing, allow your body to relax. Let your out-breath be a little longer and slower than your in-breath.

3 Allow peaceful openness and acceptance to flow through you.

4 Permit your consciousness to transcend the earthly level.

5 Summon Archangel Chamuel and the angels of love to surround you with their hallowed pink light. Feel the atmosphere around you becoming warm and intimate.

6 Gently touch your Heart Chakra with your left hand. Visualize the 12 petals of your Heart Chakra opening and, as they open, see your in-dwelling altar (your most sacred point of consciousness).

7 In the centre of your altar see your pink heart flame. Begin to sound the *bija* mantra 'YAM'.

8 Invite the angels of love to dwell in your heart; see the flame change into a beautiful golden-pink six-pointed star. Allow this wonderful energy to flow through your body and aura and then outwards into the world, sending love to everyone who is willing to receive it.

9 Allow yourself sufficient time to come back to everyday waking consciousness once the meditation is over.

ANGEL MEDITATIONS

Meditation Posture

Sit cross-legged in a comfortable steady posture with the spine and neck held erect but not tense, especially if you are meditating for long periods. Put a small, firm cushion beneath the base of the spine so that the psychic current can flow unimpeded from the base of the spine to the top of the head.

You can also lie on your back on the floor. Keep your arms and legs straight but relaxed and cover yourself with a light blanket if you feel cold.

If sitting on a chair, choose a straight-backed chair, place your feet flat on the floor, hands resting palms up on your knees. Do not let your head roll forward because this will restrict your breathing.

Grounding yourself Some people like to ground themselves before and after meditating as it gives a clearer perception of the experience and allows for greater self-control. Ground yourself when sitting in a chair by placing your feet flat on the floor; then visualize strong roots growing out of the soles of your feet anchoring you firmly to the Earth. When sitting in a classic meditation posture, imagine strong roots growing out of the base of your spine and growing down deep into Mother Earth.

Sit upright with your feet placed flat on the floor, hands on knees and your spine erect.

Meditation Space

We all need space to shut out the world. Your room or meditation space should be comfortably warm but well aired, especially if you use candles or incense. Keep it clean and simple; this will heighten your concentration. Colour is very important to the ambience of the room in which you meditate; many people favour the classic simplicity of white, but you might prefer a pale blue, for instance. Create a simple angel altar as a useful spiritual focus, or perhaps have something from nature such as a beautiful crystal close to hand.

Have a regular time and place for your meditation practice; the most conducive times are dawn and dusk. Make yourself comfortable with pillows, cushions, rugs or even a cosy chair. Ensure that you are warm enough; use a blanket to cover yourself if you get cold. Make sure you will not be disturbed during the meditation – allow at least an hour.

A sacred circle Some people create a sacred circle as protection while meditating since it prevents outside unwanted energies influencing the meditator. Place four candles in secure holders in each of the four compass directions, making sure they are placed away from fire hazards. You can use more candles to define the circle, or use the appropriate coloured candles to represent the angel with whom you are working.

Crystals may be used instead of, or as well as, candles. Some people like to stand in the centre of the circle and use their finger or Clear Quartz crystal to draw a circle of light; go clockwise (deosil or sunwise) to create the circle and anti-clockwise to close it.

Preparation

Once you have dedicated a room or a corner of a room as your sacred space, you can begin to make preparations for meditation. There are a number of suggestions below, some or all of which you may find helpful:

- You may wish to light an appropriate coloured candle.
- Purify your energy space with incense, angel sprays or essential oil diffuser.
- Place a drop of essential oil onto one of your palms; then gently rub your hands together. Inhale the fragrance to swiftly transport yourself into an altered state of awareness.
- Play soothing angelic music if it does not distract you too much.
- Flowers are very acceptable as energy offerings to the angels, who also like bells; sounding a small bell at the beginning and end of a meditation is a useful way of acknowledging your sacred time.
- Hold an angelic crystal such as Seraphinite, Angelite, Celestite, Seriphos Green or Angel Aura Quartz.
- Purify your physical body by taking a shower or bath and putting on clean clothes; this can make you feel more receptive and in tune with angels.
- Wear loose cotton clothes which are comfortable and allow freedom of movement. Keep them especially for meditation because each time you wear them it signals to your

Purify your meditation space with angel of light aura essence mist; or light a candle of an appropriate colour.

subconscious mind that you are going into meditation practice.

- Avoid synthetic fabrics since they interfere with the energy flow of the meridian channels, as well as potentially holding negativity within the energy system. Black, dark or drab-coloured clothing will interfere with the meditation session by lowering your vibrational rate.
- Practise mental clarity by clearing away 'psychological debris' and adopting clarity of purpose.

The more you prepare for your meditation sessions the quicker you will attune to the angelic realm. Once you are used to communicating with your angels, you will be able to go instantly to your heart centre and consult with the angels many times a day.

Angelic Alignment

This meditation can bring you into contact with your guardian angel. It is an attunement which will allow you to open up to your angelic guardian. This relationship will place your feet firmly on the road towards enlightenment.

HOW TO PRACTISE THE MEDITATION

WHAT TO DO

1 Sit in a comfortable meditation posture. Relax your body by focusing on your breathing.

2 Once relaxed, imagine you can breathe energy up and down your spine.

3 On the in-breath move Earth energy from the Root Chakra to the Crown Chakra, and on the out-breath move spiritual energy from the Crown to the Root. This technique cleanses and removes energetic blockages.

4 Once you have mastered this technique and your 'spiritual' spine feels clear, bring the energy up your spine as you inhale and send it up to Heaven. With it send gratitude for all the good things in your life. As you do so imagine an overcast day. See the clouds part, as a ray of brilliant white light comes through and settles directly on your head.

5 Absorb that brilliant light into your being through the top of your head. This is your link with the angels.

6 Allow celestial light to pour in through your body; feel it nurturing every cell.

7 Bring in the angelic blessings that are meant for you. Feel this positive energy coursing through your body. Allow it to bathe you internally and externally.

8 Now focus your awareness on your Heart Chakra where the angels most strongly connect with you; visualize it as rose-pink.

9 Allow your consciousness to transcend the ordinary senses and go into a state of heightened awareness. This is your link with an unlimited realm of angelic wisdom.

10 It is now time to make full contact with your angelic guidance. From the deepest centre of your heart where your divine spark dwells, send out your longing for an angel to be your guide.

11 Feel your angel drawing closer. Experience the change as you link into the higher consciousness of the angelic realms.

12 Imagine your angel standing beside you and enfolding you in its wings. Experience the unconditional love your angel is directing towards you.

13 You may wish to ask for guidance or even your angel's name; be still and wait patiently for an answer.

14 To close the session, bring yourself back to everyday waking reality.

Angel Wings Meditation

Those who frequently tune into the angelic realm develop a spiritual aura. This often appears to clairvoyant vision as wings of light. Once we have unfurled our angelic wings they have a number of uses. They attune us instantly to the angelic realm and lighten our vibrational rate, which helps us rise above our troubles. We can wrap ourselves in our wings to give ourselves comfort and protection from unkind energies.

Everyone's wings are different and they are a direct radiance from the divine spark of light which dwells in your Heart Chakra. Some wings appear as feathers, while others have wings of ethereal fibres resembling shimmering starlight. Some wings are huge, extending the full length of the spine (this is normally a sign that all the chakra centres embedded within the spine are in balance). These spinal wings can extend beneath the feet and above the head.

Some people experience their etheric angelic wings as white feathers while others may have wings of fibre like starlight.

HOW TO PRACTISE THE MEDITATION

This meditation is best done standing up.

WHAT TO DO

1 Stand with your bare feet planted firmly on the floor.

2 Raise your arms high above you. As you do so, visualize yourself with your feet standing firmly on the Earth and your head in the highest Heaven. Feel your body connecting Heaven and Earth.

3 Stretch your fingers upwards and, as you do, feel the angelic hands of your guardian angel come downwards; allow them to place their hands in yours. This is a special experience and you may wish to bask in the contact for a few moments as it opens your Heart Chakra.

4 When you are ready, allow your angelic wings to grow out of the space between your shoulder-blades. Feel them growing upwards and outwards. Sense how they feel, and what they look like.

5 Let your wings unfurl fully. However you sense them, allow your body to adjust to the experience of having wings. Often you will feel a shift in your overall energy field as your vibrational rate is raised and you grow accustomed to the experience of having wings.

6 See if you can move your wings.

7 Ask for a blessing to be placed on your wings.

Unfurl your wings and wrap them around you for protection. You may feel a shift in balance as you become familiar with them.

Angel Halo Meditation

This meditation begins to activate the transcendental chakras situated above your head. It begins with the Soul Star Chakra, also known as the 'seat of the soul' or Halo Chakra. Situated about a hand's length above your head, it is sometimes referred to as the eighth chakra. The Soul Star Chakra contains information relating to your soul; once this first transcendental chakra is activated you will automatically define yourself through *gnosis* (enlightenment) rather than external religion and dogma.

The Soul Star Chakra is Moon-white in colour or crystal clear. When fully open and activated it links in a spiral fashion to the other six transcendental chakras situated in a line above your head. The next chakra, the Star Gateway, is known as the ninth chakra. It resembles a starburst of energy and is situated at the highest point your hands can reach above your head.

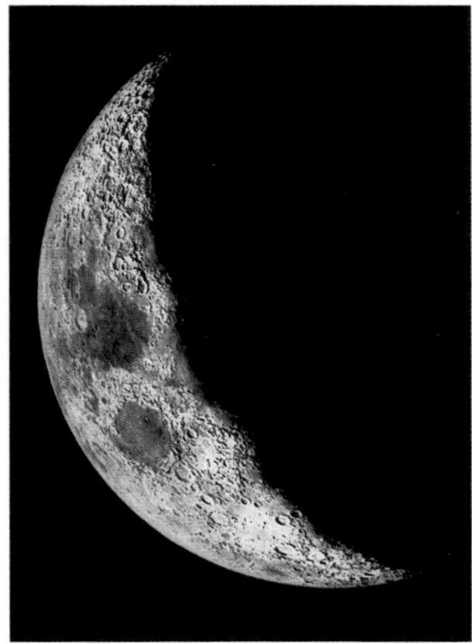

Moon-white, the Soul Star Chakra is situated just above your head and is related to your soul.

HOW TO PRACTISE THE MEDITATION

WHAT TO DO

1 Sit in a comfortable meditation posture. Relax your body by focusing on your breathing.

2 Focus your awareness on your Crown Chakra; visualize the thousand-petal lotus flower opening. The thousand petals are arranged from left to right in 20 layers containing 50 petals. The Crown Chakra, normally violet when open, changes to white. The pericarp (seed-vessel) is pure gold.

3 Look deep into the Crown Chakra; see the circular Moon sphere radiating soft reflective light. In the centre of the Moon sphere is a luminous downward-pointing triangle of soft golden light. In the centre of the triangle is what appears to be a red dot of light.

4 As you gaze at the red dot of light, you see it contains two red crescent moons (one above the other). A white circle is above the first and a red circle of red fire is above the second. Above them is another white circle containing a red dot of light and a white dot of light.

5 As you continue to gaze at these, become aware of a spiral of light coming out of your Crown Chakra that forms a halo of soft crystal-clear light around and above your head. This activates and forms your Halo Chakra.

6 To end the meditation, bring yourself back to everyday waking reality.

Angelic Temple Meditation

Archangels and their spheres of influence

Archangel Michael	*– Empowerment, protection, strength and truth*
Archangel Jophiel	*– Wisdom, illumination and energy renewal*
Archangel Raphael	*– Healing arts and knowledge of science*
Archangel Haniel	*– Working with group energies, communication*
Archangel Gabriel	*– Guidance, awakening and purification*
Archangel Zadkiel	*– Transformation and transmutation with the Violet Flame*
Archangel Uriel	*– Life-path, peace and unity among nations*
Archangel Metatron	*– Ascension and Light Body activation*
Archangel Chamuel	*– Relationships, love, beauty and compassion*
Archangel Melchizedek	*– Christ-consciousness and spiritual evolution*
Archangel Seraphiel	*– Karma clearing and cosmic purification*
Archangel Sandalphon	*– Earth-healing, prayer and absent healing*
Archangel Tzaphkiel	*– Cosmic Mother, contemplation, nurturing*
Archangel Raziel	*– Cosmic Father, secret mysteries of the universe*
Archangel Auriel	*– Divine feminine, Moon magic, phases of life*
Archangel Muriel	*– Self-reflection, working with dolphins and other sea creatures*

Each archangel has a spiritual home or Temple of Light anchored in the etheric realms over the Earth's various 'power' vortexes. These were established by the 'Spiritual Hierarchy' under the guidance of the archangels. Each temple has a different purpose that will help you on your spiritual path. The focus of each temple relates to a 'cosmic virtue' that each archangel enshrines. When spiritual seekers visit the temple during meditation they are nourished and inspired.

HOW TO PRACTISE THE MEDITATION

WHAT TO DO

1 Sit in a comfortable meditation posture. Relax your body by focusing on your breathing; allow your breathing to become slower and deeper, with the out-breath being slower than the in-breath.

2 Summon the archangel whose temple you wish to visit and ask for your conscious awareness to be transported there during the meditation.

3 Feel the archangel you called upon drawing closer; allow yourself to be surrounded by their energy and transported to their 'spiritual home'.

4 When you reach the temple, state what you wish to study, or by what you wish to be inspired and nourished.

5 The archangels will signal to you when it is time to return from your meditation and will bring you safely back to your body and everyday waking reality.

Sword of Archangel Michael Meditation

Each archangel has a temple 'anchored' in the etheric realm (see pages 40–41). The Temple of Light you wish to visit during this meditation is the retreat centre of Archangel Michael, which is anchored near Lake Louise in Canada.

HOW TO PRACTISE THE MEDITATION

WHAT TO DO

1 Sit in a comfortable meditation posture. Relax your body by focusing on your breathing.

2 Once relaxed, call on Archangel Michael, using this invocation:

Mighty Archangel Michael empower me. I acknowledge I have free will, so I now choose a life-path of joy and freedom. If it is appropriate to my spiritual path give me my sword of freedom. I promise to use it only for the highest good of all.

3 Feel yourself enveloped by the energy of the Archangel Michael; allow yourself to be raised upwards on a spiral of pure light. Slowly the light spiral raises you higher and higher; you feel yourself held perfectly safely in angelic arms.

4 You will find yourself in the temple and will be guided to the door of the sword room.

5 Archangel Michael will take you inside the sword room, where

you will see rows and rows of swords; each is already assigned to those who are meant to be sword-bearers. These are the ones who agree to carry the sapphire-blue flame of freedom. Each sword is very different in appearance, just as each being on the planet is an individual. But each sword is identical in respect of the authority it carries, in bringing freedom and protection.

6 Archangel Michael hands you your sword: the name of your sword will be written on it in the 'language of light'. He will also give you the authority to use it. You will be given a special secret symbol that is placed within your energy field; this 'crystalline' symbol must be in balance in your energy field, or your sword will be rendered useless.

7 Archangel Michael will let you stay in the sword room as long as you need to. It is a very special moment on your evolutionary path. When you are ready, Archangel Michael will gently guide you back into your physical body.

Archangel Michael's temple is anchored somewhere over pristine Lake Louise in Canada.

Discover Your Life-path with Archangel Uriel Meditation

Uriel is the archangel to call on for inner peace and tranquillity of spirit. Archangel Uriel's Temple of Light is over the Tatra mountains of Poland (see page 40). He saves us from spiritual confusion by illuminating our path through life. His glyph is the lightning flash that he uses to bring flashes of inspiration. We are all born with a special 'gift', which is our reason for incarnating. Each being on the planet has a special place in the world scheme and the Earth's evolution.

The powerful energy of the lightning flash is symbolic of Uriel's ability to bring inspiration and insight.

HOW TO PRACTISE THE MEDITATION

WHAT TO DO

1 Sit in a comfortable meditation posture. Close your eyes and relax your body.

2 Summon Archangel Uriel, using this invocation:

Archangel Uriel, bring peace to my mind and spirit. Dissolve all obstacles on my spiritual path by showing me my true path in life so I can fulfil my Dharma.

3 Let yourself be enveloped in the energy of Archangel Uriel. Allow yourself to be raised upwards on a spiral of ruby-gold light. Slowly the light spiral raises you higher and higher, and you feel yourself held safely in angelic arms as you are transported to Uriel's temple.

4 You stand before Archangel Uriel, who will ask you if you wish to visit the scroll room. Here are stored billions of scrolls, one for each person incarnate on the planet. Your scroll is here written in the 'language of light' and contains your Dharma, your soul agreement. This agreement was made before you were born, at a higher level of your being. It is your true path in life.

5 Archangel Uriel will let you know when it is time to leave, bringing you safely back into your body.

The Tatra mountains of Poland provide the anchor for Archangel Uriel's temple.

Angels of the Morning Meditation

Attuning to the angels of the Sun at the birth of each new day helps you accept happiness into your life and appreciate the simple pleasures, joys and blessings you already have in your life.

Archangel Michael is the angel most closely associated with the Sun, but you may find other angels are attracted by your renewed joyful sunny disposition. This meditation is designed to bring balance and harmony and is similar to the 'Salute to the Sun', a Hatha yoga exercise, which is designed to activate and energize each chakra. This meditation should be performed just as the first rays of the Sun bless the Earth with their glorious awakening. It brings harmony to your world and awakens you to the Earth's beauty and bounty.

Summoning the angels of the morning to fill your body with optimism and joy for the day ahead is similar to performing the yogic 'Salute to the Sun'.

HOW TO PRACTISE THE MEDITATION

WHAT TO DO

1 Begin by spending several minutes breathing deeply.

2 Stand up straight and bring your hands together (palms touching) in the prayer position at your Heart Chakra.

3 Take several more deep breaths and allow your body to relax. Be aware of the weight of your body and your feet on the floor. Make sure the weight of your body is evenly balanced on both feet and allow your knees to relax so that there is no tension in your body and your energy is flowing smoothly.

4 On the next in-breath, raise your arms (palms still together) above your head. Lean back slightly to stretch your spine and look upwards towards your hands.

5 On the out-breath, bend forwards from the hips, with the intention of touching the floor with your hands or fingertips (bend your knees if you have to) and connect with Mother Earth.

6 On the in-breath, stand upright again and open your arms outwards – imagine you are embracing the world.

7 With the next in-breath, allow the energy of the angels of the Sun to flood your whole body and aura with light, warmth and optimism.

8 Stay in this energy as long as you like; feel the angelic blessings flowing into you bringing nourishment to every cell in your body.

9 When you are ready, lower your arms to your sides on an out-breath.

Angels of the Evening Meditation

Close your day by welcoming the angels of the evening. As the sunlight fades, ask the angels of the Moon to wrap their mantle of silvery protection around you, the Earth and all the children of the Earth. Archangel Auriel, the angel of destiny, and Archangel Gabriel, the angel of guidance, are most closely associated with the Moon, but you may find other angels blessing you with their peaceful moonbeams and inspirational dreams. The Moon angels help us view the workings of the unconscious mind and deep memory, especially while we sleep. They teach us that by sealing ourselves in their light we gain a command of the hidden depths of our psyche which, if not unified, causes fragmentation.

HOW TO PRACTISE THE MEDITATION

WHAT TO DO

1 Begin by spending several minutes breathing deeply.

2 Stand up straight and bring your hands together (palms touching) in the prayer position at your Heart Chakra.

3 Take several more deep breaths and allow your body to relax. Be aware of the weight of your body and your feet on the floor. Make sure the weight of your body is evenly balanced on both feet and allow your knees to relax so that there is no tension in your body and your energy is flowing smoothly.

4 On the next in-breath, open your arms outwards to embrace the energies of the moon. Feel your body flooded with the peaceful but powerful energies of the angels of the Moon.

5 Ask the angels for protection throughout the night. If you desire insightful dreams ask that these be sent to you.

6 On the next in-breath, raise your arms above your head and bring your hands together (palms almost touching). Imagine or feel a sphere of brilliant moonlight between your hands – cradle it gently, and see it becoming sparkling moondust.

7 On the next out-breath, bring both of your arms downwards in a circular movement. As you do this, imagine or feel your aura completely covered in shimmering moondust.

Summon the angels of the evening to protect your sleep and inspire your dreams.

Star Alignment Meditation

Many ancient people believed that the stars watched over them, representing their divine 'starry' origins. By aligning ourselves with 'our' star, we allow the higher dimensional energies or codes of light from our higher self to be downloaded into our cellular memory. Each star, like each person, has its own resonance. Aligning with our star leads to the union of flesh with spirit. As we align the white-light spiral from the heart of the Creator, it anchors the energy within our Heart Chakra, which in turn opens our consciousness to the higher dimensional stargates. (A stargate is an opening to another dimension or reality.) Many people who work with the angelic realm send their conscious awareness through the stargates to receive higher knowledge, wisdom and understanding.

HOW TO PRACTISE THE MEDITATION

WHAT TO DO

1 Begin by spending several minutes breathing deeply.

2 Stand up straight and bring your hands together in the prayer position at your Heart Chakra.

3 Take several more deep breaths and allow your body to relax. Be aware of the weight of your body. Make sure it is evenly balanced on both feet and allow your knees to relax so that there is no tension in your body and your energy is flowing smoothly.

4 Visualize a clear starry night sky. See the billions of stars twinkling above; one seems to be shining more brightly than the rest. This is your star. As you gaze upon it, it seems to grow even brighter and lighter, becoming more dazzling by the moment.

Aligning yourself with your star will help open your consciousness to stargates.

5 Raise your arms above your head and call on the angels of light to assist you in bringing down your own star energies.

6 See the light spiralling downwards towards you. See it aligning at the transcendental chakras above your head and then guide this energy downwards with your hands. Allow it to flow into your Crown Chakra and the whole of your body.

7 See yourself twinkling with white starlight. Experience how much lighter you feel.

8 Take several deep breaths, and become aware of the weight of your physical body; begin to move your toes and fingers, then get up and stretch. Ask your angels to suitably ground, close, seal and protect you.

ANGELS OF MANY LANDS

Old Testament Angels and Their Roots

The first historical records of winged beings come from Zoroastrianism, one of the world's oldest religions. The prophet Zarathustra, who lived in Persia (now Iran) no earlier than 1700 BCE and no later than 600 BCE, reformed the religious practices of the region, some of which were parallel to the ancient Vedic religion of northern India. Zoroastrianism has dualistic undertones, with a series of seven beings who had the status and function of angels with good qualities, and another seven beings with evil qualities.

Zoroastrianism is uniquely important in the history of religion because of its formative links to both Western and Eastern religious traditions. Central to Zoroastrianism is the emphasis on moral choice, and of life as a battle between the forces of good and evil represented by *Ahura Mazda* and his antithesis, the Satanic *Angra Mainya*. These opposite forces may have emerged from the Indo-Iranian distinction between two forms of spiritual being – *ahuras* and *daevas*. In Zoroastrianism, *daevas* are portrayed as demonic and *ahuras* as angelic. Additionally, there are some 20 abstract terms that are regarded as emanations or aspects of *Ahura Mazda*. In later literature, they are personified as an archangel retinue of the Wise Lord.

Old and New Testament angels In the Old Testament, angels play an important role as messengers from God. In the New Testament, angels are present at all the major events in the life of Jesus, acting as God's agents on Earth. From the

Annunciation (Luke 1:26–38) to the nativity (Luke 2:8–14), amd finally to the resurrection and ascension into heaven (Luke 24:6; John 20:12; Matthew 28:6) to sit at the right hand of his father, there are angels in attendance.

Early depiction of winged beings, such as this protective spirit from the 9th-century BCE Assyrian palace of Ashurnasirpal II, appear throughout the ancient world.

Jewish Tradition

Founded by the prophets Abraham and Moses, Judaism emerged some 3,500 years ago in the Middle East. Today there are 12 million Jews around the world, mostly living in Israel or the USA. The Jewish holy book is the Hebrew Bible or *Tanakh*, especially the first five books, called the *Torah*.

Abraham is regarded as the first patriarch of the Jewish people; the covenant with God is a common thread running throughout the early part of the Bible and one of the vital pillars of Judaism. God gave the first covenant to Abraham and the second covenant to Moses on Mount Sinai when he received the Ten Commandments. Moses is one of the most prominent figures in the Bible and one of the most influential prophets in Judao-Christian theology. His vision of 'one God' and the ten commandments given to Moses by God, have been a cornerstone of human morality for 3,000 years. The manna that fed the children of Israel as they fled into the desert was the bread of angels and the whole of the Jewish faith is based on their patriarchs' encounters with God's angels.

The Archangel Michael is the guardian angel of the people of Israel and Jews believe that they are the chosen people of their one God. But angels are not just a Jewish concept – the Jews borrowed their ideas about angels from their neighbours, particularly from the Babylonians while the Jews were in exile in Babylonia. Many of the Jewish angels could be Babylonian gods in disguise. Ancient Babylonian carved reliefs depicting winged beings guarding temples and other important buildings can be found in museum collections scattered around the world.

A 15th-century detail of Moses with the Ten Commandments *by Joos van Gent.*

Angels of the Kabala

One of the richest sources of angelic lore is the Jewish mystical tradition known as the Kabala (see pages 68–99). The Kabala is a body of information rather than a single manuscript or source, although two early texts were the *Zohar,* or 'Book of Splendour', and the *Sepher Yetzirah, or* 'Book of Formation'. The latter was traditionally credited to Melchizedek, a priest-king of Salem (later Jerusalem), and was believed to have been passed down to Abraham, father of the Jewish nation, in a revelation.

For centuries the Kabala has been used by mystics as a way to experience the different aspects of creation, and has been assessed by them (either by direct personal experience or through spiritual revelation) as a path, map or route to God. The Kabalist mystics understand that the vision is a manifestation of a cosmic core reality that underpins the various elements symbolizing the structure of existence as it was created. The divine energy descends from above and gives birth to the ten sephiroth. The expression 'Tree of Life' was popularized in the Middle Ages and is a powerful image that has captured not just the Kabalist tradition but that of other cultures as well, surfacing in Australian rock art, and in Hopi and Celtic traditions.

The mystical aspect of the Kabala is the *Shekinah,* the female manifestation of God in man. The Shekinah is known as the 'Bride of the Lord' or 'Angel of Love and Blessings'. As the feminine aspect of God, she is also known as the 'liberating' angel. To the average Christian or Jew, this was blasphemy. Perhaps for this reason, the study of the Kabala was limited by the rabbis to married men over

The Tree of Life incorporates an aspect of Shekinah, the Liberating Angel in the Kabala.

the age of 40. Today it is widely acceptable for both men and women of any age to study the Kabala.

The expression 'the Shekinah rests' (or resides) is used for a paraphrase in Genesis 48:16 for 'God dwells' as uttered by Israel (Jacob) 'in the angel that redeemed me from all evil'. In the Christian tradition the Shekinah is the lost female aspect of God. In the Eastern Orthodox Church many cathedrals are dedicated to her as 'Holy Wisdom'; she is one of the archangels: winged, dressed in white, seated on a throne, holding a scroll (2 Enoch).

Christian Angels

Angels are represented throughout the Catholic Bible as intermediary spiritual beings, forever travelling between God and man. As St Augustine and St Gregory explained, 'angel' is the name of the 'office' and it expresses neither their essential nature nor their essential function. This means that angels are the attendants of God's throne in the court of Heaven. The function of the angelic host is to act as assistants to God and more than once the seven angels of the Presence are described.

Catholics are very clear about angels being God's instrument of communication. In Jacob's vision, angels are witnessed ascending and descending to Heaven. An angel of God found Agar in the wilderness and angels drew Lot out of Sodom; an angel announces to Gideon that he is to save his people. An angel announces Samson's birth and the Archangel Gabriel instructs Daniel, although he is not called an angel in either of these passages, but 'the man Gabriel'.

The same messenger announces the birth of St John the Baptist and the incarnation of the Redeemer, while tradition says that he is the messenger of shepherds and the angel who strengthens Jesus on the cross. The prophet Zachariah gives the revelation that the angel is speaking in him; this is an important point because it clearly defines the angelic guidance as coming from within and not an outside vision speaking to him.

Throughout the Bible, it is repeatedly implied that each individual soul has a tutelary angel; this is a point of faith to many Catholics. Catholic doctrine also dictates that our guardian angel can intercede with God on our behalf.

St Ambrose said: 'We should pray to the angels who were given to us as our guardians.' Catholics have a hierarchy of angels – Cherubim feature in the Bible, as do the Seraphim. Archangels are mentioned only in St Jude, but St Paul gives lists of other heavenly groups. He tells us in Ephes. 1: 21 that Christ is raised up 'above all principality, and power, and virtue, and dominion', and in Colossians 1:16 he says: 'In Him were all things created in heaven and on earth, visible and invisible, whether thrones or dominions, or principalities and powers.'

Detail from a 14th-century fresco by Giusto Menabuoi in the Baptistery at Padua. This angel appears to have two sets of wings.

Buddhist and Hindu Angels

Buddhism is based on the teachings of the Buddha, the 'One who has awakened'. The Buddha, Sidhatta Gotama (Siddhartha Gautama), was born around 563 BCE. His teachings – the Tripitaka – form the basis of the many different forms of Buddhism. Buddhists do not believe in a personal creator God. The primary Buddhist belief is that through rebirth we learn to release our desires and attachments, which ultimately leads to enlightenment.

The Buddhists believe that angels are bodhisattvas, or 'enlightened ones' – beings whose Buddha-hood is assured but who have postponed entering Nirvana in order to help others to attain enlightenment. Bodhisattvas often reveal themselves to humans as forms of light emanations or through meditation. Many bodhisattvas are revered.

Hinduism Although some of its elements are much older, Hinduism originated some 3,000 years ago. The Vedas are the most sacred Hindu religious texts. Hinduism is not a single unified religion – it has no founder, no prophet or single teacher. Hindus believe in a Universal Soul or God called Brahman. All other Hindu deities, such as Vishnu (preserver), Shiva (destroyer) and Krishna, are aspects of Brahman the creator. Brahman is the sole reality and is present in all things. Brahman has no form and is eternal; he is creator, preserver and transformer of everything. Brahman appears in the human spirit as Atman or the Soul.

In Hinduism there are no references to angels, but there are spirits who perform similar functions. Gandharvas are often portrayed as having wings; they are well known for their musical skills and the

This Indian miniature depicts Shri Krishna, one of the Hindu deities who is an aspect of Brahman the creator.

power to cast illusions. They were sometimes the attendants of Devas (angelic beings called the 'shining ones') who help men on their spiritual quests.

There is a direct reference to angels in the *Introduction to the Jataka*; when Queen Maha Maya conceived the future Buddha, she was carried to the Himalayas by four guardian angels, and after conception the queen was guarded by four angels with swords. Four Maha-Brahma angels attended the Buddha's birth.

Dharmapalas are protectors of the Dharma and they can often appear as angelic beings. In Tibetan Buddhism celestial beings are called Devas and they often appear before humans as emanations of light.

Islamic Angels

Islam has a vast hierarchy of *mala'ika* (angels), having inherited the concept of angels from Judaism and Christianity. Indeed, belief in angels is one of the six pillars of Islamic faith. In descending order of importance, the angels of the Islamic faith are:

A 16th-century Turkish depiction: an angel brings Abraham a ram to sacrifice rather than his son.

- The Four Throne Bearers of Allah (*hamalat al-arsh*), symbolized by a bull, a man, a lion and an eagle (which was inspired by the Revelation of St John in the New Testament).

- The Cherubim (*karubiyum*) who praise Allah constantly.

- The four archangels: Gabriel (Jibril also spelt Jabra'il), the revealer, who revealed the Koran to Mohammed; Michael (Mikal), the provider; Izrail, the angel of death (who separates mens' souls from their bodies); and Israfil, the angel of the last judgement of Allah.

- There are also lesser angels, known as the *hafazah* or *hafza*, who are guardian angels.

In Islam, Jibril acts as a messenger between God and man, as bearer of revelation to the prophets of God. Mohammed mentions Jibril by name three times in the Koran and it is Jibril and Mikal who purify the prophet's heart in preparation for his ascension into Heaven. Jibril guided Mohammed through the various levels of Heaven to reach the throne of God. Jibril also helped Mohammed by coming to his aid at the battle of Badr (624 CE) with thousands of angels telling him to attack the Jewish tribes of Banu Qaynuqa and Banu Qurayzah. As-Shaitan is the 'evil one', the Islamic devil, who is prince of the evil angels or bad spirits. The Koran says that angels were created from light and the jinn (evil angels) were created from smokeless fire. Malik is the angel who is the keeper of hell.

Islamic angels have wings and are beautiful in appearance; they are also vast because the prophet Mohammed described Jibril as filling the space between Heaven and Earth. He also saw Jibril's true form – he had 600 wings that covered the horizon and pearls and rubies fell from his wings. The number of angels is not known in Islam; only Allah knows how many angels there are.

Mormons

The Church of Jesus Christ of Latter-day Saints, the Mormon church, was founded in 1830 in New York by Joseph Smith (1805–1844) and developed by Bingham Young (1801–1877). The church is centred on Christ, but has substantial differences in belief to the Catholic, Protestant and Orthodox Christian churches. Mormons believe people can be baptized into their faith even after they have died. They also believe that Joseph Smith was a prophet of God and that humans can become gods in the afterlife.

Scripture – the Mormon holy books – includes: the Holy Bible (King James version); the Book of Mormon: Another Testament of Jesus Christ; Doctrine and Covenants: a compilation of revelations and writings; and The Pearl of Great Price: a selection of revelations, translations and writings of Joseph Smith. The Book of Mormon is at the centre of the Mormon faith. They believe that this book tells the story of God's dealings with the ancient inhabitants of the American continent, including a visit by the risen Jesus to the people of the New World.

Mormon was an ancient American prophet who compiled the history of the ancient civilization from old records. The document was inscribed on plates of gold which Mormon's son Moroni buried for safety in what is now New York State. Moroni returned in 1823 as an angel and showed Joseph Smith (founder of the church) where the plates were hidden. Smith translated the plates into the Book of Mormon, which was first published in 1830. Joseph Smith received his vision in the spring of 1820 while praying in the woods. He saw a pillar of light, within which were two glorious figures.

Joseph Smith received his vision of the angel Moroni while praying in the woods.

Celtic Angels

Celts are defined as a group of Indo-European people, originally from central Europe, who spread to western Europe, the British Isles and southeast to Galatia (Turkey) during pre-Roman times, especially the Britons and Gauls. The pre-Christian Celts had a well-organized social hierarchy and culture. They produced little in the way of literary output, preferring the bardic, story-telling tradition. Druid priests in ancient days were given the secrets of the universe in visions. The priests were not allowed to write down their secrets, so all mystic knowledge had to be passed from master to pupil, which meant that a long apprenticeship was required to become a Druid priest.

The Celts believed in reincarnation and the continuity of the soul. They interpreted the world using the Celtic Tree of Life. For the ancient Celts their Anamchara (angel or soul-friend) was part of their daily life. Celtic angels are spiritual beings who take a very special interest in humans, especially those who are spiritually aware or just developing their spirituality. Celtic angels play the role of guardians or companions very much like the totem animal does in other shamanic traditions. The New Age movement and interest in native cultures has brought about a huge upsurge of interest in Celtic angels.

Celtic angels dwell on several levels. The highest level has those angels who are in constant contact with the God-force, very similar to the Buddhist bodhisattvas – enlightened beings who delay entering the heavenly realm in order to assist the spiritual development of others.

The next level is full of angels who are ascending to God and the third level holds the angels that are closest to us and our physical world. The Anamchara closest to us is the easiest to contact and meditating in natural places such as groves, woods, waterfalls or by lakes produces great results as these places are full of Anamchairde (plural of Anamchara). Like other angels, your Anamchara can appear in any form that is appropriate, even occasionally taking on the human form; and if it is appropriate it will have wings.

Celtic angels (Anamchara) take a special interest in helping those who are evolving spiritually.

First Nations Legends of North America and Shamanism

The Thunderbird is a mythological creature found in the spiritual lore of many First Nations in North America. This mythical creature's name derives from the idea that the movement of its huge wings caused thunder. The Lakota name for the Thunderbird is *Wakinyan* from the words *kinyan* meaning 'winged' and *wakin* meaning 'sacred'. The Kwakiult called it *Hohoq* and the Nootka named the creature *Kw-Uhnx-Wa*.

The Thunderbird is enormous with a two-canoe-length wingspan which can create a storm as it flies. Clouds are bundled together, causing thunderclaps, and streaks of lightning issue from its eyes as it blinks. It carries glowing snakes of lightning bolts within its beak. It is depicted in masks as many-coloured, two-horned and with teeth in its beak.

Thunderbirds are sometimes thought to be solitary creatures living on mountaintops or travelling as a group. The mountaintop Thunderbirds were

The Thunderbird carries messages from the 'Great Spirit' to humans on Earth.

servants of the Great Spirit and flew about only to carry messages from him. The Kwakiult and Cowichan tribes believed that the non-solitary Thunderbirds took on human form by tilting their beaks backwards (like a mask) and throwing off their feathers like a blanket. There are stories of these 'human' Thunderbirds marrying humans.

Is the mythical Thunderbird an angel (it does carry messages and bring light), a crypto-zoological bird or related to the roc or *rukh* from Persian legend? The *rukh* was reported to be able to carry off an elephant and eat it. The Thunderbird could also be related to the phoenix of Egyptian mythology – the fabulous bird that periodically regenerates itself. It is used in literature to symbolize death and resurrection. According to legend, when it reached the end of its 500-year life span, it burned itself on a pyre of flames, and from the ashes a new phoenix arose.

Shamanism In shamanic cultures, the healer often takes the form of a bird to travel through the different worlds in search of his patient's soul fragment. The

This Thunderbird totem pole stands in Stanley Park, Vancouver. It is a replica of an early 20th-century house post carved by Charlie James.

ritual coats of present-day Siberian shamans are produced to resemble birds with feathers. And, although in all the forms of shamanism across Asia there is little interest in the production of concrete images of winged humans, the belief that the shaman can fly is universal.

Ancient Egypt and Ancient Greece

There appear to be no distinctly angelic beings in Egyptian mythology, although there is the sacred phoenix which was the symbol of immortality. The phoenix represents the Sun, which dies each night and rises again each morning. At the end of its life cycle the phoenix builds a pyre of cinnamon twigs, which it ignites, burning itself to ashes from which the new bird emerges. The new phoenix embalms the ashes of the old one in an egg made of myrrh which it deposits in Heliopolis, located in Egypt.

The goddess Isis used her wings to breathe life into Osiris and to conceive her son Horus.

Originally the phoenix was a stork or heron-like bird called a *benu*, known from the *Book of the Dead*; it is closely associated with the Sun-god Amun-Ra. Religion in ancient Egypt was a very important part of everyday life. Daily, the priests attended to the images of their gods (who were thought to be manifest in the image). The Egyptian gods and goddesses often had animal heads; Anubis, the jackal-headed god of the dead, is an example. Though the Egyptians had many deities, only a few appear to have wings; Isis on one occasion used her wings to breathe life into her dead husband-brother Osiris and to conceive Horus. The goddess Nut was portrayed as a woman with a pot on her head with vulture wings, or a woman covered in stars, bending over the Earth.

Greek angels The word *daemon* in ancient Greek meant an inspiring spirit. The Goddess Nike and her son Eros served as angelic images for later depictions of angels.

The Winged Victory of Samothrace *(c.220–190 BCE) is the Goddess Nike (Victory).*

New Age

The New Age movement is a free-flowing spiritual transformation that differs from all other religions. It has no prophets, no holy texts or sacred books, no membership, no religious centres, no creed, no priests, nuns, clergymen and, importantly, no hidden agenda.

The New Age movement does, however, use some 'mutually' accepted terms, such as chakra, aura and chi, and many New Agers believe in reincarnation and the continuation of the soul after death. All New Agers define themselves

The New Age movement has no prophets or gurus; we are all aspects of God.

as seekers of personal truth, knowledge and wisdom as they seek to live a balanced lifestyle, usually by acknowledging and developing the spiritual aspect of their psyche.

A new golden age Belief in angels and other highly evolved spiritual beings is increasing as the Age of Aquarius unfolds. Most New Agers believe a new golden age will develop in which gender, race, religion, age, social status and other forms of discrimination will end. Ego, tribal and national attachments will be replaced by global responsibility as the Earth's inhabitants seek to eradicate war, poverty, hunger and disease.

Belief in angels is not confined to the New Age movement; in fact the belief in angels goes back to the dawn of civilization. But many New Agers feel that the movement is angelically led, through personal contact with their own guardian angel. Currently there are many books available on angels and everything angelic seems to be on the increase.

Some New Age seekers add on New Age beliefs to their existing religious affiliations or backgrounds and all seekers believe in a divine intelligence which underpins the fabric of the universe. The New Age movement started in the late 1960s, but early signs of its birth appeared in the 19th century with writers such as Elena Blavatsky (1831–1891) who started the Theosophy Society. Astrology, Buddhism, channelling, Hinduism, Gnostic traditions, Paganism, Spiritualism and Wicca have also had an impact on the New Age movement.

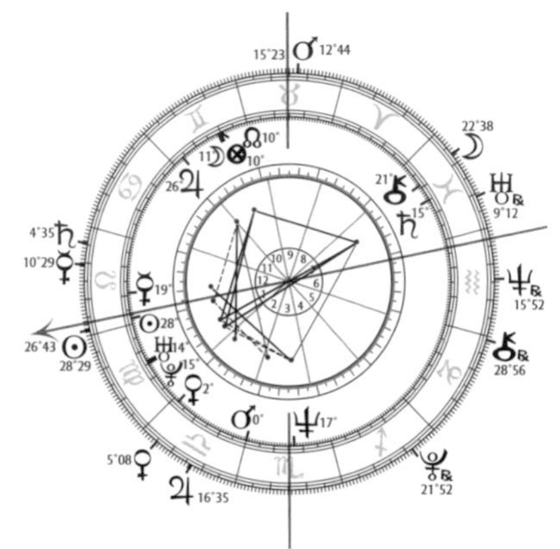

A new angelically led golden age will emerge as we move into the Age of Aquarius.

ANGEL VISIONS

Famous Historical Angel Visions

Within this section are accounts of some of the most famous angel visions through the ages, taken from the words of Ezekiel, Enoch, St John and Daniel. They include visions of the highest heaven containing the throne of God.

DANIEL

As I looked, thrones were set in place, and the Ancient of Days took his seat. His clothing was as white as snow; the hair of his head was white like wool. His throne was flaming with fire, and its wheels were all ablaze. A river of fire was flowing, coming out from before him. Thousands upon thousands attended him; ten thousand times ten thousand stood before him.

Daniel 7:9–10

A 12th-century illustration of Daniel's vision of the Four Beasts and God enthroned, from a commentary by Asturian monk Beatus.

ENOCH

And I looked and saw therein a lofty throne: its appearance was as crystal, and the wheels thereof as the shining sun, and there was the vision of the Cherubim. And from underneath the throne came streams of flaming fire so that I could not look thereon. And the Great Glory sat thereon, and His raiment shone more brightly than the sun and was whiter than any snow. None of the angels could enter and behold His face by the reason of the magnificence and glory and no flesh could behold Him. The flaming fire was round about Him, and a great fire stood before Him, and none could draw nigh Him: ten thousand times ten thousand (stood) before Him.

1 Enoch 18b–23a

ELIJAH

As Elijah and his son Elisha were walking and talking together, suddenly a chariot of fire and horses of fire appeared and separated the two of them, and Elijah went up to heaven in a whirlwind. Elisha saw this and cried out, 'My father! My father! The chariots and horsemen of Israel!' And Elisha saw him no more.

2 Kings 2:11–12

The prophets Elijah and Enoch were both blessed with visions of God and the heavenly host.

EZEKIEL

The chariot throne of God (Hebrew Merkavah) was first described in Ezekiel, which was written shortly after the first Jewish exiles arrived in Babylon (587 BCE).

...the fire was what looked like four living creatures. In appearance their form was like that of a man, but each of them had four faces and four wings. Their legs were straight; their feet were like those of a calf and gleamed like burnished bronze. Under their wings on their four sides they had the hands of a man. All four of them had faces and wings, and their wings touched one another. Each one went straight ahead; they did not turn as they moved. Their faces looked like this: Each of the four had the face of a man, and on the right side each had the face of a lion, and on the left the face of an ox; each also had the face of an eagle. Such were their faces. Their wings were spread out upward; each had two wings, one touching the wing of another creature on either side, and two wings covering its body...The appearance of the living creatures was like burning coals of fire or like torches. Fire moved back and forth among the creatures; it was bright, and lightning flashed out of it. The creatures sped back and forth like flashes of lightning.

Ezekiel 1:5–14

A 17th-century woodcut of Ezekiel's vision of the chariot throne of God.

ST JOHN

St John's vision of the throne of God is the only one to appear in the New Testament.

At once I was in the Spirit, and there before me was a throne in heaven with someone sitting on it. And the one who sat there had the appearance of jasper and carnelian. A rainbow, resembling an emerald, encircled the throne. Surrounding the throne were 24 other thrones, and seated on them were 24 elders. They were dressed in white and had crowns of gold on their heads. From the throne came flashes of lightning, rumblings and peals of thunder. Before the throne, seven lamps were blazing. These are the seven spirits of God. Also before the throne there was what looked like a sea of glass, clear as crystal. In the centre, around the throne, were four living creatures, and they were covered with eyes, in front and in back. The first living creature was like a lion, the second was like an ox, the third had a face like a man, the fourth was like a flying eagle. Each of the four living creatures had six wings and was covered with eyes all around, even under his wings. Day and night they never stop saying: 'Holy, holy, holy, is the Lord God Almighty, who was, and is, and is to come.' Whenever the living creatures give glory, honour and thanks to him who sits on the throne and who lives for ever and ever, the 24 elders fall down before him. They lay their crowns before the throne and say: 'You are worthy, our Lord and God, to receive glory and honour and power, for you created all things, and by your will they were created and have their being.'

Revelation 4:2–11

HILDEGARD OF BINGEN

Hildegard of Bingen (1098–1179) was a great Christian mystic and writer who had 26 visions of divinity.

Then I saw the lucent sky, in which I heard different kinds of music, marvellously embodying all the meanings I had heard before. I heard the praises of the joyous citizens of heaven, steadfastly preserving the ways of truth...

Vision Thirteen

JOAN OF ARC

When Joan of Arc (1412–1431) was 12 years old, she began to hear heavenly voices inspiring her to save France. One of these voices belonged to Archangel Michael. Joan was reluctant to speak of her voices. She said nothing about them to her confessor, and at her trial constantly refused to be inveigled into descriptions of the appearance of the saints and to explain how she recognized them. None the less, she told her judges: 'I saw them with these very eyes, as well as I see you.'

An 18th-century painting of Joan of Arc being watched over while she sleeps.

WILLIAM BLAKE

William Blake (1757–1827) was a British poet, painter, visionary mystic and engraver who illustrated and printed his own books. Blake has recorded that, from his early years, he experienced visions of angels and that he saw and conversed with the Angel Gabriel. His 'prophetic books' are the *Book of Thel*, the *Marriage of Heaven and Hell*, the *Book of Urizen, America, Milton* and *Jerusalem*. In these prophetic books, Blake expressed his lifelong concern with the struggle of the soul to free its natural energies from reason and organized religion. Among Blake's later artistic works are drawings and engravings for Dante's *Divine Comedy*.

PÈRE JEAN LAMY

The saintly priest Père Jean Lamy (1853–1931) had many visions of angels. He conversed regularly with his guardian angel and had visions of the past and future.

Their garments are white, but with an unearthly whiteness. I cannot describe it, because it cannot be compared to earthly whiteness; it is much softer to the eye. These bright Angels are enveloped in a light so different from ours that by comparison everything else seems dark. When you see a band of 50, you are lost in amazement. They seem clothed with golden plates, constantly moving, like so many suns.

Modern Angelic Encounters

Visions of angels have not been restricted to times long past – there have been many more recent reports of angel visions.

Angel of Mons During the First World War, a legend arose out of the Battle of Mons. Although eyewitness accounts concerning the 'Angel of Mons' do vary, something mystical happened that day and amazingly it seems that more than one person witnessed the event!

The Battle of Mons took place on 23 August 1914 in Belgium. During the first desperate clash with the advancing German troops, St George and a host of phantom bowmen stopped the Kaiser's troops. Other soldiers claimed to have seen Archangel Michael leading an angelic army. Some soldiers saw three glowing beings with wings, while others claimed angels threw a protective curtain of light around the British troops. With so many witnesses to the divine intervention it is not surprising the accounts varied so much. Even German prisoners claimed to have seen the mystical event and been rendered helpless by the apparition.

It is true that the British were heavily outnumbered and their plight was a desperate one; so the angel story at the very least lifted British spirits. However, the debate regarding the legend's authenticity still rages over 90 years later.

Angelic perception Angels are a bridge into the heavenly realms. They convey a world beyond our normal sight, which is around us and within us. Angelic contact varies greatly and, in fact, not many people are lucky enough to literally 'see' an angel.

Angelic 'vision' also varies: some people see angels complete with wings

The Angels of Mons *by W. H. Margetson illustrates the extraordinary vision witnessed by many soldiers at Mons on 23 August 1914.*

Children often see angels and can describe them in great detail.

with their eyes wide open, while others see angels with their 'mind's eye'. Some people see coloured swirling lights dancing around their bed at night, while others encounter angels through their subconscious mind, in their dreams or meditations; still others are surrounded by a beautiful energy signature or feel angelic wings encircling them. Profound angelic encounters often happen when people have a near-death experience or are at the bedside of a loved one who is seriously ill or dying.

Childhood visions Children often see angels and can describe them in great detail. I know I have always seen angels: my earliest memories are of being surrounded each night by angels, but I didn't know they were angels. I called them 'beautiful ladies' who sang me to sleep every night.

I know my nightly angelic encounters greatly disturbed my mother, but my grandmother, who was a spiritualist, was completely at peace with the situation. In fact, after she came to live with us, she would often ask me if I had been in her room at night, as she had seen an angelic figure at the bottom of her bed. I tried to explain to her that my angels were just looking in on her. I am sure she knew they were angels and not me, but I think she liked to let me know she saw angels too.

I know I am not alone in this childhood experience of angels as one of my students recently shared her first angelic encounter with me. Her encounter happened when she was nine years old and going through a very bad time at home; her early life had been difficult. One night as she lay on her bed she said the ceiling dissolved and she saw before her the most exquisite angel carrying a sword of blue flame. The sense of protection and guidance from this beautiful being changed her young life and she has been able to grow to adulthood whole and healthy despite many negative family situations.

The amazing thing is that I knew she had experienced an encounter with Archangel Michael even before she told me, because she carries his angelic signature within her energy field. I noticed it the moment she walked into the room, I could feel it, we smiled and instant angelic recognition passed between us. I say amazing, but in truth when you open your heart to the angels your life can be filled with wonder, love and miraculous joy.

Celestial vision I have never lost my celestial vision and my angelic encounters have been witnessed by others who actually saw or felt the angels around me. My angelic encounters have been featured in other angel books, women's magazines and on television – if I was to recount them all it would fill this book. I have run angel seminars for nearly 20 years and in many countries so I have witnessed thousands of people making strong angelic connections, especially during the meditations and healing sessions. I also asked my crystal course students for some of their angelic experiences; here are three from the hundreds I received.

Opening our hearts to the angelic realm fills us with joy and gratitude.

FRAN'S ANGEL STORY

In 2001 my 17-year-old son was rushed to hospital with suspected appendicitis. While sitting in a cubicle to go onto the ward with my son who was very scared, I called on the angels to help him and be with him. I immediately felt the energy change. I could sense (but not see) an angelic being at the bottom of his hospital trolley. My son then totally unprompted said, 'there is a huge golden angel at my feet'. He then became very calm and peaceful about the operation. The angel stayed with him throughout the night making it easier for me to leave.

MARC'S STORY

Marc, an art student, had a temporary job as a night security guard. One night he and another guard were alerted to the fact that there were intruders on the premises. Marc and the other guard ran to the building where the intruders were and saw something that made them feel that they could not believe their eyes. Just above them floating in the clear starry night sky was a vast luminous being, an angel. It hovered above them for a few seconds before moving very slowly over several of the outer buildings; then it vanished from sight.

Marc was shaken by his experience of the angel (not the intruders) and was still in a shaky state when he got home. His family could tell something amazing had happened to him as he excitedly recounted his experience, but his mother just smiled and said: 'I did ask for angelic protection for you, as I was worried about you.'

TANIA'S STORY IN HER OWN WORDS

My first conscious experience of angels was when my father was taken ill suddenly. I received a phone call from my mother to say he wasn't well and that she had called the doctor, but I wasn't to worry. Twenty minutes later she called back crying, saying his heart had stopped. I told her I was on my way, so my partner and I got in the car and drove to my parents' house. During the drive I was consciously asking Archangels Michael and Raphael to help both my mother and father. My own heart was racing as I wanted to get to them [her parents] as quickly as possible without breaking the speed limit too much!

I came to a set of traffic lights which were on red. As I stopped my car, my heart slowed and an immense sense of peace came over me and I knew my father was all right. Five minutes later I arrived at my parents' house and was told my father had passed away five minutes earlier. I came to understand that these wonderful angels had helped my father, but not in the physical sense. It was time for his spirit to move on and Archangels Michael and Raphael had guided him on his way. I also thank the angels for this experience because, although it tore me apart losing my father in this sudden way, it set me on my spiritual path.

As she drove to see her ill father, Tania asked Archangels Michael and Raphael to help both her mother and father.

ANGEL HEALING

Causes of Disease

Conventional medicine focuses on the physical systems of the body, and uses tests and physical symptoms to diagnose the problem. It aims to cure the disease with surgery or drugs. Before conventional medicine became so pervasive, people sought natural remedies for their ailments. They knew that their lives were greatly influenced by different energies, some of which – the subtle energies – cannot be seen or sensed by most people and therefore are dismissed as non-existent.

Health can be viewed as the continuous harmonious flow of energy between the body, mind, spirit, soul and the universal web of life. When we become diseased or ill at ease with any aspect of ourselves, we block the flow of vital energy on all levels of our being. We are all in a constant state of change and personal growth; remaining in harmony with our soul is a constant balancing act.

When we become stressed, we block the flow of vital life-energy.

Redirecting the life-energy Any form of healing or therapy allows *qi* (vital life-energy) to be redirected by the healer, which clears the patterns of disease that have blocked the harmonious flow within yourself in relation to the universe. Disease is your spirit's way of communicating with you through your physical body, your thoughts, your emotions and your feelings. Disease should never be viewed as a negative experience; it is your spirit's way of attracting your attention. When we are healthy we tend to take life for granted, we become complacent and delude ourselves that we are physically immortal. This delusion is stagnation to your soul and the death of spiritual growth and soul harmony.

Each disease and the crisis it brings as the instigator of change within your life creates a sacred space for your spirit to teach you about yourself. Your disease is unique to you. If you grasp the opportunity of working with your soul to heal your imbalance, you free yourself from a place of stagnation and move forward into a more spiritual and harmonious life.

Good health is something we take for granted, but we should not forget that we are physically mortal.

Angelic healing aims to weave us back into unity with the soul. It is focused not just on well-being, but on so much more. It requires us to listen to the whisperings of our souls, feel our emotions, develop our intuition and nurture our spirits. This holistic state brings contentment, allowing us to function peacefully in connection with others in the flow of life.

The Path of Growth

Our journey through life can sometimes feel painful as our soul searches for its authenticity and maturity. I hear over and over again from people attending my angel seminars that they experience feelings of coming home, of feeling themselves, of being connected, of remembering who they truly are. Frequently during the angel seminars, tears of release flow; these tears are always a positive experience.

We know that we are achieving true angelic communication when we can acknowledge that we no longer feel alone. Protection, guidance, support and nurturing are not only there for us in abundance, but are actively flowing in our direction, influencing and improving all areas of our life.

Although the angels are definitely not a quick fix, some people experience immediate and permanent change. Through attuning to the angels, you will find your true purpose in life and your pathway home. It is also true that working with the angels may challenge outworn patterns and belief systems and shake you out of your comfort zones. It takes courage to open doors to healing, and even the most beneficial life changes can be challenging.

As part of the transformation process you have to integrate yourself once more into your surroundings and current lifestyle. This includes the people closest to you – your partner, children, family, friends, work colleagues. They may not always feel comfortable with the 'new' you; it means that they might have to change too and they may not be ready for this change. Think back to a time in your life when change was forced upon you;

perhaps this change was due to bereavement, divorce or job loss. Remember how uncomfortable the process was.

It is important to be self-reliant and single-minded through your transformation, since others may even perceive you as selfish. It is important that you seek out those who will support you and encourage your spiritual growth and health renewal.

As part of the transformational process, you need to integrate yourself back into your current lifestyle and your family and friends.

Preparing for an Angelic Healing Session

Even the most naturally gifted healers acknowledge the importance of meditation for stilling the mind before they open themselves to the higher energies of the angelic realm – otherwise they run the risk of becoming overwhelmed by the experience.

It is also vitally important that, before you begin to help others, you yourself go through a process of self-healing and angelic attunement. Attuning to the angelic realm could not be easier to do, especially if you follow the meditations in this book.

Always remember that we need to prepare ourselves physically, mentally, emotionally and spiritually before we offer therapy of any kind to others.

HOW TO PREPARE FOR ANGELIC ALIGNMENT

The way you prepare yourself and your client before an angelic healing session will have an enormous effect on the quality of the experience, and also on the outcome. Adopt these guidelines to help make the best of your healing sessions.

WHAT TO DO

1 Wear loose white cotton clothing that allows freedom of movement for both giving and receiving treatment. Synthetic fabrics interfere with the energy flow of

the meridian channels, as well as holding potential negativity. Dark or drab-coloured clothing will lower your energy field and that of your client.

2 Ask your client to drink plenty of water before and after each session to ease the removal of energy blocks and toxicity. Drink plenty of water yourself to cleanse your energy field before and after giving a healing session.

3 Avoid heavy meals immediately before and after a session as blood will be diverted to help with the digestion process.

4 Wash your hands in cool flowing water before and after each client to remove residual energies.

5 Relax and be confident before starting a healing session: if you are tense, your client will feel it and also become tense.

6 Ask your client to remove contact lenses, glasses, all jewellery, belts and any metal objects such as keys or change from their pockets.

7 Your client should lie on a massage table or therapy couch with a pillow supporting the head for comfort. Your couch needs to be wide enough and long enough to accommodate your client so that their arms can relax easily at their sides and their feet are on the couch.

8 Ask your client not to cross their arms or legs during the therapy process as this will block the energy flow.

9 Cover your client with a white blanket if at any time during the session they feel cold.

10 Allow time to attune to the angels you will be aligning with for the session.

11 Allow yourself plenty of time to gain energetic rapport with your client. If you feel threatened or drained by something attached to your client, such as lower entities, immediately ask Archangel Michael for protection.

Palm and Mental Body Activations

PALM CENTRE ACTIVATION

It is important to raise the receptiveness in your hands before giving an angelic healing treatment as this will help you develop sensitivity to subtle energies. Also, your hands and arms are an extension of your Heart Chakra (think about when you embrace someone and give them a hug). To help others with angelic healing we need to have an open Heart Chakra (see page 146, Pink Flame Heart-star meditation).

WHAT TO DO

1 Wash your hands in cool water and dry them thoroughly in order to cleanse your hands and open your heart before giving angelic healing.

2 Shake your hands vigorously to sensitize them; this releases blocked emotional energy and opens your Heart Chakra.

3 Rub your palms together rapidly in a circular motion several times to build up the surface *qi*.

4 Alternatively, you can open and close your hands rapidly and simultaneously until you feel the surface *qi* building up; or roll a Clear Quartz crystal between your palms to achieve activation.

Clear Quartz crystal

MENTAL BODY ACTIVATION

This exercise will increase your perceptive power by energizing your mental body, connecting you with the sunshine Yellow Ray of Archangel Jophiel, which allows you to experience the energy field of your client with ease. This is especially important when you are first learning to sense the chakras. In time you will not need to energize your mental body and your Palm Chakras will develop an amazing energetic structure.

WHAT TO DO

1 Raise the receptiveness in your hands by washing them in cool water and drying them thoroughly. Sensitize your hands by shaking them vigorously. Then rub your palms together rapidly in a circular motion several times to build up the surface *qi*.

2 Hold your hands with palms facing each other, about 22 cm (9 in) apart. Feel the energy radiating and vibrating between your hands; then play with this energy. (It will feel like sticky toffee.)

3 Begin to form this energy into a sphere and visualize it as bright yellow in colour. When it feels strongly pulsing with life-force, place this sunshine-yellow sphere into the solar plexus area. This quickly energizes your mental body.

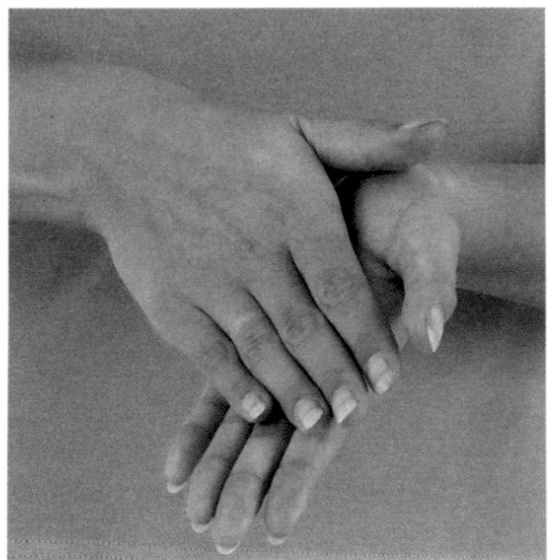

Roll a Clear Quartz crystal between your hands to activate your Palm Chakras.

Sensing the Chakras

The seven master chakras lie in the centre line of the body. These funnel-shaped vortexes of energy absorb and distribute life-force or *qi*. You will need to become aware of each chakra in order to work in the subtle-energy fields.

HOW TO SENSE THE CHAKRAS

For those of you who are new to sensing subtle-energy fields and making an intuitive energetic diagnosis, here is the basic chakra-sensing exercise. You will need a partner to work. Your partner should lie face up on a therapy couch.

WHAT TO DO

1 Invoke Archangel Raphael to increase your intuition.

2 Take a deep breath, and relax. Release all negative thoughts and emotions and focus on the energy field of your partner. Remain non-judgemental and positive.

3 Place your hands on your partner's shoulders and allow yourself several minutes to gain energetic rapport: this attunement process is vital.

4 When you feel ready, start to scan your partner's chakras (see pages 102–103).

5 Begin about 20 cm (8 in) above the top of your partner's head in the crown area. Raise your hands

upwards, palms facing each other about 50 cm (20 in) apart.

6 Slowly lower your hands towards the top of the head, at the same time bringing your hands together. Stop if you feel resistance. With your hands, explore the Crown Chakra energy field. Often the Crown Chakra is sensed at about 15 cm (6 in) from the head, but it depends on sensitivity and spiritual development.

7 Move to the Third Eye Chakra and position your hands as high as you can above the brow area; your hands should be about 50 cm (20 in) apart. Slowly bring your hands down and together until you feel a resistance. With your hands, explore the Third Eye Chakra energy field. Do this very gently, as most people on the spiritual path have a very sensitive third eye.

8 Repeat the process, sensing all the chakras in this manner until you feel you have located all the seven master chakras.

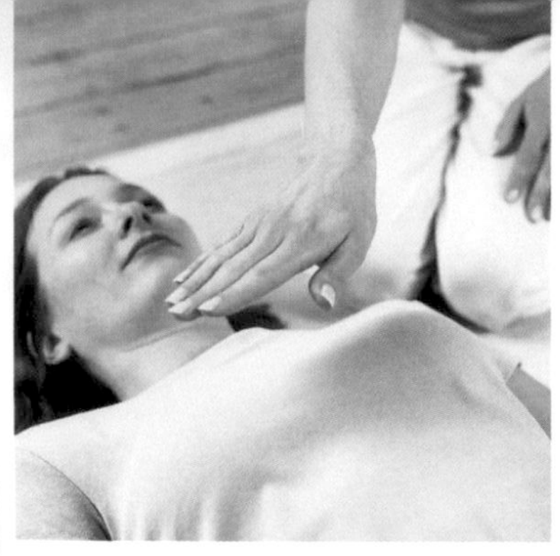

Sense the Throat Chakra by bringing your hands down and together until you feel resistance.

9 The Root Chakra is the slowest energy and the easiest to sense. You may need to stand at your partner's feet. Position your hands just beneath and between your partner's feet. Very slowly move your hand towards your partner until you feel a resistance.

10 At the end of the session allow yourself to detach from your partner's energy and ground yourself by asking the Archangel Raphael to ground, close, seal and protect your chakra centres and aura and those of your partner. You can make notes and, if appropriate, share with your partner what you perceived.

Chakra Dowsing

Many techniques exist for working on the chakras, but using a Clear Quartz pendulum is one of the easiest. A simple Clear Quartz crystal pendulum of about 5 cm (2 in) long, symmetrically cut and balanced, and suspended on a silver chain, is the best because it has a broad spectrum of healing energies and can be suitably cleansed, dedicated and programmed for working with the angelic realm.

Because it is quartz, you will quickly find one that has natural entrainment with your energy field, and by holding it near your solar plexus you will feel the resonance very strongly. Your pranic energy flows into the Clear Quartz pendulum to energize it.

Before you begin dowsing, you need to establish the 'yes' and 'no' pattern of your particular pendulum. Clear Quartz is easy to use.

HOW TO ESTABLISH 'YES' AND 'NO' ANSWERS FOR YOUR PENDULUM

As a beginner you will need to establish that the pendulum of your choice is resonating with your energy field or you may find it impossible to establish your 'yes' and 'no' answers. This dialogue with your pendulum will be unique to you. Some people find their pendulum swings clockwise for 'yes' and anti-clockwise for 'no'. But yours may be different; as long as you know what is your 'yes' and what is your 'no', that is all that really counts. You must also check at the beginning of each dowsing session that your 'yes' and 'no' pendulum movements have not changed.

YOU WILL NEED

Clear Quartz pendulum on a silver chain

WHAT TO DO

1 Hold the pendulum's chain between the thumb and forefinger of your right hand. Hold your left hand directly underneath your pendulum. Make sure that your pendulum is perfectly still; if you have the correct pendulum for you it should start to 'tremble'. Going into resonance is a direct sign that it is in entrainment with your energy field.

2 If it does not immediately go into resonance, try holding it just in front of your Solar Plexus Chakra. If that does not work, move it up towards your Heart Chakra.

3 Still your pendulum and ask mentally or aloud for your pendulum to show you the 'yes' movement. Take a few moments for this movement to become firmly established.

4 Still your pendulum and then ask it to show you the 'no' movement. This will be different from your 'yes' signal.

Chakra Cleansing

Chakra cleansing is possible using many techniques, but using a Clear Quartz pendulum is one of the easiest, especially when you are tuned into the healing angels. The angels will guide the pendulum to seek out areas of imbalance within the chakra. Chakra dowsing can be used to cleanse, energize, strengthen, align and harmonize the entire chakra system within the body.

Clear Quartz and Amethyst pendulums provide a broad spectrum of healing energies.

HOW TO CLEANSE THE CHAKRAS

YOU WILL NEED

Clear Quartz pendulum on a silver chain

WHAT TO DO

1 Invoke Archangel Zadkiel and his Violet Flame of Transformation. This will transform into positive energy any energy blockages or negative energy that is removed or released.

2 Established your pendulum's 'yes' and 'no' answers, then simply hold your pendulum over each chakra centre in turn and ask if the chakra needs cleansing.

3 Start at the Crown Chakra and work downwards in order. If a chakra does need cleansing, hold your pendulum over it and allow the pendulum to cleanse the chakra – usually anti-clockwise (unwinding). Visualize the Violet Flame over the chakra centre as the blockage is removed.

4 Once you have worked through all the chakra centres, you are ready to put positive healing energy into them to bring balance and alignment (see pages 228–229, Chakra Balancing).

5 Another useful method of cleansing the chakras is to hold your hands about 20 cm (8 in) apart, palms towards your partner over each chakra centre in turn. Continue as above from step 3.

One of my favourite ways of cleansing the chakras is to use a feather fan and an gem essence made from the beautiful purple crystal Amethyst (see page 283 for how to make a gem essence; see also page 312, Amethyst). Spray each chakra centre that your intuition or scanning tells you needs cleansing with the Amethyst essence. Then use the feather fan to cleanse each chakra – use upward sweeping movements with the feather fan.

Chakra Balancing

Balancing the chakras is possible using many techniques; two techniques are outlined here.

Dowsing over the Heart Chakra quickly cleanses and realigns emotional imbalances.

HOW TO BALANCE THE CHAKRAS WITH A PENDULUM

YOU WILL NEED

Clear Quartz pendulum on a silver chain

WHAT TO DO

1 Invoke Archangel Raphael and his healing angels before you begin.

2 Hold your pendulum over your partner's chakra centres, starting at the Crown Chakra, and work downwards in order.

3 Allow the healing energy directed by Archangel Raphael to flow into each chakra in turn – this normally takes place in a clockwise movement of the pendulum.

4 Move on to the next chakra centre when your pendulum has finished placing the healing energy into the chakra. You will know that this has happened when it stops moving.

HOW TO BALANCE THE CHAKRAS WITH YOUR HANDS

WHAT TO DO

1 Invoke Archangel Raphael and his angels of healing. You will normally feel this energy streaming into the top of your head and downwards to your Heart Chakra, before flowing down your arms into your hands and flowing out of your Palm Chakras.

2 Once you feel the healing energy flowing strongly, hold your hands about 20 cm (8 in) apart, palms towards your partner, over each chakra centre in turn. Start at the Crown Chakra and work downwards.

3 Your intuition will tell you when to move on to the next chakra centre.

The Aura

The peoples of ancient cultures knew and understood that the human body, beyond its physical form, is a pulsing, dynamic field of energy. Through observation they developed knowledge of these fundamental subtle energies that surround and permeate the human form.

In Sanskrit this subtle-energy field is called *kosas* (body sheaths), while in modern complementary medicine it is known as the biomagnetic energy field or aura. The word 'aura' comes from the Greek *avra* meaning 'breeze'. The aura consists of seven levels that correlate to the seven master chakras. These levels begin with the seen (the physical body) and progress to more subtle refined vibrations as we go further away from the physical. All auras are different and change constantly as our thoughts, moods, environment and health change.

Auric damage and depletion may be caused by ill health, negative thought patterns, environmental pollutants, bad dietary habits, addictive substances and stress. Auric imbalances cause a loss of vitality that weakens the energy field. Energy blockages appear as dark areas in the aura.

Auric levels Each auric level has its own function and energy awareness. Alternate layers of the aura are either fixed or moving. The first, third, fifth and seventh layers are fixed, while the second, fourth and sixth layers are moving. The level closest to the physical body is the etheric level. This is an exact fixed copy of the physical body and it is pale blue or light grey. It has pinpoints of light within it and moves rapidly. It holds memories of the physical body's formation.

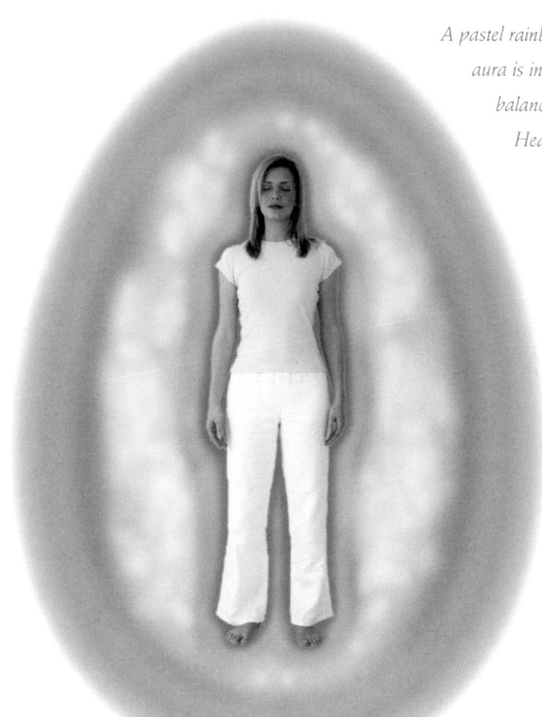

A pastel rainbow-coloured aura is indicative of a balanced, joyful Heart Chakra.

The second level relates to emotions and is a constant swirling mass of colours that change as our emotions change. The third level relates to the mental body and is a fixed layer of yellow that holds our thought processes. The fourth level relates to our heart energy. It appears as pastel colours and, when fully developed, as a pastel rainbow.

The fifth, sixth and seventh levels appear as bright blue, gold and silvery-blue to shimmering gold. These higher levels relate to spiritual development, so are not easily observable in most people.

Aura Sensing

It takes practice to become aware of auras. This technique will help you learn to sense another person's aura.

In order to sense the Third Eye Chakra, ask your partner to lie down on a therapy couch or table.

HOW TO SENSE ANOTHER'S AURA

YOU WILL NEED

A willing partner

WHAT TO DO

1 Ask your partner to stand with their feet about 30 cm (12 in) apart, knees relaxed and slightly bent. This keeps their energy flowing smoothly and the person 'grounded'. Breathing should be relaxed and normal.

2 Stand at least 2 metres (6 ft) away from your partner and energize your Palm Chakras (see page 220). Take a deep breath and relax; release all negative thoughts and emotions and focus completely on your partner's energy field.

3 Face your partner, hold your hands up in front of you, palms forwards, and begin to walk slowly towards them. Use your focused intent and try to place your awareness into your Palm Chakras. Imagine it as another set of 'eyes' you can see through.

4 Hold your focused intent on your partner and try to sense the 'edge' of their aura. This is normally oval in shape, but can be distorted. As soon as you are aware of their energy field (if you feel a resistance, change in temperature or tingling) begin moving around your partner, defining the edge of the aura with your hands.

5 Move your hands upwards above the head and downwards to the feet. Go all around your partner; sensing their energy field and make mental notes of how it felt, and its shape.

6 Allow yourself and your partner to relax, then try to feel the next auric layer. Work through all the levels, relaxing for a few moments between layers.

7 You may be aware of areas that seem too hot or cool. At the end you can make notes and, if appropriate, share with your partner what you perceived.

Aura Balancing

Many techniques exist for working in the aura, but using a Clear Quartz crystal pendulum is one of the easiest and most effective because it has a broad spectrum of healing energies. The quartz pendulum naturally seeks out areas of imbalance in the aura and removes old energy blocks. Dowsing can be used to cleanse, energize, strengthen, align, harmonize and integrate each level of the aura. It will fill holes and stop energy leaks as well as giving protection.

Practise this technique with a friend or companion, taking it in turns to sense any problems and to provide healing.

A Clear Quartz pendulum on a silver chain can be used to heal auric imbalances.

HOW TO BALANCE THE AURA USING A PENDULUM

YOU WILL NEED

Clear Quartz pendulum on a silver chain

WHAT TO DO

1 Ask your partner to lie down, then hold the pendulum just above their body.

2 Start to swing the pendulum gently backwards and forwards in a neutral fashion. Whenever the pendulum varies from the neutral swing, it has found an imbalance.

3 Allow it to move over the imbalance until it either returns to the neutral back-and-forth movement or it stops altogether. A clockwise movement usually means an input of energy and an anti-clockwise one a release of energy.

4 Start dowsing with the centre line of the body, working from beneath the feet upwards to finish above the head. Allow the pendulum and your intuition to guide you. Be ready to move your pendulum upwards or downwards as you work through the auric layers.

5 Move to the side of your partner's body and, following the natural outline, go completely around them in a clockwise manner.

6 Work around your partner's outline once more, still in a clockwise manner, but this time about 45 cm (18 in) from the outside of the body.

7 At the end of the session allow yourself to detach from your partner's energy and suitably ground yourself by asking the Archangel Raphael to ground, close, seal and protect your chakra centres and aura and those of your partner.

Self-healing

You may feel guided to begin the process of self-healing. You do not have to be ill or in pain to begin self-healing; in fact many physical ailments and common disorders have a psychological source. The following technique is beneficial for relieving emotional or mental pain as well as physical discomfort. It can also be used for acute pain or stress.

Archangel Raphael, as the over-lighting angel of healing has the capacity to guide all healers. He is known as the physician of the angelic realm, the divine healer for healing ourselves and others.

HOW TO BALANCE AND HEAL YOUR CHAKRA CENTRES

WHAT TO DO

1 Repeat steps 1–3 opposite.

2 Starting with the Root Chakra, place your hands gently on your body and allow it to fill with healing energy. When your intuition tells you to, move on to your Sacral Chakra and repeat the process.

3 Work through all your chakra centres, finishing with your Crown Chakra. As you place your hands on the top of your head, link with your higher self.

4 To finish, breathe in the emerald light. When you feel ready, bring your awareness back to everyday waking consciousness.

HOW TO PRACTISE SELF-HEALING

YOU WILL NEED

Soothing CD or tape and player

WHAT TO DO

1 Begin by invoking Archangel Raphael and asking him to guide your hands.

2 Sit in a comfortable chair and make sure you will not be disturbed. Playing soothing music helps with the initial process of self-relaxation.

3 Ask Archangel Raphael to send you a sphere of emerald green healing energy. Sense the healing energy floating above your head.

4 Allow this energy to flow into your Crown Chakra; feel it flowing down your body and anchoring in your Heart Chakra.

5 Allow the healing energy to flow down your arms, feel it flowing out of your Palm Chakras and filling your aura.

6 Allow your hands to be guided and place them wherever you feel needs healing. If you have painful areas in your body, placing your hands over the area for several minutes will relieve, ease or release the pain.

Healing Others

Ask your client to drink plenty of water before and after each healing session to ease the removal of energetic blocks and emotional toxicity. You should do the same. Prepare yourself by relaxing and becoming aware of your breath.

HOW TO HEAL OTHERS

WHAT TO DO

1 Ask the client to lie on their back with pillows or cushions under the head and knees.

2 Ask Archangel Raphael to send you a beautiful sphere of emerald green healing energy. See the healing energy floating above your head. Allow it to flow into your Crown Chakra, down your body, anchoring in your Heart Chakra.

3 Allow the energy to flow down your arms and out of your Palm Chakras. You will be placing your hands on your client – the length of time you keep your hands in

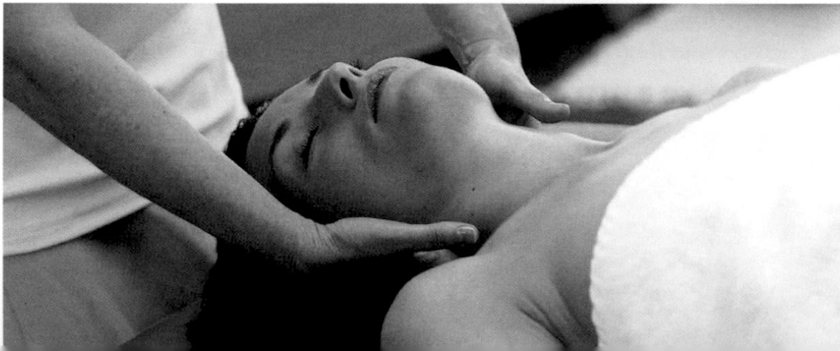

each position is up to your intuition, but three to five minutes is normal.

4 Position yourself at your client's head. You can sit for these first five hand positions.

5 Place the palms of your hands gently on the crown of the head and rest them there.

6 Place your hands over the eyes.

7 Cradle the head by placing your hands underneath it.

8 Place your hands with the heels of your palms on each side of the neck and your palms and fingers lightly on the throat.

9 Place your thumbs just below and aligned with the collarbones and with your palms towards the breastbone.

10 Move to your client's side to treat the heart, solar plexus and stomach areas. Place both hands over the ribcage in a straight line across the base of the sternum.

11 Place both hands in a straight line just above the waist.

12 Place both hands just below the waist, level with the hips.

13 Move to the legs. Move down the legs in stages. Work on each leg separately or both at the same time.

14 Move to the feet and position yourself at the end of the therapy couch. Treat the tops of both feet; then place your hands on the soles of the feet.

15 Move your hands off the feet and place your palms about 10 cm (4 in) beneath the soles of the feet. Use your intuition to observe your client's male-female polarity balance. The right foot represents male polarity and the left foot female polarity. Hold your hands in this position until all energy movement ceases. This strengthens the skeletal structure and draws your client fully back into the physical body, which signals the end of treatment.

Distant Healing

Distant or absent healing is an excellent way to begin practising angelic healing. It is also a very powerful way of working with Archangel Raphael and has validity in its own right, as you do not need all the 'paraphernalia' of the third dimension (therapy room, couch). Distant healing is also a great way of developing your multi-dimensional awareness of the healing energies that surround us all on Earth. In its simplest form, distant healing can be a prayer said for the person who has asked you for help. Keep the prayer simple and unconditional.

ARCHANGEL RAPHAEL'S EMERALD SPHERE OF ANGELIC HEALING ENERGY

WHAT TO DO

1 Decide to whom you are sending the healing.

2 Wash your hands in cool water and dry them thoroughly.

3 Sit quietly in a comfortable chair, take several deep relaxing breaths and summon Archangel Raphael.

4 Begin to sensitize your hands by shaking them gently. Then rub your palms together rapidly in a circular motion several times to build up the surface *qi*.

5 Hold your hands with palms facing each other about 20 cm (8 in) apart. Feel the energy

radiating and vibrating between your hands; play with this energy (it will feel like sticky toffee).

6 Begin to form this energy into a sphere and visualize it as emerald-green in colour.

7 Ask Archangel Raphael to bless and charge the emerald sphere with his powerful healing energy.

It is a good idea to get permission to do distant healing on someone. If this is impossible, direct the energy to be used for the highest good of all.

8 When it feels as if it is strongly pulsing with healing energy, send the sphere to the person; picture them absorbing it. See them smiling, healthy and strong.

Planetary Healing

Many people express the desire to help others, especially after seeing the terrible situations that plague our world. They feel burdened by these visions of unimaginable suffering and are guided to ask the angels to help.

Archangel Sandalphon is guardian of the Earth, in charge of planetary healing. When sending planetary healing, do not suppress your emotions since this causes blockages and affects your health. Instead, focus on the feelings and emotions that the haunting images created within you. This eases feelings of distress you are holding and directs the energy to where it is needed most.

When we view the Earth from space it is easy to feel the interconnectedness of all life.

HOW TO PRACTISE PLANETARY HEALING

WHAT TO DO

1 Sit comfortably in a chair with your feet on the ground.

2 Visualize roots growing out of the soles of your feet to ground and strengthen you. Breathe naturally so that your own energy circuits are open and flowing smoothly.

3 Summon Sandalphon and align yourself with his energy. You will feel energy flowing in through your Crown Chakra, coursing downwards into your Heart Chakra, before flowing down your arms into your hands and then flooding out of your Palm Chakras.

4 Allow yourself to be surrounded by this energy, which is often perceived as a sphere of rainbow light. You are now ready to transmit angelic healing energy.

5 Visualize the swirling rainbow moving outwards from you towards the area of distress you have chosen. See the situation and all the people involved absorbing this energy; you will see the area become illuminated with iridescent rainbow light.

6 As you continue watching, become aware of all the other healers and planetary healing groups who are also sending out rainbows of hope. They are the children of light – the rainbow warriors. Allow your energy to fuse with theirs and feel how the power intensifies.

7 Many 'lightworkers' meditate every day sending out healing energy in the form of rainbows; they know that the planet and those in need will receive it in whatever form is appropriate to them. You will now feel as if you are part of this powerful angelically guided energy.

8 To close, detach from the energy. Ground yourself by asking the Archangel Raphael to ground, close, seal and protect your chakra centres and aura.

Balancing the Emotions

Our emotions are associated with the fluid element of water. Water has a unique significance to us, since most of our body weight is made up of water and it carries the nutrients essential for life.

Likewise our emotions should nurture us, allowing us the fluid movement necessary to explore our full potential – physically, mentally and spiritually. Our emotions, like water, change constantly, ebbing and flowing, bringing growth to our body, mind and soul. Sometimes emotions become frozen and we become stuck in a space that is restrictive and often destructive, and which blocks our full potential for joy and creativity.

Water boils when heated, then turns to steam and evaporates; this too, can be reflected in the emotions of anger, loss and emptiness. Emotional turbulence is caused when we suppress or deny our emotions. Many people have significant amounts of unresolved emotional energy which is a major cause of stress and tension in their lives.

Chamuel relieves the pressure The Pink Ray of Archangel Chamuel takes the 'heat' out of emotional stress. It restores equilibrium without suppressing the release process. It promotes relaxation and acceptance of where you are in life and what you have to deal with without allowing false views to harden into anger, hatred and resentment. It is also motivational, which stops feelings of complacency, transforming them into peaceful tranquillity.

HOW TO BREATHE OUT EMOTIONAL TURBULENCE

WHAT TO DO

1 Sit in a comfortable chair where you will not be disturbed for some time.

2 Invoke Archangel Chamuel and ask him to send you a pink sphere of emotional healing energy to release emotional stress, tension and turbulence.

3 See or feel the pink sphere descending onto the part of your body that is holding emotional pain (if you are not sure where the emotional pain is stored, ask him to position it over your Heart Chakra).

4 As you take a deep slow inward breath, imagine or feel that the air is focusing directly through the pink sphere. With each in-breath, the pink sphere will gradually dissolve the stress, turbulence and tension.

5 With each out-breath, feel the stored emotions melting away.

6 To finish the process, feel nurtured by angelic healing love by seeing yourself surrounded in a warm golden-pink glowing sphere of light. Allow yourself to stay with this energy as long as you feel appropriate. To end the session, ground, close, seal and protect yourself.

When working on emotional issues, trust the process and breath deeply and slowly.

Harmonizing Relationships

Archangel Chamuel and the angels of love help you renew and improve your relationships with others by assisting you to develop your Heart Chakra. This is accomplished through his beautiful Pink Ray, which represents our ability to love and nurture others, to give and receive love unconditionally, free from all self-interest. It is a love that transcends and transforms the self and moves us through compassion towards the divine state of understanding.

Chamuel has an important role to play on our path to enlightenment. Even if you work with no other angel, Chamuel has the ability to guide you home to the 'One-heart' on his wings of infinite love. Many people are afraid of opening their hearts. Those who have been able to overcome this fear have charismatic warmth that others find reassuring, soothing and uplifting.

He assists in all our relationships, especially through life-changing situations such as divorce, bereavement or job loss. Archangel Chamuel helps us to appreciate the loving relationships we already have in our life.

Archangel Chamuel's message is: 'It is only the love energy within any given purpose that gives lasting value, beauty and benefit to all creation. Once you have true love and compassion for yourself, you have the power to love unconditionally; instantly this transforms negative energy into positive beneficial healing energy.'

HARMONY TECHNIQUE

WHAT TO DO

1 Sit in a comfortable chair where you will not be disturbed for some time.

2 Invoke Archangel Chamuel and ask him to send you two spheres of his beautiful pink heart-healing energy.

3 Keep one for yourself and send the other to the person with whom you wish to strengthen, improve or renew a loving, harmonious relationship.

4 Hold your own pink sphere in your hands and gaze into it. It will help you see yourself more clearly; look into it not only with your eyes but also with your heart.

5 Use Archangel Chamuel's pink spheres in any situation that is aggressive or threatening or contains the energy of conflict. Simply ask Chamuel to surround everyone involved; this will reduce tension and bring about peaceful resolution.

Inspiration and Illumination

Angelic healing energy has a 'natural intelligence' which flows to where we need help the most – the wisdom of angels is beyond our understanding.

Archangel Jophiel's sunshine ray illuminates our path through life by helping us look beyond the obvious to gain an understanding of the current life situations we may be caught up in. He is very good at problem-solving – he helps us look at life from a deeper level.

His energy can be used any time you need mental clarity, especially when you have to take an examination, start a new job or absorb new information and skills.

There are a few key points to remember when we are helping others with angelic healing energy. Trust the process and allow the angels to guide the healing energy. Stay connected to your breathing when giving a therapy session. The person in need of the healing is the healer, the practitioner is merely a channel for the angelic healing energy.

PRACTISING ILLUMINATION/ INSPIRATION TECHNIQUE

YOU WILL NEED

A partner to practise with

WHAT TO DO

1. Before beginning, discuss with your partner what they want the illumination/inspiration technique to shed light on. Perhaps they feel blocked creatively, lacking energy and enthusiasm, or need flashes of insight into a current problem.

2. Ask your partner to lie face up on a therapy couch. Place pillows under the head and knees for comfort. Have a blanket ready in case they feel cold.

3. Seat yourself in a straight-backed chair beside the couch, close to your partner's head.

4. Once you are sitting down comfortably with your feet on the floor, invoke Archangel Jophiel and ask him to send a golden sphere of energy for inspiration and illumination.

5. The golden sphere will descend and rest just above the top of your head. Feel your connection to Archangel Jophiel; be aware that he will guide the process.

6. Place your hands on your partner's head with your right hand under the head at the base of the skull (slightly above the back of the neck) and the left hand on the top of the head on the Crown Chakra.

7. See or visualize the golden sphere moving from above your head and entering your partner's head. Use your focused intent and see it spreading through the whole of their body and aura, surrounding them completely in a golden glow.

8. Allow 20 minutes for the process to take place. Share with your partner any insights you gained during the healing session.

Protection

Archangel Michael is the protector of humanity. He is the supreme commander-in-chief of all the archangels and he leads the heavenly forces, his 'legions of light', against evil (the demonic-inspired human vices of anger, hatred, negativity, cruelty, hostility and conflict). He can be viewed as our supreme guardian angel.

Archangel Michael is a being of magnificent, awe-inspiring glory and radiant light, who is frequently depicted riding a white horse (representing pure, pristine, spiritual power), thrusting a lance into a writhing serpent. This is Archangel Michael symbolically slaying the lower aspect of the human personality, our self-destructiveness where fear and restriction reside, and allowing for the higher-mind connection of the soul to emerge phoenix-like, as the winged dragon of ultimate wisdom.

Summon protection Before you begin an angelic healing session, it is normal to summon the protection of Archangel Michael and his legions of light. For healing to take place, your client frequently has to release painful conscious and subconscious memories. During an angelic healing session this often begins to occur spontaneously. Sometimes this involves your client reliving emotionally the whole experience and this can feel as painful to them as when the event actually occurred.

Because we encourage our clients to acknowledge their emotions and accept pain so that they can control and release it for healing, they can sometimes become angry, agitated or defensive. The protection of Archangel Michael allows us to remain open, but still balanced and anchored in unconditional love.

ARCHANGEL MICHAEL'S CLOAK OF PROTECTION

WHAT TO DO

1 Summon Archangel Michael at any time to give you immediate protection. He will place his cloak of protection around you.

2 Use the following phrases: 'Archangel Michael. Help me! Help me! Help me! Help me! Archangel Michael. Protect me from all harm.'

3 Imagine Archangel Michael's cloak of protection around you. Visualize a deep blue cloak with a hood covering you (or a loved one) completely from head to foot.

A white horse represents pure pristine spiritual power which is used with wisdom.

Harmonizing Male and Female Polarities

The Chinese use the concept of yin and yang to express balance within the body's energy flow. They are complementary qualities, constantly interacting. Neither can exist in isolation from the other. Their affinity to each other has a direct effect on health and harmony.

Yin is feminine, negative, cold, interior, soft, downward, inward, dark, yielding and reaction. Yang is masculine, positive, active, exterior, hard, upward, hot, light, forceful and action. We are able to balance or harmonize these two apparently conflicting opposites by understanding that for every action there is a reaction, and the natural laws of matter are transcended – we are in the 'moment'. We are not our past (action); we are not our future (reaction); we just are.

Yin/Yang is the Taoist symbol of universal force – Yin is receptive cool female force while Yang is active hot masculine force.

Understanding eternity Once we have grasped the 'moment' for even a brief second, we gain an understanding of eternity, the eternal moment of 'now'. We transcend the Newtonian laws of physics and step into quantum physics where all is unity, the ancient mysteries are unlocked and we see wisdom in the ultimate truth.

To transcend duality and step into the moment, we need to petition Metatron, who will open our Crown Chakras, and integrate our transcendental chakras above our head, bringing unprecedented spiritual growth and cosmic alchemy.

When you are ready to work with Archangel Metatron you are ready for the 'ultimate' angelic healing. This alignment with Metatron will reconcile the opposites that must be harmonized before balance is established.

HOW TO BALANCE THE POLARITIES

WHAT TO DO

1 Sit comfortably and breathe easily and naturally so that your energy circuits are open and flowing smoothly.

2 Ask Archangel Metatron to send you his sphere of pure white light. As you align yourself with this energy, visualize or feel it very high above your head as a column of light.

3 As you allow the light to descend to encompass the whole of your body in a pillar of light, each of the transcendental chakras above your head is activated, integrated and aligned. This causes a download of information that will over time and with continuous use activate your 'Light Body' and bring the 'ego's' illusion of duality to an end.

Promoting Spiritual Growth

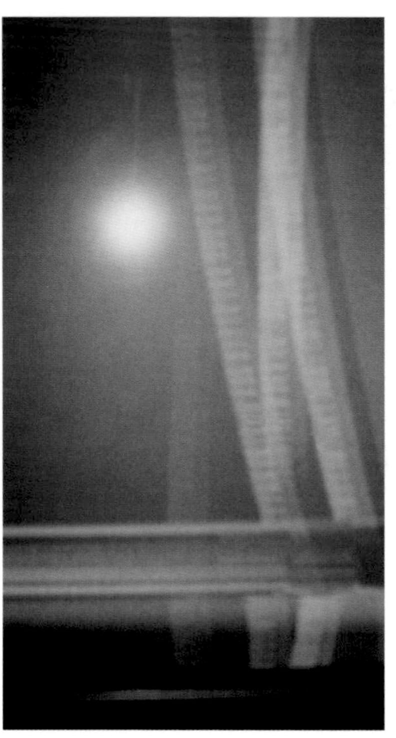

We need to raise our consciousness in order to increase our awareness of angels. When we work with Archangel Gabriel he teaches us to seek angelic help through invocation, ritual, meditation and dreams. Some people get bogged down with intellectualizing about angels, trying to understand them through logic. Gabriel's planet is the Moon; he uses this passive feminine intuitive energy to help you interpret your dreams and visions. He also uses the Moon's magical energy to inspire humanity while it sleeps.

Since the dawn of time the Moon has been revered as a symbol of guidance. In myth the Moon is said to have a profound influence on all living things. The fuller the moon, the more influence she exerts over the mind and psychic power.

HOW TO CREATE A MAGICAL MOON AMULET

This amulet creates a powerful energy field around you when you wear, carry or sleep with it. It seals and protects the aura.

YOU WILL NEED

Blue Moonstone
White tea-light (in a jar if you are outdoors)

WHAT TO DO

1. Choose a Monday, the day dedicated to the Moon, to work this angelic ritual. Choose a time when the Moon is waxing or growing larger, since this favours spells for growth and attraction (you are looking to attract spiritual growth). It can be performed outdoors, but if you choose to do it indoors make sure you can see the Moon through an open window.
2. Light the tea-light before you begin the ritual. Ask Archangel Gabriel to empower you and to oversee the process.
3. Hold your Moonstone in your feminine, intuitive left hand.

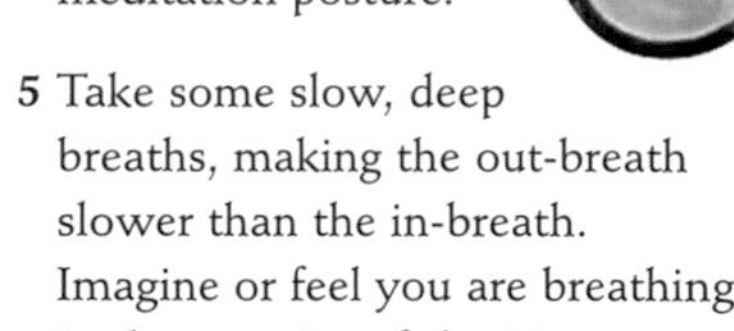

4. Sit in a comfortable meditation posture.
5. Take some slow, deep breaths, making the out-breath slower than the in-breath. Imagine or feel you are breathing in the energies of the Moon.
6. Feel your body filling with the Moon's light.
7. When your intuition tells you, breathe this energy into your Moonstone.
8. Hold the Moonstone to your Heart Chakra and ask Archangel Gabriel to empower it with his magical energy; move it to your Third Eye Chakra and ask for Archangel Gabriel's blessings.
9. Wear, carry or sleep with the Moonstone on a daily basis to increase spiritual growth.

Letting Go of the Past

We need to let go of past pain in order to find inner peace. If we continually look backwards and only remember the difficult times in our lives, we stunt our spiritual growth and restrict our capacity for future happiness. Any feelings of nostalgia, homesickness, remorse for having missed out on an opportunity, unfulfilled dreams or ambitions will also tie up your life-energy.

In the negative emotional state of permanent loss, the past can sometimes be over-idealized, weakening your connection with your current life situation. If you are at a low point in your life through a great personal loss, or have suffered a great emtional trauma, the following ritual and invocation to the four great archangels will allow you to stand once more in the centre of the circle of your being.

This crystal circle is a symbol of the Earth where all living things are equal and sacred.

SACRED ANGELIC CIRCLE

The circle is sacred in most traditions and represents the journey of life. It forms a circle of power, much like the 'Medicine Wheel' in the traditions of North American First Nations tribes.

WHAT TO DO

1. Create a circle of tea-lights or crystals, or simply define the circle with your imagination – visualize it as a circle of fire.
2. Sit in the centre of your circle facing east.
3. Call in each of the four great archangels in turn, silently or aloud, and wait until you feel each is anchored before calling in the next one.
4. Use the following words: 'Before me Raphael, Angel of the East' (visualize a green light with a gold aura); 'Behind me Gabriel, Angel of the West' (visualize an orange light with a white aura); 'On my right hand Michael, Angel of the South' (visualize a yellow light with an indigo-blue aura); 'On my left hand Uriel, Angel of the North' (visualize a red light with a violet aura).
5. Now focus on your Heart Chakra and see there the Star of David – two interlocking triangles (the symbol of the Heart Chakra and balance).
6. Mentally petition the four archangels, asking them to help you let go of the past; this allows you to build a positive 'present' and 'future' life. Give thanks and allow the energies to 'dissolve'.

Transformation

The healing energy of Archangel Zadkiel and his angels of joy help us transform past painful memories, limitations, energy blockages, negative personality traits and addictions. Decide what you want to free yourself from, then invoke Archangel Zadkiel and ask him to send his Violet Flame of Transformation. The Violet Flame is high-frequency spiritual energy (violet is the shortest and fastest light and symbolizes a transition point between the visible and the invisible). It transforms lower energies into positive life-affirming energy. Violet has always represented divine alchemy and transmutation of

Ask Archangel Zadkiel to send you his Violet Flame of Transformation while you sleep.

energy from the gross physical level into the unmanifested divine level.

Using the Violet Flame The Violet Flame is used in numerous ways in angelic healing, not just on ourselves but also on our clients. It ranges in colour from palest silver-lilac to deep amethyst. Use it to cleanse and purge all areas of the mind, body and emotions, and to purify all the chakra centres and aura during a healing session. It amplifies other healing and spiritual energies and transforms any negative energy that has been released during a healing session.

Use it to cleanse, calm and free the mind before meditation or to ease insomnia and nightmares.

SELF-HEALING TECHNIQUE

WHAT TO DO

1 Sit comfortably where you will not be disturbed.

2 Breathe easily and naturally, allowing yourself to release any tension from your physical body.

3 Mentally ask Archangel Zadkiel to send you his Violet Flame of Transformation.

4 See or feel your whole being surrounded and engulfed by the Violet Flame. As the Violet Flame diminishes and finally dissolves, the session is over.

HEALING OTHERS

At any point during a therapy session, mentally invoke Archangel Zadkiel and ask him to cleanse and purify any area (this can be the physical, emotional, mental or spiritual body, as well as any chakra centre or auric level). See the area surrounded by the Violet Flame, and allow the flame to completely consume and transform any negative energy or blockage.

Akashic Angels: Exploring Past Lives

Accessing the Akashic records is a powerful way of empowering the human spirit and connecting to your higher self. It helps you explore your past lives, Dharma, life purpose and parallel lives.

It also helps you receive impressions of your past and future lives, as well as planetary evolution and religious and other prophecies. In his role as lesser YHVH (the Tetragrammaton), Archangel Metatron is the keeper and guardian of the Akashic records.

Akasha is Sanskrit meaning primary substance or 'planetary record cell'. These archives can also be called the 'Book of Life', 'Cosmic Mind', 'Library of Life', 'Library of Light', 'Collective Unconscious', 'Universal Mind of God/Goddess' or 'Souls' Records' (see pages 56–57). It exists beyond time and space and contains information on all that was, is, or will be.

Consulting Metatron Our guardian angels have the capacity to consult Archangel Metatron and the Akashic records on our behalf. As these records are nature's complete memory of every event on Earth and every person's actions and all parallel universes (according to ancient teachings, there are billions of universes) the Akasha is cosmos not chaos.

Most humans only access the Akasha through the mental and astral worlds (Jung's 'collective unconscious'), but when we work with our higher self and our guardian angel we have access to all the levels, realities and dimensions the Akasha penetrates and transcends. Only with guidance from higher-level beings can we unlock the 'codes of light' from which the Akasha are formed.

Even with the help of your higher self, guardian angel and Metatron, the 'light

codes' will often be perceived by the human mind as symbolism or a library in which books or scrolls are stored. Yet, as we transcend the human mind, the codes of light will be downloaded into the Heart Chakra and DNA where they will be decoded and stored as a higher form of 'intelligent energy' which will bring about personal evolution, clarity and guidance. It will also influence the collective unconscious of the planet, and aid planetary evolution.

Archangel Metatron is the keeper of the Akashic records, the Universal Mind of God. Accessing these records can help you on your spiritual path and allow you to explore past and parallel lives.

Journey into Past Lives

To journey into past lives we link with our higher self and guardian angel to give us access to Archangel Metatron who will consult the Akashic records on our behalf. As the Akasha is nature's cosmos, we begin to understand the unity of all life – the 'Law of One'. The Akasha exists so that we can each journey without prejudice and without judgement into the reality of oneness.

Most people when they 'tune' into the Akasha normally access past lives and events that have the greatest amounts of emotional energy attached to them. These will be greatly influencing their present life.

Remember the future is not fixed, and by changing our behaviour and thought patterns we can influence it. What we focus on personally and planetarily we bring into manifestation.

Allow your guardian angel to surround you with protective love and light when you wish to gain access to Metatron and the Akashic records.

HOW TO JOURNEY INTO PAST LIVES

WHAT TO DO

1 Make yourself comfortable where you will be undisturbed.

2 Concentrate on your breathing, relaxing your body by making the out-breath longer and slower than the in-breath. Continue with relaxing breathing for several minutes to bring your mind to a state of calm.

3 Invoke your guardian angel and feel your connection to your higher self.

4 Allow your guardian angel's wings to surround you and enfold you with their loving protection and support.

5 Release all judgemental attitudes and prejudices you may have about yourself and others. Ask your guardian angel to help you do this if you find it difficult.

6 Once you feel a space of emotional clarity, ask your guardian angel to link in with Archangel Metatron.

7 Once you feel this connection (as a pillar of light surrounding you), ask to be shown a past life that is greatly influencing your present life.

8 Allow yourself to see or perceive this lifetime; remember you must not allow self-judgement to cloud your awareness or you will block your perceptive abilities and access to the information.

9 Once you have a clear perception of the past life, allow yourself to return to normal everyday waking reality; bring yourself gently back from this altered state of awareness.

10 Remember to be patient with yourself – it takes practice to be able to achieve spectacular results.

11 Write down your experiences in your angelic journal for future reference and meditation.

Releasing Spirits

A damaged aura leaves you open to the misery of spirit attachments (also known as negative entities or parasites). This damage can be caused by disease, negative thought patterns, pollutants, addictions, stress, psychic attack, emotional turmoil, poor breathing techniques or poor spiritual cleanliness. Holes, gaps and tears within the aura are also very common, much more so than most people realize, and they may even result in multiple energy leakages, causing debilitation.

If the integrity of your aura becomes damaged, you may attract entities that drain your life-force. This attachment of disincarnate spirits to the body that influences both the mind and behaviour of the host is recognized in every religion and is documented in every 'holy' book as well.

Out of character Attachments may cause you to behave out of character. Changes can be subtle or dramatic, and often involve a 'new' addiction. Addictions and negative thought patterns may take on a life of their own and act as a form of possession.

Symptoms of attached entities are: unexplained exhaustion, nightmares, sudden anxiety attacks or depression, hearing voices inside your head, suicidal impulses, mood swings or personality changes, indecision, confusion, poor concentration, memory gaps, impulsive behaviour and unexplained physical symptoms or illness. None of these is a sure sign of attachment, but if you have several of them it could indicate that you have made room for an uninvited guest.

Once an individual has attracted a disincarnate spirit as an attachment, that

person is more open to attracting more disincarnate spirits. These disincarnate spirits need not only to be removed, but also to be helped to the 'light' by the angels. They are often confused. Some are misguided, having realized too late that they are responsible for their behaviour, and they fear the wrath of God and so avoid the light.

Spirit attachments, energy implants and other energetic blocks, as well as binding ties that drag your energy down and lower your consciousness, can all be released with the help and support of Archangel Michael and his 'legions of light'. These angels include ones that specifically guide lost or misplaced souls back to the 'Source' to receive healing.

Ask Archangel Michael to help you release spirit attachments, other peoples' negative thought patterns and other energy blocks.

Cutting Ties with the Help of Archangel Michael

Archangel Michael and his 'legions of light' specialize in cutting binding ties, removing energy implants and releasing spirit attachments. Some attachments are designed to control us emotionally, others sexually, physically, mentally or spiritually. Energy vampirism is common and they feed off our energy – we all know people whose company leaves us feeling exhausted. Normally vampire attachments are through the Solar Plexus Chakra, but any chakra can be affected. Some attachment hooks may begin by going into one chakra but are then woven into several more.

We can also tie ourselves up in emotional knots by holding on to old relationships, past suffering, trauma or abuse. This binds a lot of our energy and

Releasing negative energy and cutting binding ties allows us to move forward with our life, bringing joy and renewal.

we need to free this energy in order to move forwards. Emotional baggage slows us down and lowers our vibrational rate (see pages 18–19); it builds up over years causing unresolved emotional stress and blockages within our energy system, which weakens our energy field. Whenever we release negative emotions or energy it must be replaced with angelic healing energy.

CUTTING TIES TECHNIQUE

During the following technique you can visualize Archangel Michael's Sword of Protection and Truth as either gold metal or a living sapphire-blue flame.

WHAT TO DO

1. Seat yourself comfortably where you will be undisturbed.
2. Visualize roots growing out of the soles of your feet to ground and strengthen you.
3. Allow your breathing to become easy and natural.
4. Summon Archangel Michael and his 'legions of light'; align yourself with this energy. Ask Archangel Michael to cut away all binding ties and cords, removing energy implants and release spirit attachments.
5. Feel or sense Archangel Michael going through each of your chakra centres and working through your aura.
6. Be aware of the process, and see or feel the ties being cut or disincarnate entities being taken up to the light by Archangel Michael.
7. To close the healing session, ask Archangel Michael to wrap you in his blue cloak, which will gently heal any holes or gaps within your aura and give protection while the healing process is completed.

Angelic Empowerment

Archangel Michael and his angels bring angelic empowerment if we seek their help. This empowerment helps us release fear and other negative emotional states that hold us back from reaching our true potential. Negative emotional states weaken our spirit. Self-limiting excuses serve to block angelic contact and stop the real you from being fully present as an incarnate being of unlimited love and light.

Receiving Archangel Michael's gift of activation of the Blue Ray (see pages 112–113) brings the attributes of courage, endurance, truthfulness, steadfastness, strength and the ability to take control of your life. Mastery of the First Ray of Divine Will and Power brings freedom from the shadows of illusion.

Empowerment helps us release negativity that holds us back, and lets us take control of our lives.

ACTIVATING THE FIRST RAY

WHAT TO DO

1 Sit comfortably where you will not be disturbed.

2 Breathe easily and naturally, releasing tension from your physical body.

3 Invoke Archangel Michael and request his gift of empowerment by activating the First Ray of Divine Will and Power within you.

4 Focus your awareness on your Heart Chakra – place your consciousness there and see the flame in your heart growing stronger and brighter. You may feel a tingling or sense of expansion and warmth.

5 Allow this flame and your conscious awareness to spiral up your spiritual spine and into your Crown Chakra.

6 Become aware of the column of light that surrounds you. This tube of light is your protection. As you gaze upwards you are aware that it seems to go on endlessly.

7 Allow your consciousness to travel upwards through the tube of light, until it comes to the pyramid of light which is the realm of your higher self and your soul family.

8 Here you see your soul family, angels and ascended beings seated around a crystal table. Take your seat at the table. Discuss with them how you can become empowered and take your divine birthright as a member of the 'legion of light'.

9 Allow the process to unfold naturally. When it is complete, bring your awareness back to the physical body and your everyday waking awareness.

Karma Clearing

Miasms are subtle-energy imprints that can lodge in any of the subtle-body systems and cause emotional or mental disease or physical illness. There are four basic types: karmic, acquired, inherited and planetary.

Karma is a Sanskrit word meaning the sum total of a person's actions in this and previous lives. The karmic principle allows each person to experience the full scope of all perspectives on life. It is central to all Eastern religions and similar principles are also found in Western religions. For example, Christianity teaches that you should 'do unto others as you would have others do unto you'.

Karmic miasms are the residue of past-life actions that lodge in the etheric body and have the potential to develop into illness, disease or suffering in the present or in future lives. This predisposition

Good actions attract good karma; by opening our hearts to angels we naturally wish to help others.

often determines our attitude and behaviour in this lifetime. They lower our state of consciousness, attracting negative people and situations into our life.

Acquired miasms are acute or infectious diseases or petrochemical toxicity acquired during this lifetime. After the acute phase of an illness, these traits settle into the subtle bodies and predispose you to illness.

Inherited miasms can also be called heredity miasms. These subtle-energy imprints are passed down to you from your ancestors. They may be genetic or can originate from infectious diseases. Planetary miasms are stored in the collective consciousness of the planet in the etheric level. They may penetrate the physical or subtle bodies.

KARMA CLEARING TECHNIQUE

The Violet Flame (see page 144) can be used to clear all types of miasms and is effective for clearing karmic miasms.

WHAT TO DO

1 Sit comfortably where you will not be disturbed.

2 Breathe easily and naturally; allow yourself to release any tension from your physical body.

3 Mentally ask Archangel Zadkiel to send you his Violet Flame of Transformation to clear your karmic miasms.

4 See or feel your whole being completely surrounded and engulfed by the Violet Flame. As the Violet Flame diminishes and finally dissolves, the session is over.

Guidance

Angels have many functions and one of the most important is to give wise counsel. People seek guidance from friends, family members or colleagues and there are people trained as counsellors and behavioural therapists who spend their lives helping others through the trauma of bereavement, redundancy and destructive relationships.

Sometimes we need to step out of the rigid third-dimension mind set and look to higher sources of guidance – we need to look larger, to explore the bigger picture. Your guardian angel links you to your higher self, where all is understood. Often we are too close to the problem and continually scrutinize each minute detail until we are emotionally exhausted.

There are times when we are not ready to discuss our problems with counsellors or we do not wish to burden our family and friends with our difficulties. This is the perfect time to seek spiritual counselling from our guardian angels.

HOW TO SEEK GUIDANCE

WHAT TO DO

1 Sit in a steady meditation posture and relax.

2 Close your eyes and take some slow deep breaths, making the out-breath slower than the in-breath.

3 Focus on your Crown Chakra and feel your connection to your higher self. Ask your higher self to send down a sphere of light to surround and protect you during this guidance technique. (The sphere can be any colour. Make a note of the colour, as often your higher self will send you the colour you most need to bring balance and healing to your life.)

4 Invoke your guardian angel and ask for spiritual guidance.

5 Visualize yourself sitting opposite an empty chair (this is for your guardian angel). Invite your angel to sit in the chair. You will be aware of a brilliant light beginning to form in front of you. See the light grow larger and take the form of your angel.

6 Feel the compassion radiating from your angel, open your heart to your angel and allow yourself mentally to tell your angel your problems and concerns.

7 Be open to receive any insights from your angel; be willing to put into practice what your angel suggests.

8 When you are ready, allow yourself to return to everyday waking reality.

Angels give wise counsel if we are prepared to listen, and allow us to look at the bigger picture.

Accepting and Developing Spiritual Gifts

If we ignore any aspect of ourselves we become fragmented. If we do not nurture our physical bodies they will quickly become unhealthy, and if we ignore our emotional needs we invite stress into our lives. If we continually ignore our spirituality and fixate on worldly possessions we develop spiritual poverty.

In recent years there has been an upsurge of interest in meditation, yoga, Reiki and other activities that reduce stress and aid relaxation. Through these techniques, many people have begun to open spiritually, started to examine

Opening and healing your Heart Chakra will allow you to accept and develop your spiritual gifts.

their lifestyles and choices, and learned how to nurture and accept all aspects of themselves. We are all born not only with a guardian angel but also with amazing spiritual gifts that are our divine birthright. In order to accept and develop your spiritual gifts, you will need to open and heal your Heart Chakra, so that you are always working from a place of love.

ACCEPTING TECHNIQUE

WHAT TO DO

1 Sit in a comfortable meditation posture and relax.

2 Close your eyes and focus gently on your breathing. Allow it to become a little slower and deeper than normal.

3 Invoke Archangel Chamuel to help you, protect you and oversee the process.

4 Touch your Heart Chakra in the centre of your chest and visualize your Heart Chakra's 12 lotus petals. As you view them, notice if any are damaged – some petals may even be closed.

5 Ask Archangel Chamuel to open the petals and repair any damaged ones. The normal colour of the heart lotus petals are green, but as we evolve spiritually they change to a beautiful shade of pink; see how many of your heart petals are now pink.

6 To close the healing session, bring yourself back to everyday waking reality. Repeat the meditation at further sessions until all your heart petals are pink, your Heart Chakra is open and you are happy developing your spiritual gifts.

Soul Rescue

Sometimes deeply traumatic events or acute or prolonged illness can make us feel ill at ease with ourselves. It is as if we have lost part of ourselves or are falling apart. Sometimes these feelings of loss of the self may be due to soul loss or fragmentation. Some people who have soul loss have memory gaps, especially from early childhood where the soul is more easily shocked into 'flipping' out. Sometimes we give away part of ourselves to others, especially during romantic relationships.

The path to recovery on a soul level has been called soul retrieval or soul rescue. By working with the angelic realms to build a bridge of light, we can summon the soul fragments back to us where they can be re-integrated. This often brings dramatic changes in overall physical, mental and emotional health.

Archangel Haniel uses the Turquoise Ray of heart-felt communication to restore your soul fragments.

SOUL-RESCUE TECHNIQUE

Archangel Haniel is the protector of your soul and will seek out your soul fragments.

WHAT TO DO

1 Sit in a comfortable meditation posture and relax.

2 Close your eyes and focus gently on your breathing. Allow your body to relax.

3 Invoke Archangel Haniel. Feel yourself connecting and aligning with his energy (turquoise). See or feel yourself completely surrounded and protected by his light.

4 Once you have made a strong connection, ask him to traverse all dimensions to seek your soul fragments.

5 If you have soul fragments that are willing to return to you (sometimes they are not), you will see them travelling back to you over a bridge of light. Often the fragment will appear to be you at the age you 'lost' this part of yourself.

6 You may feel the need to have a dialogue with the fragment, especially if it is reluctant to come back to you. If you find the emotions around the loss overpowering, or you are unable to express yourself eloquently, ask Haniel to assist you. He uses the Turquoise Ray of heartfelt communication so he can be very persuasive.

7 Once you have integrated all your soul fragments that are willing to return to you or you are willing to integrate, bring yourself back to everyday waking reality.

ANGELS AND CRYSTALS

Crystal Magic – Connecting with the Spirit World and Heaven

Crystals and gemstones have been used for thousands of years for decoration, physical adornment, healing, protection, magic and religious ceremonies. They are the most organized and stable examples of physical matter in the natural world and represent the lowest state of entropy (disorder) possible. All crystalline structures are made up of a mathematically precise three-dimensional arrangement of atoms. This is the crystal lattice, which confers a high level of stability. It also gives crystals their unique colours, hardness and physical, geometrical and subtle energetic properties.

Gemstones and crystals have an amazing capacity to absorb, store, reflect and radiate light in the form of intelligent fields of stable energy that increase the flow of vital life-force within the human physical body and subtle body. By applying this stable energy or crystal resonance in a coherent, focused way to dysfunctional energy systems, they restore stability and balance.

Malachite, used to make many objects, was ground into a healing powder by the ancient Egyptians.

Aligned with Heaven Crystals were born from the womb of Mother Earth, which gives them their unique aura of mystery and magic. They never lose colour, brilliance, beauty or value, and in many ancient civilizations this aligned them with the spirit world and Heaven. According to the evidence, the use of gemstones as jewellery at least dates back to the Palaeolithic Age. Perhaps the first written accounts of crystal healing came from the ancient Egyptians who gave detailed recipes for using gemstones such as Malachite for healing.

We still have the written knowledge of the Ayurvedic and Tantric scholars of the Indian subcontinent who knew the amazing potential of precious stones. They were 'prescribed' as protection from negative planetary

influences and either worn as jewellery or taken orally as pastes or oxides to influence the aura, as well as working through the nervous, lymphatic and *nadis* systems (channels through which prana flows).

Crystals are mentioned many times in the Bible, and in metaphysical circles it is believed that certain crystals are naturally attuned to the angelic realm. This alignment is due to their colour, angelic appearance or name such as Angelite or Celestite. It can also be due to the very high resonance they carry, which naturally attunes the wearer to the highest spiritual realms.

Selection, Care and Cleansing

Choosing a crystal to use may seem a daunting task, because there are so many to choose from. However, since all gemstones and crystals are attuned to a particular resonance and have their own particular properties, it is possible to look them up in a book and find out which is the most appropriate to use in particular circumstances.

Alternatively, see which crystal attracts you; trust your intuition. You can confirm your intuitive choice by dowsing with a pendulum, kinesiology (muscle strength reaction) or by passing your hand over the crystal to see if you can feel a subtle-energetic connection with it.

If you make a strong energetic connection, you may feel an 'electric' charge or tingling on your skin, a pulsing or twitching in your fingers or hands, sensations of heat or cold, a flush or wave of heat through your body or feelings of being enclosed by the crystal's energy field. If you are still unsure which crystal to choose, then opt for Clear Quartz, the 'master healer', since you can programme this crystal to perform almost any function you wish.

Care Do not allow other people to touch your personal crystal or jewellery at any time, since this will result in them becoming contaminated with foreign vibrations that may not be compatible with your energy field.

Store your crystal carefully, separately wrapped – if stones of differing hardness are kept together the harder ones will scratch and damage the softer ones, even if they are all tumbled stones. Some crystals such as Celestite or Kunzite can lose their colour in strong sunlight.

Cleansing It is important to purify your crystal before and after use. This ensures that any residual disharmonies are removed and your crystal is filled with positive energy. Choose a safe cleansing process for your particular type of crystal.

Smudging is an excellent ancient form of purification, for you and for your healing or meditation space. Allow the smoke to pass around the crystal to remove residual disharmonies. If you are indoors, keep a window open to let the stagnant energy out. Using sound to cleanse your crystal is very effective, especially for purifying several at the same time. Use a crystal singing bowl, a bell, ting-shaw (small Tibetan cymbals) or a tuning fork.

There are specialist products available for cleansing crystals. These crystal, angelic or aromatherapy cleansers come in atomizer bottles and are used to cleanse crystals and the environment.

Making a gem essence Gem essences contain nothing more than subtly energized water. Use a crystal of your choice, distilled water, brandy, clear glass bowls, large amber bottle and a smaller bottle with a dropper. Cleanse your crystal and sterilize equipment. Place crystal in a bowl of distilled water, or if dissolvable in water, place crystal inside empty bowl and put that bowl inside a water-filled bowl. Allow to stand in sun for 2–3 hours. Pour water into the main bottle and add twice as much alcohol. Using a dropper, put 7 drops into small bottle, fill this bottle with ⅔ distilled water, ⅓ alcohol. Use this as your gem essence. Label both bottles.

Even tap water can be used to cleanse your crystals in an emergency, though it is not ideal.

Dedicating Your Crystal

After you have chosen and cleansed your crystal, it is a good idea to dedicate it to protect it from negative energies. In order to dedicate a crystal or gemstone, simply hold it in your hand and state clearly in your mind: 'Only positive high-level energy may flow through this healing tool.'

Programming Normally, only Clear Quartz crystals are modifiable or 'programmable', as other crystals automatically contain their own specific resonance or natural signature. To programme your crystal, simply hold it to your Third Eye Chakra and concentrate on the purpose for which you wish to use it. Remain positive while you allow the crystal to fill with this energy. You could also state the intention of the programming out loud; for example, 'I programme this crystal for healing' (or for love, abundance, meditation, dream recall or other purpose of your choice). Once you have programmed a crystal it will hold your intent until you or someone else reprogrammes it.

Energizing All crystals and gemstones can be energized, which makes it a much more powerful healing or meditation tool. Some crystals naturally prefer to be energized with sunlight while others respond to moonlight. Most crystals accept being energized with Reiki. Some crystals like to be energized with sound, thunderstorms, colour or angelic energy. You can even place your crystal inside a pyramid to energize it. You may also enact a simple ceremony, asking the angels of light, love and protection to place their energy within the crystal.

Programme for protection the crystal you use to block negative energy from your computer.

Angel Aura Quartz

- **Colour** *Opalescent*
- **Appearance** *Natural quartz crystals scientifically bonded with platinum; produces shimmering play of pale rainbow colours*
- **Rarity** *Readily available*
- **Source** *Manufactured coating on natural quartz crystal*
- **Angel** *Your guardian angel and the 'crystal angels', a group of celestial beings dedicated to guiding and assisting those who work with crystals in their meditations and therapy sessions*

Natural crystal formation of Angel Aura Quartz.

Attributes: Angel Aura Quartz is also known as Opal or Pearl Aura Quartz. The shimmering shades of iridescent colours that play within this crystal swiftly attune the senses to the angelic realms of love and light. They purify and uplift your spirit, which floods your energy field with 'sweet' sparkling rainbow bubbles of protection. This crystal transports your awareness to the 'inner temple' of the higher self where knowledge of your guardian angel is stored.

Psychologically: Attunes you to beauty. Opens you to the energies of nature spirits and fairies. Brings lightness and spontaneity to all your activities. Awakens spiritual awareness.

Mentally: Used to counteract mental stress, confusion, apathy, inflexibility, rigidity, bewilderment and intolerance.

Emotionally: Releases inhibitions. Heals stress and stress-related illness. Brings peaceful resolution of emotional issues and discord.

Physically: Used to purify the physical body and to enhance the detoxification process undertaken when people begin to attune to higher frequencies.

Healing: Can help to heal all conditions, especially chronic or degraded conditions that have not responded to other complementary or orthodox medical treatment. Increases physical stamina and stops 'burn-out'.

Position: Wear to protect and strengthen the aura and to become a beacon of love and angelic light. Place on any chakra as your intuition guides you. It is especially powerful when placed in the Crown Chakra and the transcendental chakra centres. Makes an excellent gem essence. Energizes in the energies of the full Moon. Store in white silk square.

Additional note: Can be set in gold, silver or platinum. Combines well with Amethyst, Morganite, Phenacite, Aquamarine and Danburite.

Seraphinite

- **Colour** *Olive-green with white streaks*
- **Appearance** *The white streaks often resemble silvery feathers*
- **Rarity** *Easily available under the name Clinochlore*
- **Source** *Worldwide occurrence, quality specimens available from eastern Siberia, Russia*
- **Angel** *The Seraphim*

A polished slice of Seraphinite

Attributes: Seraphinite is the New Age name for Clinochlore. The origins of the mineral name are from the Greek *klino* (oblique) and chloros (green). The name Seraphinite is derived from the white streaks which often appear as angelic silvery feathers, angel wings or angelic beings. Because Seraphinite cuts and polishes easily, it is often formed into spheres, cabochons (oval shapes), healing wands and pendants. Seraphinite is one of the premier healing stones of our time. It activates angelic contact to the highest realms of healing. It is also a dynamic purifier of the two major conduits – the female Ida and male Pingala – through which energy rises up the spine, bringing yin-yang balance and stability to the Heart Chakra which allows alignment with and opening of the Crown Chakra.

Psychologically: Aids discrimination in matters of the heart. Helps you feel that it is good to be alive, helps you succeed without struggle by harmonizing the desires of the heart into perfect alignment with your soul's true desires.

Mentally: Removes thought forms that have become imbedded within the mental body and is excellent for helping those who feel either disconnected or disorientated.

Emotionally: Helps dispel negative emotions. Especially useful during stormy periods in a relationship as it helps you understand which emotions are yours and which emotions are being projected onto you.

Physically: Brings healing to all levels of the body as it purifies the blood. Relaxes the shoulders and upper chest, which increases oxygenation of the blood due to increased lung function.

Healing: Acts as a catalyst to heal all long-standing degraded physical conditions.

Position: Place on the Heart Chakra or wear as a pendant for prolonged periods. Makes an excellent gem essence.

Celestite

- **Colour** *Sky-blue, white or bi-coloured, can have tints of red or yellow*
- **Appearance** *Tabular blades, geode or pyramidal shape*
- **Rarity** *Common strontium mineral of the Barite group*
- **Source** *USA, Madagascar, Sicily, Germany*
- **Angel** *Celestial Guardians*

A geode of Celestite

Attributes: Celestite's name derives from the Latin *cealestis* which refers to its heavenly pale blue colour. It is also called Celestina or Celestita. It is used for conscious attunement to the angelic realm. It brings inner peace, tranquillity, calm and focus to the highest realms of heavenly light. It is a 'master' teacher for the New Age bringing spiritual expansion and soul harmony. Celestite links very strongly with the Celestial Guardians, who are vast beings of light that guide the cosmos.

Psychologically: Those who work with the very high vibration of Celestite are blessed with a sunny, harmonious, joyful disposition. You can clearly see their connection to the angelic realms. It brings them everyday flowing connection and they are in constant angelic communication.

Mentally: Nullifies ego-led desires and creates new mental pathways, especially where creativity has been blocked. Celestite makes those who wear it or work with it charming, amusing and wonderful to be with. Enhances communication skills and brings visions of humanity in harmony – world peace.

Emotionally: Celestite has a strange power over the emotions; it is so calming and soothing that it is almost soporific. Helps those people who suffer inner conflict due to absorbing other people's emotional stress and discord. These human 'sponges' often become allergic to people – which cuts them off from others and so brings isolation and withdrawal into fantasy worlds.

Physically: Lowers blood pressure. Eases stomach problems. Eases all nervous stress conditions.

Healing: Dissolves pain, eliminates toxins and eases fiery conditions.

Position: Place on the Throat, Third Eye or Crown Chakras or wear as a pendant. Makes an excellent gem essence (use the indirect method – see page 283). Never place in sunlight for prolonged periods as it will quickly fade and become clear.

Angelite

- **Colour** *Pale to sky-blue, violet*
- **Appearance** *Opaque and veined with white wings*
- **Rarity** *Common as Anhydrite*
- **Source** *Germany, Mexico, Peru and New Mexico*
- **Angel** *Heavenly Realms*

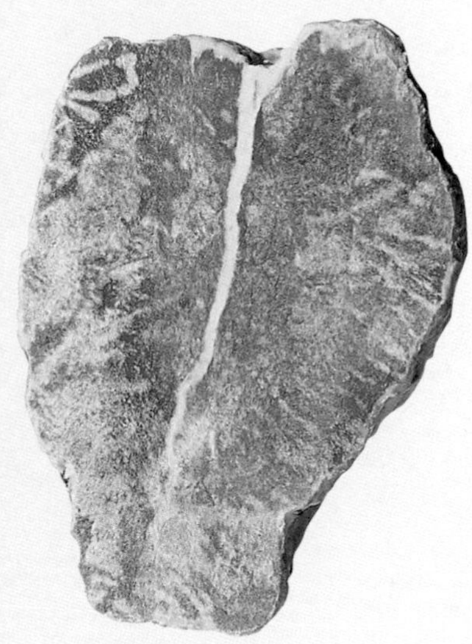

A polished face of Angelite

Attributes: Angelite is also called Anhydrite. The name is of Greek origin and means 'without water'. Angelite is formed from Celestite that has been compressed and the water extracted over millions of years. It is a New Age Aquarian stone that first came to prominence during the 'Harmonic Convergence' of 1986 in Peru when the 'keepers of days' gathered to welcome the 'new golden age'. Angelite is used for conscious connection to the angelic realms via attunement to the heavenly vibration of this pale sky-blue stone. Angelite brings inner peace, tranquillity, calm and focus to the highest realms of heavenly light.

Psychologically: Combats the fear of speaking the truth. Enhances kindness and gives you a social consciousness and emotional depth. It is not a frivolous crystal as it can be very down-to-earth and solid. Instils wisdom and counteracts cruelty and brutality.

Mentally: Teaches acceptance of the self and so is helpful for bringing calm acceptance of personality traits that have caused mental anguish. Grounds you in the present moment, which allows you to release that which no longer serves your highest good.

Emotionally: Enhances telepathic skills, which helps you interact with others at a higher emotional level.

Physically: Lowers blood pressure, soothes sunburn and balances overactive thyroid. Balances fluid functions of the body and thereby releases excess body weight. Eases bloating and lung problems.

Healing: A massage stone of Angelite applied to the feet and hands unblocks the meridians and swiftly clears any energy blockages.

Position: Place on the Throat, Third Eye or Crown Chakras or wear as a pendant. Makes an excellent gem essence (use the indirect method – see page 283). It enhances sound healing and chanting exercises that are designed to balance the chakras.

Azeztulite

- **Colour** *Colourless or white*
- **Appearance** *Opaque or clear*
- **Rarity** *Rare*
- **Source** *North Carolina, Vermont*
- **Angel** *Angels of the Azez*

Azeztulite in its raw state

Attributes: Azeztulite is a type of quartz but its energies are far more potent than those of ordinary quartz. This repatterned quartz carries an amazing light energy which is said to have been activated by an angelic entity known as the Azez. This group of inter-dimensional angelic beings aligns with the 'Great Central Sun' and they have 'anchored' their presence over many major power vortexes within the etheric realm of the Earth – including the Andes, Himalayas and other mountain ranges. The Azez carry and serve an energy signature known as the 'Nameless Light'. Azeztulite is the vessel and conduit for the Azez. It is a powerful stone that brings about shifts in consciousness as well as conscious inter-dimensional travel. Those who wear, carry or meditate with it are imbued with this energy and become an integral part of the network of 'Nameless Light' that will cause the consciousness of all humanity to be raised.

Psychologically: Awakens us to altered states of reality and elevates the consciousness. Activates the ascension points – allows us to open to the other realms and multitude of realities that inhabit the same energetic space. The ascension points are at the base of the spiritual spine, hara (energy focus point) and centre of the brain (pineal gland).

Mentally: Causes a quantum leap in the mental processes, so should only be used when you have completed a thorough cleansing of the mental body. This should include deprogramming yourself of mental clutter and energetic implants, past-life and ancestral miasms.

Emotionally: Dissolves old patterns of negative emotions when you feel the time is right for your ascension into cosmic awareness and enlightenment.

Physically: Can be used to bring light and healing energy to every cell in the body. Can improve all degraded conditions of the physical body, especially when used as a conscious channel for healing.

Healing: Can be used for any physical ailment which requires structured repatterning of the body.

Position: All chakras.

Moldavite

- **Colour** *Bottle-green*
- **Appearance** *Transparent, smooth, scarred, pitted or fern-like patterns*
- **Rarity** *Rare*
- **Source** *Czech Republic*
- **Angel** *Angels of Transformation*

Natural Moldavite

Attributes: Moldavite is a tektite (stone of extra-terrestrial origin) that was formed from a meteorite impact in what is now the Bohemian plateau of the Czech Republic. The meteorite crash happened some 15 million years ago, so Moldavite comes from only one place in the world. Moldavite's chemistry is unique and there are several theories regarding its formation. Many strange events occur during a meteorite impact, because of the tremendous heat and pressure produced. Tektites may be fused glass formed during the impact of the meteor on the Earth's surface. Archaeologists have discovered tektite shards and pieces in cave dwellings dating back some 25,000 years.

Psychologically: Moldavite is the 'Holy Grail', the 'emerald of enlightenment' that fell from the sky of spiritual transformation; it produces profound and lasting shifts in consciousness.

Mentally: Metaphysically, we have within us the 'Light Body' (see page 128) which contains encoded information like files. When we hold Moldavite this data is released causing mental repatterning or reprogramming.

Emotionally: Moldavite has a very 'hot' and 'fast' energy which quickly brings up emotional debris – often through tears or other emotional outbursts or flushes of energy. It also emotionally awakens 'star children' (beings from other planetary systems who have taken physical incarnation on this planet to help with its spiritual evolution), who long for the security of their cosmic home.

Physically: Assists in healing all physical conditions.

Healing: Moldavite is a diagnostic tool. An aversion to Moldavite or the colour green indicates dis-ease with emotions. It shows a deep fear of opening our hearts to unconditional love. Moldavite unlocks these hidden fears that cause our psychological and physical disease; once fears are acknowledged and released with unconditional love, true healing can begin.

Position: Heart or Third Eye Chakras.

Kunzite and Hiddenite

- **Colour** *Pale pink, lilac (Kunzite); pale green (Hiddenite)*
- **Appearance** *Transparent or translucent with striations*
- **Rarity** *Readily available*
- **Source** *USA, Brazil, Madagascar*
- **Angel** *Shekinah*

Kunzite in its natural state

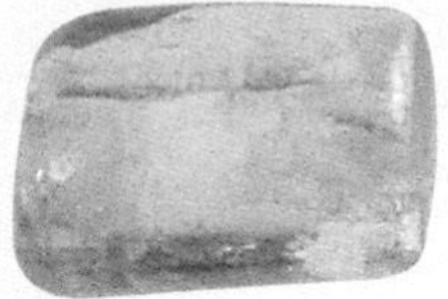

Tumbled Hiddenite

Attributes: Kunzite carries the pale pink to lilac ray of spiritual love – the true love of the mother for her child – which is always unconditional and bypasses the ego-centred love of the self. Hiddenite carries the pale green ray of tender heart healing. It is not the powerful emerald-green ray, rather the ray of fragile new beginnings. It is soft and gentle, like a whisper that holds the promise that all will be well. Both Kunzite and its sister Hiddenite display the qualities of Shekinah, the Queen of Heaven (see page 77), who is also called the angel of deliverance. The Shekinah is the feminine side of Archangel Metatron or the female manifestation of God in man, the divine in-dwelling. She is also called the 'Bride of the Lord'. In the New Testament sense, the Shekina is the glory emanating from God.

Psychologically: Combined Hiddenite and Kunzite allows us to get in touch with the part of ourselves that has always been in contact with the Divine. It activates the in-dwelling spirit of God which leads us out of the shadowland of illusion towards wholeness and unity.

Mentally: Combined use of Hiddenite and Kunzite allows us to feel safe and cosseted which helps us discover who we truly are and why we are here. Eases depression and all manic disorders.

Emotionally: Combined use of Hiddenite and Kunzite allows the emotions of the innermost heart to be healed. Together they support new beginnings and facilitate deep healing. Reminds us that change brings positive opportunities to release inner blocks.

Physically: Heals the nervous system. Stops panic attacks.

Healing: True healing on all levels of our being – allows us to simply be 'ourselves' regardless of all outside influences and physical restrictions. Our in-dwelling divinity, the Shekinah, is only awaiting our call; as the divine mother she waits with patience in the sure knowledge that one day we will awaken from our trance state and seek bliss.

Position: Heart Chakra.

Opal

- **Colour** *Precious Opals have flashes of colour. Common Opal can be any colour but has no opalescence*
- **Appearance** *Opaque with flashes of colour*
- **Rarity** *Readily available but expensive*
- **Source** *Worldwide, best specimens are found in Australia*
- **Angel** *Pistas Sophia (angel of faith and wisdom)*

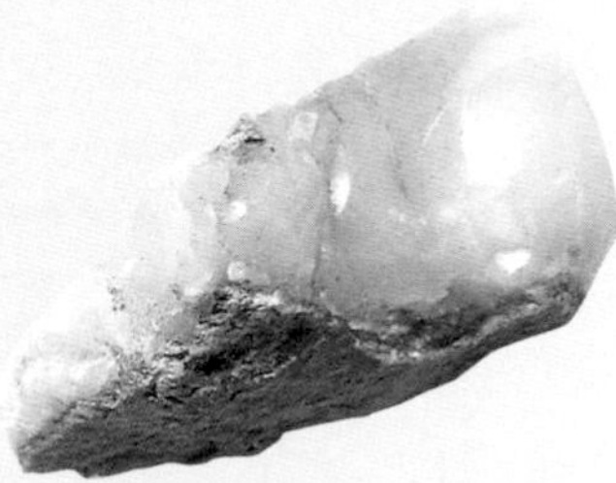

Fire Opal

Tumbled Pink Opal

Attributes: Opal is not strictly a crystal as it has no crystalline structure (regular arrangement of atoms). There are two kinds of opal – common and precious. Common Opal does not have flashes of colour, but can be any solid colour from transparent or white through to black. Precious Opal, which has flashes of colour (preferably rainbow), is the stone that resonates with the angel Pistas Sophia. She is said to be the mother of the superior angels according to Gnostic lore. The superior angels are the angels of the rays who stand before the throne of God. In India, Opal is thought to be the goddess of rainbows turned to stone when fleeing from the romantic advances of the other gods.

Psychologically: Opal can intensify emotional states. Mysterious Opals contain the wonders of the sky – sparking rainbows, fireworks and lightning. They are inspirational and have been used by artists to gain heavenly divine flashes. Precious Opal is very motivating and is a wonderful aid to visualization, especially if you are using visualization as a healing tool. Precious Opal also activates our Soul Star Chakra which is the first of the transcendental chakras above our head.

Mentally: Opals will show you exactly what past mental states have caused your present emotional imbalance. Brings light to your darkness and alignment through movement.

Emotionally: Opal opens doorways to the wonder of healing – it shows you how to manifest miracles in your life. Cleanses and heals old emotional wounds.

Physically: Heals hormonal imbalances. Strengthens, alleviates physical exhaustion and emotional or mental 'burn-out'.

Healing: Strengthens will-power, renews the will to live, dissipates fevers, and aids physical and spiritual sight and insight.

Position: Place or wear over the Heart Chakra or as your intuition guides you. Opal also makes an excellent gem essence (see page 283 for how to make a gem essence).

Seriphos Green Quartz

- **Colour** *Pale to deep green*
- **Appearance** *Long, slender opaque to transparent quartz points*
- **Rarity** *Rare, specialist shops*
- **Source** *Greek island of Seriphos*
- **Angel** *Archangel Seraphiel*

Natural Seriphos Green Quartz

Attributes: Seriphos Green Quartz comes from the beautiful Greek island named after the highest order of angels. The delicate pale to deep green crystals bring harmony, balance and emotional stability. They are a 'paradise' crystal and swiftly attune the senses to the healing potential of the angelic realms. They are used for opening, cleansing and activating the heart centre, which allows you to experience love and compassion for yourself and others. Seriphos Green Quartz is soothing and comforting to the emotions which helps heal a broken heart. These crystals are also an excellent aid for those people who are not comfortable being in their physical body, since these crystals bring you into a constant state of awareness of the higher angelic realms.

Psychologically: Excellent for clearing miasms on all levels. Quickly attunes the senses to the healing potential of the angelic realms.

Mentally: Clears mental imprints which may cause physical disease.

Emotionally: Heals emotional imbalances by attuning the senses to nature, which brings joy. Especially good for clearing the emotions of grief, abandonment and betrayal.

Physically: Heals by helping those who feel uncomfortable in the physical body adjust to the earthly vibration. Helps you to embrace life and enjoy being in a physical body.

Healing: Strengthens the will to live. Ameliorates heart and lung conditions. Strengthens the immune system and aids cellular regeneration.

Position: Place over the Heart Chakra.

Diamond

- **Colour** *Clear white, yellow, brown, pink, blue, green, mauve and black*
- **Appearance** *Clear when faceted, commonly occurs as octahedral crystals*
- **Rarity** *Common but expensive, even in natural state*
- **Source** *Africa, Brazil, Australia, India, Russia, USA*
- **Angel** *Archangel Metatron*

Raw Diamonds

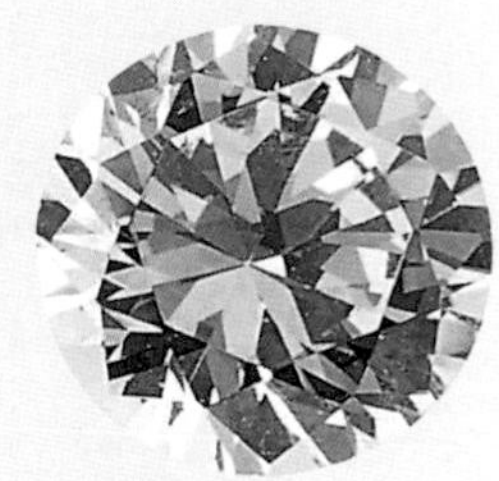

Faceted Diamond

Attributes: The name comes from the Greek word *adamas* meaning 'invincible' and alludes to the hardness and durability of the Diamond. Reputed to endow the wearer with purity, love and joy, the Diamond is traditionally the emblem for fearlessness. The Italian words *amante de Dio* mean 'lover of God'. Diamond is the hardest of natural substances and in ancient times it was used to counteract poison. Its energy and brilliance will indeed protect your subtle-energy fields from the poisonous energy of others.

Psychologically: Swiftly attunes the senses to the celestial realms by dispelling darkness within the aura. Amplifies the soul's light, which allows our light to shine brightly in the world. Diamonds aid success in all endeavours by increasing the brightness of the aura, making you more attractive, so more opportunities flow your way.

Mentally: Clarifies the mental processes and increases the ability to hold positive thoughts. Diamond also amplifies the power of your thoughts and prayers.

Emotionally: Emotional mirror – becoming cloudy when you get angry. It shows you your true emotional health and helps you work through your emotions, refining your vibrational rate.

Physically: Is a 'cure-all', improving all ailments. Clears allergies and all chronic conditions related to immune system dysfunction.

Healing: Strengthens the body.

Position: Place or wear as your intuition guides you. Diamonds can be set in either white gold or yellow gold. They combine well with the other gems: Rubies, Emeralds and Blue Sapphires.

Tanzanite

- **Colour** *Blue to lavender, deeper violet lights within*
- **Appearance** *Clear*
- **Rarity** *Rare, expected to be mined out within the next 10 years*
- **Source** *Merelani Hills, Tanzania*
- **Angel** *Archangel Tzaphkiel*

Tumbled Tanzanite

Attributes: Tanzanite is trichroic: that is, it reveals different colours when viewed in different directions. One direction shows blue, another lavender and another bronze. This colour change facilitates altered states of reality, allowing for radical shifts in consciousness. Because Tanzanite raises the vibratory signature of the user, it expands their personal *mandala*, allowing for 'downloads' of information from the Akashic records. Tanzanite is used for inner and outer journeys. Your raised vibratory rate will cause you to see a thinning of the veil between the various planes of consciousness, allowing for clear communication with angels, Ascended Masters, spirit guides and other enlightened beings from dimensions not usually available to your normal conscious awareness.

Psychologically: Enhances spiritual perception. Increases faith and understanding of universal truths by imparting wisdom and balanced spirituality.

Mentally: Tanzanite casts out all that is superficial to spiritual development. It increases insight, mysticism and discernment, by helping to fully develop the feminine intuitive side of your nature. This in turn allows your heart to open fully and your soul's purity to be made manifest on Earth for the freedom and salvation of all.

Emotionally: Tanzanite's healing energy takes you beyond the confines of the Earth plane into a space where you learn to nurture yourself by letting go of the past to find inner peace.

Physically: Reverses the ageing process.

Healing: Strengthens and renews.

Position: Place on the Third Eye Chakra.

Rutile Quartz

- **Colour** *Clear through to smoky with needles of gold, reddish or brown strands*
- **Appearance** *Threads of rutile with quartz*
- **Rarity** *Common, especially tumbled stones*
- **Source** *Worldwide*
- **Angel** *Archangel Melchizedek*

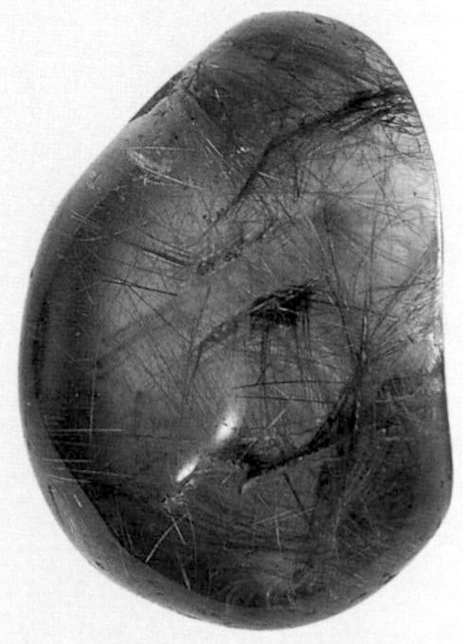

Tumbled Rutile Quartz

Attributes: Rutile Quartz is also known as Angel Hair Quartz due to the inclusion of fine golden needles of rutile. This crystal has been used as a potent talisman since ancient times, and is known as the 'illuminator of the soul'. It clears the pathway for necessary action by exposing flaws and negativity. By sustaining vital life-force it restores vibrancy and vitality. It breaks down barriers, fears and phobias which have held up spiritual progress. Use Rutile Quartz to bring about a change, rejuvenation and new directions. It cleanses the aura, filling it with spiritual light.

Psychologically: Perfect balance of cosmic light which promotes spiritual growth and energy integration.

Mentally: Clears the pathway for necessary action by exposing negative emotional states that have become deeply rooted in the neural pathways.

Emotionally: Provides the energy needed to break down barriers that have blocked your emotional growth.

Physically: Sustains life and the vital life-force. Is used to restore vibrancy and vitality which will lead to the resonance of perfect health.

Healing: Clears up and modifies any condition, including allergies, lung conditions, chronic conditions and negative entities.

Position: Place on any chakra. Has a special affinity to the Solar Plexus Chakra.

Iolite

- **Colour** *Indigo, blue or honey-yellow*
- **Appearance** *Small; clear or translucent*
- **Rarity** *Readily available from specialist shops*
- **Source** *Sri Lanka, Madagascar, Burma and India*
- **Angel** *Archangel Raziel*

Tumbled Iolite

Attributes: Iolite is the gemstone variety of Cordierite, also called Water Sapphire or Star Stone. Pleochroism (the ability to transmit different colours in different directions) is very pronounced in Iolite and three different colour shades are seen in the same stone. Iolite is the New Age prophecy and vision stone. It gives full psychic activation and integration, but only if the five lower chakras are fully balanced; otherwise there is a danger of disorientation.

Psychologically: Iolite and the secret mysteries of Archangel Raziel are not for everyone; they take the recipient into the heavenly realm where science and mysticism are one and the same – the quantum universe.

Mentally: These 'mind-blowing' encounters with Iolite and Archangel Raziel need time to be fully integrated into all levels of your being; otherwise you can find yourself becoming completely unbalanced.

Emotionally: Releases discord and co-dependency. Helps you overcome your addictions.

Physically: Eases bronchitis, asthma and other chronic lung conditions. Lowers high blood pressure. Eases back problems, sciatic, lumbago and other spinal or neurological complaints. Transmutes and purifies negativity.

Healing: Improves brain function. Reducing headaches and insomnia.

Position: Place on the Throat, Third Eye or Crown Chakras, or wear as a pendant or a ring. Iolite is most potent when worn for extended time periods. It can be set in yellow gold.

Amethyst

- **Colour** *Various shades of purple*
- **Appearance** *Geode, transparent, single point or cluster*
- **Rarity** *Readily available*
- **Source** *Africa, Germany, Italy, USA, Mexico, Brazil, Canada, Uruguay*
- **Angel** *Archangel Zadkiel*

Amethyst point

Attributes: Amethyst is the purple variety of quartz. The name 'amethyst' comes from the Greek *amethustos*, which means 'not drunken'. This may have been due to a belief that Amethyst would ward off the effects of alcohol, but most likely the Greeks were referring to the almost wine-like colour of some. Its beautiful colour is unparalleled; although it must always be purple to be Amethyst, it has a wide range of purple shades.

Psychologically: High vibration used to enhance meditation.

Mentally: Calms and focuses an overactive mind. Deepens understanding of underlying issues.

Emotionally: Soothing; used to ease stress and emotional exhaustion. Also eases addictions and addictive traits within the personality.

Physically: Amethyst has a wide spectrum of healing energies so is an effective healer of most conditions. Neutralizes pain, so it can be placed over any painful area. Eases headache and migraine – those people who suffer from frequent headaches often keep a few Amethyst crystals in the fridge, ready for when they are needed. Place the cold Amethyst on the temples.

Healing: Has a broad spectrum of applications and so is a 'master' healer. Can be used for sending absent healing.

Position: Place on the Third Eye or Crown Chakras to balance them. Place anywhere on the body or in the aura as your intuition dictates. Place under pillow or on a bedside table to prevent nightmares and insomnia. An Amethyst geode or cluster will cleanse the environment of large amounts of stagnant energy. Use in a room after many people have been present.

Blue Topaz

- **Colour** *Various shades of blue*
- **Appearance** *Transparent pegmatite crystals*
- **Rarity** *Readily available*
- **Source** *Africa, Germany, Italy, USA, Mexico, Brazil, Canada, Uruguay*
- **Angel** *Archangel Haniel*

Tumbled Blue Topaz

Attributes: Legend has it that Blue Topaz dispels enchantment and improves the eyesight. Topaz was also said to change colour in the presence of poisoned food or drink. Its mystical curative powers waxed and waned with the phases of the Moon: it was said to cure insomnia, asthma and haemorrhages. The ancient Greeks believed that it had the power to increase strength and make the wearer invisible in times of emergency. In Mexico it was used as a truth stone. It is still worn today to detect the 'poisonous' thoughts of others.

Psychologically: Topaz facilitates the deep understanding and acceptance of universal laws. It inspires and uplifts. It aids clear communication, allowing the rational mind to win even under the severest provocation.

Mentally: Soothing, calming and inspiring. It stops the build-up of anger, resentment and bitterness.

Emotionally: Defuses emotional deadlock. Lifts you above the stressful situation, which allows new behavioural patterns to be formed.

Physically: Blue Topaz aids clear communication. It is used to balance the Throat Chakra, so will ameliorate sore throats and thyroid imbalances.

Healing: Encourages balance and calm in the physical and subtle bodies.

Position: Place on the Throat, Third Eye or Crown Chakras. Blue Topaz can be worn as a pendant or ring, set in white or yellow gold. Natural pale-blue Topaz is a wonderful channelling gemstone which connects you to secret knowledge and ancient wisdom.

Rose Quartz

- **Colour** *Pink*
- **Appearance** *Transparent to translucent*
- **Rarity** *Readily available*
- **Source** *Brazil, Madagascar, USA, India*
- **Angel** *Archangel Chamuel*

Natural Rose Quartz

Tumbled Rose Quartz

Attributes: Rose Quartz is the pleasantly seductive variety of quartz – it is the colour of love. It transmits a soft, soothing energy that teaches the true essence of love. It has a natural affinity with the Heart Chakra and the emotions; it deals with all the emotions of the heart, so assists us in developing all kinds of loving relationships. It is used as a talisman to attract a soulmate.

Psychologically: Can strengthen our empathic links with others and assist us in all our relationships, especially through traumatic life-changing situations such as divorce, bereavement or job loss. Helps us to appreciate the loving relationships we already have in our life.

Mentally: Soothing and comforting; stops the build-up of feelings such as hatred, anger and hostility.

Emotionally: When you first use Rose Quartz it can sometimes bring up a lot of suppressed emotions, which it helps you acknowledge and release. Quickly dissolves the negative emotions of self-condemnation, low self-worth, self-loathing and selfishness. Releases aggressive behaviour patterns.

Physically: Opens the heart, which supports healing. Aids fertility.

Healing: Releases emotional stress that has become locked in any area of the physical body. Is good for the newborn, and those yet to be born.

Position: Place on the Heart Chakra or any area of the body that has stored stress or pain. Wear Rose Quartz as a ring, pendant or necklace to see you through times of crisis.

Emerald

- **Colour** *Green*
- **Appearance** *Transparent to translucent*
- **Rarity** *Readily available*
- **Source** *Brazil, India, Colombia, Zimbabwe, Madagascar, Russia*
- **Angel** *Archangel Raphael*

Natural Emerald

Faceted Emerald

Attributes: Emerald has been treasured for its remarkable colour and mystical properties for at least 4,000 years. In Revelations in the Bible it says that the throne of God is made of Emerald. The legendary mystical knowledge of the Egyptian god Thoth was engraved on Emerald tablets. In fact, Emerald is steeped in mystic lore.

Emerald is linked to the planet Mercury, the messenger of the gods in Vedic astrology. In other cultures it was dedicated to the goddess Venus. Cleopatra prized her Emeralds more than any other gem. Egyptian mummies were often buried with an Emerald carved with the symbol for verdure, flourishing greenness, to symbolize eternal youth. Emeralds are still prized the world over and rightly so, since no other gemstone attracts such potent healing energy.

Psychologically: Promotes unity and unconditional love. Improves the intellect and strengthens the character as well as promoting harmony and abundance.

Mentally: Improves the memory; it is a stone of wisdom and discernment.

Emotionally: Aids emotional resilience and adaptability. Releases jealousy, resentment, selfishness and hypochondria.

Physically: Opens the heart to healing and aids recovery. Eases claustrophobia.

Healing: Eases biliousness, releases toxins, which improves the liver and kidney function, and in turn tones the physical body. Emerald is a 'spring' tonic, a breath of fresh air; it eases heart and lung conditions and helps us absorb pranic energy.

Position: Place on the Heart or Third Eye Chakras. It is traditionally set in yellow gold and worn as a ring on the little finger of the left hand to aid communication and to overcome shyness.

Citrine

- **Colour** *Transparent*
- **Appearance** *Geode, transparent, single point or cluster*
- **Rarity** *Natural Citrine is rare*
- **Source** *Brazil, India, USA, Madagascar, Russia, France*
- **Angel** *Archangel Jophiel*

Citrine geode

Attributes: Most of the yellow and brownish-yellow quartz which in the past was often sold under the misnomer 'Topaz' is heat-treated Amethyst. Citrine gets its name from the French word *citron*. Most natural Citrine is pale lemon or smoky lemon. In ancient times Citrine was carried as a protection against snake venom and the evil thoughts of others. Citrine is a lustrous gemstone that balances the Solar Plexus Chakra and cleanses and strengthens the mental body. Citrine is the colour of sunshine and as such it promotes and enhances positive energy. It gives those who use it a 'sunny, joyful disposition'.

Psychologically: Use Citrine if your energy is low and you have lost your *joie de vivre* or when you feel unclear, confused or scattered. If you need joy and laughter in your life and you feel burdened by worries and cares, or have lost your personal power and sense of self, Citrine quickly boosts your confidence, enthusiasm and self-esteem.

Mentally: If you feel constantly drained of energy and even the smallest task becomes an insurmountable obstacle, use Citrine. It is also helpful if you need to release negative thought patterns or addictive behaviour traits or when you are fearful and full of self-doubt.

Emotionally: Brings stable uplifting feelings, freedom, laughter and joy, Increases self-control. Raises self-esteem and brings feelings of total well-being. Stimulates conversation and enhances communication. Prevents shyness and gives courage.

Physically: Works on the pancreas, liver, gall bladder, spleen, middle stomach, nervous system, digestive system and skin.

Healing: Fortifies, brightens, tones, stimulates, reinforces energy.

Position: Solar Plexus Chakra, or wear as a pendant or ring for prolonged periods.

Lapis Lazuli

- **Colour** *Ultramarine blue with flecks of golden pyrite*
- **Appearance** *Opaque*
- **Rarity** *Easily obtained*
- **Source** *Afghanistan*
- **Angel** *Archangel Michael*

Natural Lapis Lazuli

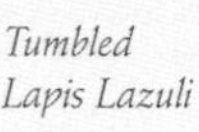

Tumbled Lapis Lazuli

Attributes: The ancient city of Ur had a thriving trade in Lapis as early as the 4th millennium BCE. The name comes from the Latin *lapis*, which means stone, and from the Arabic *azul,* which means blue. Lapis is a high-intensity etheric blue stone. It contains the energies of truth, wisdom, patience, inspiration, integrity, loyalty, revelation and contemplation.

Psychologically: Lapis helps to develop the virtues of truth, honesty and faith. If you need immediate protection from low-energy entities, or feel you are under psychic attack or have been cursed or feel a victim of the evil 'eye', Lapis will give a cloak of protection and safety.

Mentally: Eases depression, aids clarity of thought and assists us in taking charge of our life. Amplifies our thoughts and stimulates objectivity. Combats fear of speaking the truth.

Emotionally: Harmonizes emotional conflict and stops vacillation, hesitation and uncertainty.

Physically: Lapis alleviates pain, especially headaches and migraine. Used to heal the throat, lungs, thyroid, thymus and high blood pressure.

Healing: Reduces fevers and regulates hyperactivity, inflammatory and derailing processes. Brings clarity and serenity. Eases ear and throat infections.

Position: Throat or Third Eye Chakras. Wear as a pendant or ring for prolonged periods to get the full benefit of this amazing gemstone. Never, however, wear Lapis for prolonged periods if you suffer from low blood pressure.

Danburite

- **Colour** *Clear, white, yellow or pink*
- **Appearance** *Transparent with striations*
- **Rarity** *Easily obtained*
- **Source** *Mexico, USA, Japan, Burma, Switzerland*
- **Angel** *Archangel Gabriel*

Natural Danburite

Natural Danburite single-terminated point

Attributes: Danburite gets its name from where it was originally found – Danbury, Connecticut. Danburite carries an extremely high vibration that swiftly and joyfully attunes the senses to the angelic domain. It speedily opens and cleanses the Heart and Crown Chakras as well as promotes lucid dreams. Danburite brings light, clarity and purity to the aura, which means it has the power to modify all conditions that have caused misery and disease. By its very nature, it is a cure-all.

Psychologically: Draws down divine light. It is used for guidance, spiritual awakening, soul purification, revelation, inspiration and insightful dreams. It is a transition crystal, so it is helpful when you are starting new projects, changing career or even thinking of starting a family.

Mentally: Alerts you to coincidences which pave the way for releasing the past.

Emotionally: Clears emotional miasms. Links you to the serenity of angles and the angelic domains.

Physically: Clears allergies, toxins and chronic degraded conditions, which in turn supports the liver, gall bladder, kidneys, pancreas and skin.

Healing: A versatile crystal which has a broad spectrum of healing energies.

Position: Any chakra. Wear as a pendant; it can be set in silver or gold. Danburite makes an excellent gem essence (see page 283).

Ruby

Natural Ruby

- Colour *Red*
- Appearance *Transparent*
- Rarity *Readily available*
- Source *India, Mexico, Madagascar, Russia, Sri Lanka*
- Angel *Archangel Uriel*

Polished Ruby

Attributes: Ruby was said to be the most precious of all the gemstones that God created. It is 'lord of gems' and was used in the breastplate of the high priest. The Bible says wisdom is more precious than Rubies. In Sanskrit it is called *ratnaraj* ('king of precious stones') and *ratnanayaka*, ('leader of precious stones'). Ruby instils in the wearer a passion for life, courage, perseverance and positive leadership qualities. Ruby is for pioneers, those who must go first, bravely, into uncharted territory. Ruby is raw power and passion for life.

Psychologically: Brings spiritual devotion through selfless service to others. Releases the soul's true potential.

Mentally: Removes inertia, procrastination and lethargy.

Emotionally: Dynamic, removes fear. Survival issues reduced, restores the will to live.

Physically: Releases energy blocks deep within the system. Gives a boost to processes that have been sluggish or stagnant. Detoxifies by removing inertia.

Healing: Warms the body and increases physical energy. Good for those who suffer from low blood pressure, circulatory problems or anaemia. Stimulates the adrenals.

Position: Root or Earth Star Chakras. Do not wear Ruby if you suffer from high blood pressure.

Moonstone

- **Colour** *White, cream, peach, pink, blue, green or rainbow*
- **Appearance** *Translucent*
- **Rarity** *Readily available*
- **Source** *India, Sri Lanka*
- **Angel** *Archangel Auriel*

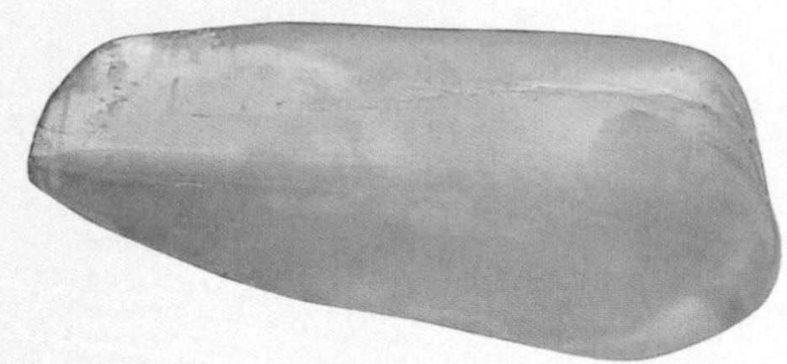

Tumbled Moonstones

Attributes: Moonstone appears mystical and magical, with a ghostly shimmering glow floating in crystalline depths. The Romans thought Moonstone was formed out of moonlight. Moonstone, as its name implies, is strongly connected to the Moon and its powers are said to change with the cycles of the Moon. At full moon its powers reach their zenith. Moonstone is especially beneficial for women of all ages.

Psychologically: Harmonizes the female aspect of your personality. Allows access to the deep subconscious. Each month our psychic power increases at the time of the full moon. The 'veil' between worlds is at its thinnest and our natural gifts of clairvoyance, clairsentience and clairaudience are all enhanced.

Mentally: Soothing. Opens the mind to serendipity and hidden opportunities. Increases intuition.

Emotionally: Soothing to the emotions. Allows positive energy to flow, which dissolves past hurts, pain and longings. Eases mood swings.

Physically: Especially beneficial for the female reproductive system. Soothes stomach upsets and digestive disorders. Calms overactive thyroid; lowers high blood pressure. Eases stomach cramps and PMT. Eliminates toxins; eases water retention and bloating.

Healing: Cools the body and releases excess energy and agitation. Soothes the adrenals.

Position: Heart Chakra. Wear Moonstone as a ring or pendant for prolonged periods to gain the best results. Moonstone must be set in silver only; wrap it in a white silk square when not in use.

Fulgurite

- **Colour** *White to dark brown*
- **Appearance** *Sponge-like texture*
- **Rarity** *Specialist shops*
- **Source** *Sahara Desert, Florida beaches*
- **Angel** *Archangel Sandalphon*

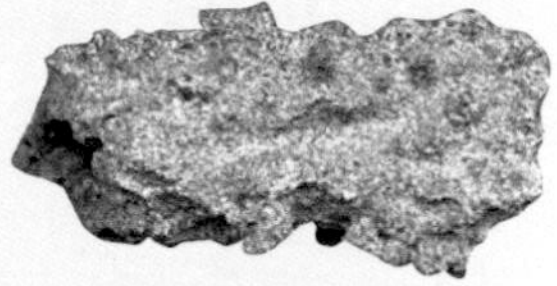

Natural Fulgurite

Attributes: Fulgurite is unique in its formation, being created when lightning strikes sand. This causes the grains to fuse into tubular glass shapes that echo the pattern of the lightning. Fulgurite is tubular because the sand at the centre vaporizes, and the surrounding sand liquefies, later hardening into the fulgurite. It vibrates with the energy of the thunderbolt and this is among the highest and fastest vibrations of the mineral kingdom. It is a catalyst crystal containing storm energy and is used for rapid spiritual transformation. Legend has it that shamans used it to send their prayers up to the Divine.

Psychologically: Focuses and grounds the power of angelic prayer and ritual. Acts like a thunderbolt; a catalyst for change. Powerfully unlocks the Third Eye Chakra and has been used to explore other realities and dimensions. Has also been used for balanced *kundalini* (psychic force) activation and past-life exploration.

Mentally: Creates an environment that is creative, allowing manifestation through the higher mind and higher mental states.

Emotionally: Increases intuition. Allows greater insight into the formation of emotional turbulence.

Physically: Creates a vortex of purified energy which raises the user's vibrational rate, and thus has the power to improve all physical ailments.

Healing: Energizing, purifying and uplifting; use when you want to make quantum leaps in healing any aspect of the psyche.

Position: Place in the Earth Star and Soul Star Chakras. Fulgurite is very fragile so handle with great care.

Aquamarine

- **Colour** *Sky-blue or greenish-blue*
- **Appearance** *Translucent to opaque*
- **Rarity** *Readily available*
- **Source** *India, Pakistan, Brazil, Mexico, Afghanistan, Russia, USA*
- **Angel** *Archangel Muriel*

Faceted Aquamarine

Natural Aquamarine

Attributes: Aquamarine, the 'gem of the sea', derives its name from sea water. Legend says that it is the treasure of the mermaids with the power to keep sailors safe at sea. The ancients also believed Aquamarine gave protection against the wiles of the devil, and that to dream of Aquamarine meant you would meet new friends. It gives freedom from the impressions and influences of others.

Psychologically: Has a strong affinity with those poeple who are highly attuned to subtle energies and acts as a stone of courage by filtering out discordant and conflicting energy. Facilitates communication with the angelic realm. Enhances psychic skill, in particular the ability to tune into images from past and other dimensions.

Mentally: Calms and focuses the mind, which sharpens the intellect. Clarifies perception, which helps us identify underlying patterns of behaviour that we may need to release in order to move forward in our lives.

Emotionally: Calming and soothing to the emotions. Swiftly releases energy blockages and washes away anger, guilt, hatred, resentment and fear. Alleviates grief and sorrow.

Physically: Relieves sore throats, swollen glands and thyroid problems. Eases fluid retention and bloating and has a beneficial effect on the kidneys, bladder, eyes and immune system. Eases panic attacks, seasickness and phobias. Helps clear hay fever and allergic reactions.

Healing: Calming.

Position: All chakras. Wear as a pendant or ring set in silver or gold. Makes an excellent gem essence to help you go with the flow (see page 283).

ANGELS AND ESSENTIAL OILS

The Use of Fragrance to Attract Angels

One of the most potent tools we can use for attracting angelic help is beautiful fragrance, especially in the form of essential oils, which are well known as mood-enhancing, mind alterants. Recently there has been a significant growth of interest in aromatherapy and the emotional well-being it promotes. Our ancestors were well aware of the etheric qualities of essential oils and they were widely used by priests and priestesses of virtually all religions. Fragrant oils were used to attract spirits, goddesses and gods, to banish evil spirits and to purify places of worship. Devotees anointed themselves with sacred scents in order to facilitate divine communication.

Essential oils Essential oils are highly concentrated, naturally occurring, exquisite aromatic substances produced by many different plants. Essential oils are distilled from certain species of plants: some are derived from flower petals,

The use of scent in ritual can be a powerful aid to spiritual development and angelic attunement.

others from fruits, seeds, stems, barks, twigs, roots, trees, resins or grasses. For example, neroli oil is produced from the flowers, ginger is derived from the root of the plant and patchouli is extracted from the leaves. Essential oils are produced in practically every country throughout the world.

Scent is a subtle etheric form of communication which heightens our consciousness because it carries the soul of the plant. By appealing to our sense of smell, plants communicate with us on a deep instinctive level. Our fragrance receptors are located in the oldest part of our brain, which is intuitive and not governed by our logical mind.

Many essential oils are distilled from flowers – as such they are the sacred spirit of that flower.

There are many different ways of using essential oils for your body, mind and spirit. There are also several ways of taking essential oils into the body. One of the most effective ways is through the skin. Essential oils are precious, highly concentrated fragrant substances. Store them in a cool dark place and avoid evaporation by making sure the lids are always tightly closed.

Carrier Oils and Safety Guidelines

Aromatherapists use a wide variety of carrier or base oils to which they add essential oils. The following base oils can be used neat on the skin and are usually employed as general base carrier oils for massage, bath or perfume blends: sweet almond, light coconut, apricot kernel, grapeseed, safflower, wheatgerm, jojoba, avocado, sunflower and evening primrose oil. Sweet almond oil is easy to obtain as are sunflower and safflower. Sweet almond is used in India to heighten intellectual ability.

When choosing a base oil, you should always try to buy organic, or the one that appears the most pure. Sweet almond, light coconut, apricot kernel and grapeseed have a fine texture and are easily absorbed into the skin. Other oils, such as wheatgerm, avocado and jojoba, are rich and thick.

Safety Pure essential oils are highly concentrated substances that must be treated with caution. Below is a list of general safety guidelines that should be observed when using essential oils. If you are interested in or uncertain about how to use a particular essential oil, refer to any reputable book on the subject; this will list the characteristics of each oil and highlight the contraindications for particularly potent or strong oils.

- Do not take essential oils orally.
- Never use an undiluted essential oil directly on the skin.
- Keep out of reach of children, pets and anyone with special needs. Be very cautious of using essential oils on children. Seek advice.
- If you are pregnant, suffer from epilepsy, high/low blood pressure or

any other specific condition please seek medical advice before using any essential oils.

- Keep products away from delicate eye areas.
- Care must also be taken with certain oils (especially citrus oils) before exposure to direct sunlight.
- When adding essential oils to bath water, dilute first in a small amount of carrier oil base.
- Try to restrict the use of any essential oil, because constant use over time may cause sensitization to the oil, nausea or headaches.
- Certain oils may cause skin sensitivity or adverse reactions in some individuals. Discontinue use immediately if this occurs.
- Do not use machinery or drive a motor vehicle immediately following a relaxation treatment, especially after using soporific oils.
- Keep products away from polished surfaces, plastic and naked flames or other sources of ignition.

A selection of bottles and droppers are useful when blending your own essential oil fragrances and massage oils.

Massage, Bathing and Steam Inhalation

There are many different ways of using essential oils for your body, mind and spirit. The quantities recommended may seem tiny and sometimes the aroma may be barely perceptible, but the aroma and the effect are there in spite of this. The scent receptors in the brain quickly get used to the smell and then we think that it is no longer there.

Massage One of the most common methods employed by aromatherapists, massage with essential oils relaxes the physical body, relieving stress and tension. The fragrance works directly on the deepest levels of the emotions while the skin absorbs the therapeutic elements of the oils.

Make a simple massage oil blend by mixing 5 drops of your chosen essential oil to 1 tablespoon of base oil such as sweet almond, apricot kernel, grapeseed, soya or sunflower. If you are using more than one essential oil in your blend, mix them together first before adding them to the base oil and adjust the number of drops accordingly. It is always wise,

Essential oils are used in massage to relax the physical body and aid detoxification.

especially if you have allergies to perfumes or cosmetics, to do a skin test 24 hours before using the oil blend for a massage treatment. (See pages 338–339 for a list of safety guidelines on using essential oils.)

Bathing Bathing with essential oils is an ancient method of personal purification. It stirs the senses and brings attunement to subtle energies. Blend up to 8 drops of your chosen essential oil to 1 tablespoon of base oil and add the mixture to a full bathtub. Agitate the water to disperse the oils through the bathwater. Remember to shut the bathroom door to stop the therapeutic vapours escaping. Soak in the bath for at least 15 minutes, inhaling deeply and relaxing. Certain essential oils should not be used in the bath: among them are ginger, thyme, peppermint, eucalyptus, basil, cinnamon and clove.

You can also use essential oils in the shower. Shower as normal, then add 2 drops of essential oil to a sponge and rub over yourself while the hot water is still running. Inhale deeply through your nose.

Add a blend of essential oils to your bath; a combination of chamomile and lavender is conducive to restful sleep.

Steam inhalation Some essential oils can be inhaled as vapour. To use this method, pour hot water into a bowl, add 2 drops of your chosen essential oil. Put your face about 25 cm (10 inches) away from the bowl, cover your head with a towel, close your eyes and inhale deeply through your nose for up to two minutes.

Diffusers

Diffusers are designed to heat the essential oils and release aroma molecules into the atmosphere. Some are made of pottery, but water bowls, candles and radiators can also serve the same purpose.

Pottery diffusers have a bowl section which is heated by electricity or a candle flame. Place the diffuser in the room you wish to fragrance. Fill the bowl with water before adding up to 6 drops of essential oil. Switch on the diffuser or light the candle beneath the bowl. Do not leave lighted candles unattended in a room.

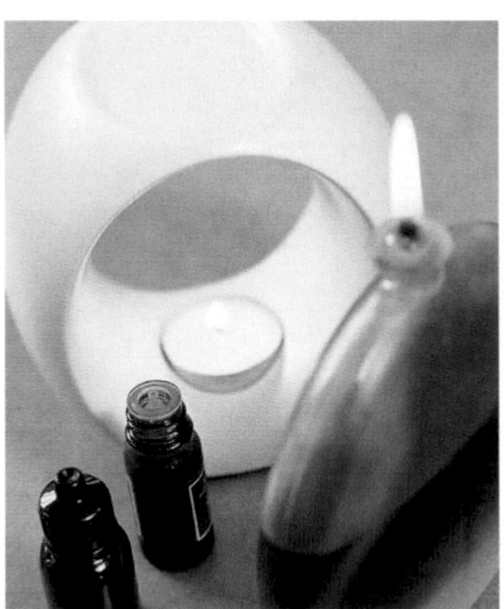

Water bowl Make sure all the windows and doors are closed in the room you wish to fragrance. Pour hot water into a heat-resistant bowl, add up to 8 drops of essential oil to the hot water and wait for 10 minutes for the aroma to fill the atmosphere of the room.

Candles Light a candle and allow it to burn until the centre wax has melted. Blow out the flame and add 2 drops of

Essential oils can be diffused using oil burners, candles, water bowls and light bulbs.

essential oil to the central pool of wax. Relight the candle.

Light bulbs You can purchase special rings made of metal or pottery which are designed to sit on top of light bulbs (table lamps or bedside lamps). The rings are hollow in the centre to hold the essential oil. With the lamp turned off, place a ring on the light bulb, then place 5 drops of essential oil on the ring. Switch on the light to release the fragrance.

Room sprays This is a heavenly way of using essential oil, as it quickly purifies and sanctifies your sacred space. Add 5 drops of essential oil to a 50 ml glass atomizer bottle filled with water. Shake the bottle well each time you use it to mix the oil and water. Spray high into the air. Avoid spraying polished surfaces and delicate fabrics such as velvet or silk.

Log fires and radiators Using 1 drop of essential oil per log, place the oil on the log an hour before you plan to burn the logs on the fire. If you do not want to light a fire or have no fireplace, put up to 8 drops of essential oil onto a cotton wool ball and place it on a radiator. You could also add the essential oil to the water in a humidifier on the radiator.

Flowers If you have silk, paper or dried flowers, place 1 drop of oil on each flower. Some essential oils are almost clear and others have strong colours, so choose an essential oil that will not damage the colour of your flowers.

Add 2 drops of your chosen oil to the pool of liquid wax in a candle then relight the candle.

Scenting Household Items

Essential oils can be used to gently scent many objects in a room. The fragrance from the items will pervade the air and introduce a wonderful healing ambience to the room. Pillows, clothing, bed linen and handkerchiefs can all be scented.

Pillows and cushions A few drops of essential oil can be sprinkled directly onto your pillows – this is especially nice when you wish to induce angelic dreams, or in your therapy or meditation room to entice angels into your space. Some oils will stain – so place the drops of essential oil onto a cotton wool ball and place it between the pillow and the pillowcase. Use the same method for cushions.

Clothing A drop of essential oil can be placed directly on your clothing; try a drop on your sleeve so you can easily breathe in the aroma as required, or on the hem of your skirt or jacket which will waft through the air as you move about. It is also possible to scent tissues or handkerchiefs with 1 drop of essential oil and inhale as required.

Lotions and flower-waters Buy pure and perfume-free pre-prepared creams or lotions and add a few drops of your favourite essential oil.

Flower-waters can be used to consecrate and cleanse magical spaces prior to ritual or meditation. They can also be used to anoint sacred objects and candles and are an old favourite in skin care. Rose, lavender, neroli and jasmine are particularly suited to skin care and are often used as perfumes. Although oil is insoluble in water, during the infusion process subtle energy and fragrance is transferred to the water. Add 30 drops of essential oil to 100 ml of spring water. Leave to infuse for a few days in a cool dark place. Filter through coffee filter paper. It can then be used in an atomizer as a perfume or as a room spray.

Anointment is the most ancient and traditional application for essential oils. Dilute essential oil following the same recipe as bath or massage. Use as a perfume or for protection. Apply to sacred objects such as candles or crystals.

Use fragrance to attract angels; scent your bedlinen to facilitate angelic dreams.

Essential Oils for Specific Problems

Certain problems respond to a number of oils. In the following pages, a comprehensive list of oils has been provided for each specific problem or situation. The list of oils is flexible and adaptable. Essential oils are complex: on average, an essential oil contains over 100 components, such as esters, aldehydes, ketones, phenols, alcohols and terpenes. You can choose just one oil from the list or design your own blend in a carrier oil. When you blend two or more essential oils together you create a new compound.

As you look at the list of oils it is possible to use a pendulum and dowse to see which oil is the most appropriate for you and your current life situation. When you go into shops that sell essential oils, smell the oils and if you like one buy it. Do, however, make sure that you are buying pure essential oils.

Several oils will be listed under more than one heading because they perform more than one function. For example, lemon brings balance, it works directly on the central nervous system and will stimulate or relax you depending on what your requirements are.

***Lemon** brings balance, sharpens the intellect and helps communication and learning.*

Clary Sage aids meditation by clearing away inner conflicts.

Chamomile opens the higher chakras, aids meditation and restful sleep.

When you use oils for meditation, divination or dream work always use the same oil or blend of oils as this quickly signals to your subconscious mind that you are shifting frequencies and moving into an altered state of awareness.

Healing – Archangel Raphael To open the Heart Chakra and attract the angels of healing, rejuvenation, regeneration and renewal use the following essential oils:
Carnation • Chamomile • Clove • Juniper • Lavender • Lemon • Mimosa • Neroli • Palmarosa • Pimento Berry • Pine • Rose Otto • Sandalwood • Spearmint • Thyme

Meditation – Archangel Tzaphkiel To open the Crown and Third Eye Chakras and to invite the angels of meditation, contemplation, reflection, introspection and soul searching, use the following essential oils:
Clary Sage • Frankincense • Lavender • Linden Blossom • Sweet Fennel • Violet Leaf

Spiritual wisdom – Archangel Zadkiel To open the higher chakra centres and summon to your presence the angels of divine spiritual wisdom, knowledge, discernment and divine understanding, you should use the following essential oils:
Benzoin • Carrot Seed • Chamomile • Clary Sage • Cypress • Frankincense • Linden Blossom • Myrrh • Rosemary • Rosewood • Sage • Sandalwood

__Jasmine__ has an exquisite aroma that opens our consciousness to the heavenly realms.

__Narcissus__ is used for inspiration, prophetic dreams and trance work.

Visions – Archangel Raziel To clear the Third Eye Chakra centre, to unveil the secrets of the universe and to quickly summon the angels of spiritual visions, prophecy and revelations, use the following essential oils:

Bay • Benzoin • Carrot Seed • Cinnamon • Galbanum • Jasmine • Lemon Verbena • Lime • Mimosa • Myrrh • Narcissus • Neroli • Rose Otto • Rosewood • Sage • Sandalwood • Tuberose

Angelic dreams – Archangel Gabriel These high-vibration oils summon the angels of destiny to send your consciousness soaring while you sleep, to give you angelic dreams and guidance. Use the following essential oils:

Angelica Seed • Anise Star • Basil • Bay • Benzoin • Cinnamon • Clary Sage • Coriander • Dill Seed • Elemi • Immortelle • Lemon Verbena • Linden Blossom • Melissa • Mimosa • Myrrh • Narcissus • Neroli • Ravensara • Rose Otto • Spearmint

Angelic communication – Archangel Haniel To form lasting bonds of angelic inspiration and enhance all your communication skills by purifying your Throat Chakra, use the following essential oils:

Bay • Carnation • Chamomile • Grapefruit • Lemon • Linden Blossom • Myrrh • Neroli • Orange • Rose Otto • Sandalwood • Tangerine

Divination – Archangel Raziel In order to more easily access higher guidance and to help induce heightened states of awareness which will enhance all your divination skills and take you to a new spiritual level (including giving angel readings), you should use the following essential oils:

Angelica Seed • Bay • Benzoin • Carrot Seed • Cinnamon • Clary Sage • Clove Bud • Frankincense • Galbanum • Lemon Verbena • Linden Blossom • Mimosa • Myrrh • Narcissus • Peppermint • Rosewood • Sage • Sandalwood • Tuberose

Inner child – Archangel Chamuel These essential oils summon to our side the angels that help us resolve, heal and strengthen all of our relationships. These loving angels help us to reconnect with our inner child to bring about deep healing, comfort and forgiveness. They help cleanse issues of past abuse, abandonment and neglect. Use the following essential oils:

Benzoin • Chamomile • Frankincense • Geranium • Hyacinth • Lavender • Mandarin • Melissa • Neroli • Rose Otto

***Myrrh** is considered one of the most holy plants, which is used for purification and for letting go of the past.*

***Geranium** balances the emotions allowing the angels of love to draw closer to us.*

Transition – Archangel Metatron
Throughout time people have burned incense around those who are making the transition from life to death. It was believed beautiful aromas would attract the angels and the smoke from burning incense or sacred herbs would carry the soul to the heavenly realms. To summon Archangel Metatron's angels of ascension, to speed the soul towards the Divine and assist them in letting go of the physical realm and to make a peaceful transition, use the following oils:

Benzoin • Cedarwood • Chamomile Roman • Cypress • Frankincense • Geranium • Jasmine • Juniper • Lavender • Linden Blossom • Mandarin • Neroli • Patchouli • Rose Otto • Sandalwood • Vetivert

Loneliness – Archangel Jophiel
Depression, loneliness, grief and melancholy can affect us all at some point in our life, often brought about through external causes, such as bereavement, job loss or the break-up of a relationship. It can last for a few days, weeks, months or even years. Anyone who feels depressed should seek medical advice as it could be a hormonal imbalance. The following oils cleanse the body, mind and spirit and summon the angels of illumination, sunshine and joy. Use the following essential oils:

Benzoin • Bergamot • Chamomile • Helichrysum • Lemon • Narcissus • Neroli

***Juniper** is used for purification, protection and to dispel negative energies; it clears past trauma. **Bergamot** elevates the spirit, aids self-confidence and clears the mind.*

Purification – Archangel Zadkiel For purification and aura-cleansing by transmutation of negative energy into positive energy, invoke Archangel Zadkiel, the keeper of the Violet Flame. Using lavender oil helps to release negative emotions, such as anger, hatred, resentment or bitterness, and repair auric damage. Negative emotions lower your vibrational rate and attract negative energy like a magnet. Use the following essential oils:
Basil • Bay • Cajeput • Camphor • Cedarwood • Citronella • Clary Sage • Cypress • Eucalyptus • Frankincense • Galbanum • Hyssop • Juniper • Lavender • Lemon • Lemon Grass • Lemon Lime • Melissa • Mimosa • Myrrh • Neroli • Niaouli • Peppermint • Pine • Rosemary • Rose Otto • Sage • Sandalwood • Spearmint • Spikenard • Tea-tree • Thyme • Valerian • Verbena

Consecration – Archangel Zadkiel For consecration of sacred objects and for creating a sacred space for meditation, ritual or dream work, summon the help of Archangel Zadkiel. To aid you in this summoning, use the following essential oils:
Anise Star • Basil • Cedarwood • Frankincense • Hyssop • Lavender • Lemon Melissa • Niaouli • Peppermint • Pine • Rosemary • Sage • Sweet Fennel • Verbena

__Eucalyptus__ is used for healing rituals where negative energy needs to be released.

__Anise Star__ is traditionally used for consecration and purification rituals.

Protection – Archangel Michael For protection, security, safety, empowerment, overcoming obstacles and releasing fear, including the nagging fear of self-doubt, summon Archangel Michael and his legions of angels. Use one of the following essential oils:

Anise Star • Aniseed • Black Pepper • Cajeput • Carnation • Clary Sage • Clove • Cumin • Elemi • Frankincense • Galbanum • Geranium • Ginger • Hyssop • Juniper • Lavender • Lime • Melissa • Mimosa • Myrrh • Niaouli • Oakmoss • Palmarosa • Pimento Berry • Pine • Rosemary • Sage • Spikenard • Sweet Fennel • Tea-tree • Thyme • Valerian • Vetivert • Yarrow

Centring – Archangel Jophiel For centring, balancing, restoring inner light and harmony. Use one of the following essential oils, which will summon the Archangel Jophiel:

Amyris • Cedarwood • Geranium • Grapefruit • Lavender • Lemon • Mandarin • Orange • Rosewood • Ylang-Ylang

Focus intent – Archangel Jophiel To focus your intent, restore mental clarity and aid memory enhancement, use the following essential oils:

Basil • Cajeput • Cedarwood • Frankincense • Juniper • Mandarin • Neroli • Oakmoss • Orange • Palmarosa • Rosemary • Spearmint • Spikenard • Sweet Fennel • Tea-tree

***Hyssop** is used for protection and consecration of ritual objects and spaces. Avoid in pregnancy.*

***Lavender** is used for meditation, protection and to repair the aura.*

Peppermint dispels negative thought forms, cleanses ritual objects and sacred spaces.

Hyacinth is used to bring inner peace and helps release compulsive behaviour patterns.

Banishing negativity – Archangel Michael To banish negativity and dispel anxiety, phobias and apprehension, use one of the following essential oils to summon Archangel Michael:

Bergamot • Camphor • Chamomile • Eucalyptus • Hyssop • Lavender • Lime • Mandarin • Neroli • Peppermint • Rose Otto • Sage • Sandalwood • Sweet Marjoram • Ylang-Ylang

Inner peace – Archangel Uriel To restore inner peace, soul harmony and attain a supported grounded reality, use one of the following oils to summon Archangel Uriel who will respond swiftly to your request:

Carnation • Chamomile • Hyacinth • Lavender • Mandarin • Melissa • Myrtle • Neroli • Petitgrain • Rose Otto • Sandalwood

Confidence – Archangel Jophiel For self-confidence, self-esteem and an enhancement of personal creativity, summon the Archangel Jophiel to your side by using one of the following essential oils :

Basil • Bergamot • Chamomile • Grapefruit • Jasmine • Lemon • Lime • Litsea Cubeba •Mandarin • Orange • Rosemary • Ylang-Ylang •

Courage – Archangel Uriel For personal courage, strength, endurance and stamina, summon Archangel Uriel by using one of the following oils to stimulate the Base Chakra. Uriel will also help to overcome irrational fear, paranoia or panic attacks:

Basil • Black Pepper • Carnation • Clove • Frankincense • Ginger • Grapefruit • Ravensara • Sweet Fennel • Thyme • Yarrow • Sweet Marjoram

Aphrodisiac – Archangel Chamuel The following oils are all great aphrodisiacs that increase sensuality. Summon Archangel Chamuel to help you with all your relationships, especially your awareness of the *kundalini* energy. Jasmine is traditionally used in Tantric rituals. Use the following essential oils:

Cardamom • Carrot Seed • Cumin • Ginger • Jasmine • Patchouli • Rose Otto • Tuberose • Vanilla • Ylang-Ylang

Marjoram *is used to open the Heart Chakra, dispel fear and promote bliss.*

Vanilla *attracts loving energies and stimulates the Base Chakra which increases energy flow.*

Attract love, joy, happiness or a soulmate – Archangel Chamuel To open and heal your Heart Chakra and attract love into your life, to discover joyful, happy loving relationships and even attract a soulmate, use one of the following oils and petition Archangel Chamuel to assist you in your quest:

Cinnamon • Clove • Coriander • Jasmine • Linden Blossom • Mimosa • Myrtle • Orange • Palmarosa • Rose • Vanilla • Yarrow • Ylang-Ylang

Attract luck – Archangel Jophiel Some people attract good luck; they have often developed a prosperity consciousness. To understand the laws of manifestation, summon Archangel Jophiel and use a combination of two or three of the following essential oils, which will clear blocks within the Base, Sacral and Solar Plexus Chakras:

Cinnamon • Clove • Cumin • Melissa • Myrtle • Oakmoss • Pimento Berry • Pine • Sandalwood • Spikenard • Vetivert

Yarrow *banishes negative energy and increases love, friendship and psychic powers.*
Cinnamon *stimulates mental powers and aids focused concentration.*

ANGELS AND ASTROLOGY

Planetary Angels

The seven classical planets, which were widely known to the ancients at least as far back as the Roman era, were each attributed to archetypal energetic beings who also ruled over their own day of the week.

In 12th-century Moorish Spain, the cross-cultural fertilization of Christian, Arab and Jewish heritages brought about the birth of the golden age of the Renaissance, heralding the end of the Dark Ages. It was from Spain during this period that the first documentary evidence of planetary angels also emerged.

This knowledge was stifled and condemned by Protestant Puritanism in Europe from the 16th century onwards, but the synthesis of astrology, religion, mysticism and alchemical magic surfaced once again. As more planets were discovered – Uranus, Neptune and Pluto – angels were assigned to them.

In ancient times the seven known planets were regarded as divine entities or gods.

Each of the seven ancient planets has an angelic being associated with it that helps manifest mankind's dreams and aspirations.

The planets and their ruling angels

Planet	*Angel*	*Planet*	*Angel*
Sun	*Archangel Michael*	*Venus*	*Archangel Hagiel*
Moon	*Archangel Gabriel*	*Saturn*	*Archangel Cassiel*
Mars	*Archangel Camael*	*Uranus*	*Uriel*
Mercury	*Archangel Raphael*	*Pluto*	*Azrael*
Jupiter	*Archangel Zadkiel*	*Neptune*	*Asariel*

Angels of the Zodiac

Planetary angels also rule over the zodiac. The zodiac is split into 12 astrological signs, associated with the 12 known constellations. Zodiac angels can help you understand your astrological birth sign personality. If you have your birth chart drawn up you can also work with other angels such as your 'rising' sign angel or Moon sign angel.

Zodiac angels

Sign	*Angel*	*Zodiac sign qualities*
Aries	*Camael*	*Assertive and confident*
Taurus	*Hagiel*	*Reliable and practical*
Gemini	*Raphael*	*Adaptable and sociable*
Cancer	*Gabriel*	*Sensitive and sympathetic*
Leo	*Michael*	*Generous and open*
Virgo	*Raphael*	*Efficient and analytical*
Libra	*Hagiel*	*Harmonious and diplomatic*
Scorpio	*Azrael and Camael*	*Intense and powerful*
Sagittarius	*Zadkiel*	*Optimistic and adventurous*
Capricorn	*Asariel*	*Careful and responsible*
Aquarius	*Uriel and Cassiel*	*Idealistic and humanitarian*
Pisces	*Asariel and Zadkiel*	*Artistic and emotional*

Angels of the Seasons

The following charts give the angels of the four seasons, the 12 months and the 28 angels who rule the mansions of the Moon. These charts help you harness angelic forces for magical use to help you achieve your goals and desires.

Angels of the four seasons

Season	*Direction*	*Archangel*	*Elemental*
Spring	*East*	*Raphael*	*Air*
Summer	*South*	*Michael*	*Fire*
Autumn	*West*	*Gabriel*	*Water*
Winter	*North*	*Uriel*	*Earth*

Angels governing the 12 months of the year

Month	*Angel*	*Month*	*Angel*
January	*Gabriel*	*July*	*Verchiel*
February	*Barchiel*	*August*	*Hamaliel*
March	*Machidiel*	*September*	*Zuriel*
April	*Asmodel*	*October*	*Barbiel*
May	*Ambriel*	*November*	*Adnachiel*
June	*Muriel*	*December*	*Anael*

Angels of the Moon

Each day of the 28-day cycle of the phases of the Moon is governed by an angel. They are in order:

1. Geniel
2. Enediel
3. Anixiel
4. Azariel
5. Gabriel
6. Dirachiel
7. Scheliel
8. Amnediel
9. Barbiel
10. Ardifiel
11. Neciel
12. Abdizuel
13. Jazeriel
14. Ergediel
15. Atliel
16. Azeruel
17. Adriel
18. Egibiel
19. Amutiel
20. Kyriel
21. Bethnael
22. Geliel
23. Requiel
24. Abrinael
25. Aziel
26. Tagriel
27. Atheniel
28. Amnixiel

Waxing and waning moon Lunar power is the basis of natural magic. For millennia those with occult knowledge have used the mysterious lunar energies that govern the tides of life and the unconscious mind to illuminate their indwelling spirit.

New and full moons are times of intense magical focus. Even today Tibetan Buddhists observe the full and new moon with silent meditations. Special prayers are used in synagogues on the Sabbath before the new or full moon. Wicca hold *esbats* at these times and Christians calculate Easter relative to the full moon after the spring equinox.

Waxing moon The waxing moon lasts approximately 15 days from new moon to full moon. The waxing moon means an increase in the Moon's size. Therefore anything you wish to increase should be blessed or started at this time.

Waning moon The waning moon lasts approximately 15 days from full moon to new moon. The waning moon means a decrease in the Moon's size. Therefore anything you wish to decrease or let go of should be done at this time.

The Moon is associated with self-reflection, dream work and astral travel, as well as psychic ability.

Angels of the Days and Hours

Each day of the week and every hour of the day and night is governed by its own angel. The boxes below outline the angels of the week and the angels of the hours.

Temperance, the winged angel of time from the Tarot deck, bears the sign of the Sun on his forehead. He pours the essence of life from one chalice to the other.

Angels of the days of the week

Angel	*Day*
Archangel Michael	*Sunday*
Archangel Gabriel	*Monday*
Archangel Camael	*Tuesday*
Archangel Raphael	*Wednesday*
Archangel Zadkiel	*Thursday*
Archangel Hagiel	*Friday*
Archangel Cassiel	*Saturday*

Angels of the hours of day and night

DAY	*Sunday*	*Monday*	*Tuesday*	*Wednesday*
Hours				
1	*Michael*	*Gabriel*	*Samael*	*Raphael*
2	*Anael*	*Cassiel*	*Michael*	*Gabriel*
3	*Raphael*	*Sachiel*	*Anael*	*Cassiel*
4	*Gabriel*	*Samael*	*Raphael*	*Sachiel*
5	*Cassiel*	*Michael*	*Gabriel*	*Samael*
6	*Sachiel*	*Anael*	*Cassiel*	*Michael*
7	*Samael*	*Raphael*	*Sachiel*	*Anael*
8	*Michael*	*Gabriel*	*Samael*	*Raphael*
9	*Anael*	*Cassiel*	*Michael*	*Gabriel*
10	*Raphael*	*Sachiel*	*Anael*	*Cassiel*
11	*Gabriel*	*Samael*	*Raphael*	*Sachiel*
12	*Cassiel*	*Michael*	*Gabriel*	*Samael*

NIGHT				
Hours				
1	*Sachiel*	*Anael*	*Cassiel*	*Michael*
2	*Samael*	*Raphael*	*Sachiel*	*Anael*
3	*Michael*	*Gabriel*	*Samael*	*Raphael*
4	*Anael*	*Cassiel*	*Michael*	*Gabriel*
5	*Raphael*	*Sachiel*	*Anael*	*Cassiel*
6	*Gabriel*	*Samael*	*Raphael*	*Sachiel*
7	*Cassiel*	*Michael*	*Gabriel*	*Samael*
8	*Sachiel*	*Anael*	*Cassiel*	*Michael*
9	*Samael*	*Raphael*	*Sachiel*	*Anael*
10	*Michael*	*Gabriel*	*Samael*	*Raphael*
11	*Anael*	*Cassiel*	*Michael*	*Gabriel*
12	*Raphael*	*Sachiel*	*Anael*	*Cassiel*

DAY	*Thursday*	*Friday*	*Saturday*
Hours			
1	*Sachiel*	*Anael*	*Cassiel*
2	*Samael*	*Raphael*	*Sachiel*
3	*Michael*	*Gabriel*	*Samael*
4	*Anael*	*Cassiel*	*Michael*
5	*Raphael*	*Sachiel*	*Anael*
6	*Gabriel*	*Samael*	*Raphael*
7	*Cassiel*	*Michael*	*Gabriel*
8	*Sachiel*	*Anael*	*Cassiel*
9	*Samael*	*Raphael*	*Sachiel*
10	*Michael*	*Gabriel*	*Samael*
11	*Anael*	*Cassiel*	*Michael*
12	*Raphael*	*Sachiel*	*Anael*

NIGHT			
Hours			
1	*Gabriel*	*Samael*	*Raphael*
2	*Cassiel*	*Michael*	*Gabriel*
3	*Sachiel*	*Anael*	*Cassiel*
4	*Samael*	*Raphael*	*Sachiel*
5	*Michael*	*Gabriel*	*Samael*
6	*Anael*	*Cassiel*	*Michael*
7	*Raphael*	*Sachiel*	*Anael*
8	*Gabriel*	*Samael*	*Raphael*
9	*Cassiel*	*Michael*	*Gabriel*
10	*Sachiel*	*Anael*	*Cassiel*
11	*Samael*	*Raphael*	*Sachiel*
12	*Michael*	*Gabriel*	*Samael*

Angels of the Four Directions

When we work with the Angels of the Four Directions to create a sacred circle to bring balance and harmony to our life, it is very much like the First Nations American Medicine Wheel or the Cross of the Celts.

Archangel Raphael Responsible for the east, the gateway to spirit, illumination, clarity and enlightenment. It is the direction of new beginnings, of inspiration, illumination and creativity, of the dawn and spring, new births and childhood.

Physical representation to place on your altar: Incense sticks, feathers or chiming bells.

Archangel Michael Responsible for the south, gateway to the physical, trust and innocence. It is the direction of vitality, of high noon and hot suns, of summer and the vigorous growth of youth and passion.

Physical representation to place on your altar: Candle, essential oil burner or image of the Sun.

Archangel Gabriel Responsible for the west, gateway to emotions, inspiration, intuition and change. The west is the direction associated with introspection, of the evening, of autumn and maturity, deepening and ripening.

Physical representation to place on your altar: Water, mirror or an image of the Moon.

Archangel Uriel Responsible for the north, gateway to the mind, knowledge, wisdom, philosophy, religion, science. It is the direction of night, of winter, of wisdom and transformation, of dropping inessentials to reveal the core.

Physical representation to place on your altar: Crystals or religious images that inspire you.

ANGELS OF ASSISTANCE

When you Need Immediate Help

This is a quick-reference guide to use when you require immediate angelic help. God is omnipotent and omnipresent, which means God is all-powerful and everywhere. There is nothing that is not God, but we sometimes forget this; so to remind us God uses angels who possess divine attributes. Angels therefore are the active presence of God in our lives, and they support everything in the universe, manifested and unmanifested. Angelic energy sustains, nurtures and protects humanity. There are angels responsible for every situation known to mankind; all we have to do is ask.

When you summon angelic assistance, think of it as a request or invitation. Invocations and letters to the angels can be formal or informal, both styles will work. Just as with those who channel the 'angels' – the 'channelling' is always 'flavoured' with the person's ego, so some styles are very formal and others are 'flowery' – there is no right or wrong way, so just follow your heart.

Physical healing Archangel Raphael is the physician of the angelic realm. You can call upon him for healing yourself and helping to find the inner guidance and inspiration to heal others. Raphael's name means 'God has healed'. He carries a cup of healing unguent.

Essential oils of Anise Star and Lavender are used to contact Archangel Raphael. Lavender brings regeneration and heals auric damage, while Anise Star is used for consecration and gives protection from negative energies.

His element is air and his planet is Mercury. Raphael's day of the week is

Wednesday. His crystal is Emerald and he works on the Green Ray. His direction is east and he rules over the physical Heart Chakra. Trees associated with Raphael are hazel, myrtle and mulberry, and good omens and signs that Archangel Raphael is responding to your request for healing are the sight of ravens or ibises, in fact most birds, or white feathers.

Mulberry, associated with Raphael, can be made into an essence to release painful emotions.

Use green or yellow candles and expect speedy results, usually within seven days. Use pale green paper to write your healing request.

Emotional healing Archangel Chamuel helps to heal emotional disease and assists in developing the higher emotions of the Heart Chakra. His colour is pink (all shades); he rules over the Fourth Dimension Heart Chakra. His element is air.

The essential oil Rose Otto is used to contact Archangel Chamuel, and is used for opening the Heart Chakra, bringing love, inner peace and emotional balance. His crystal is Rose Quartz. The best day to contact Archangel Chamuel is Friday, which is ruled by the planet Venus. Animals associated with Chamuel are deer, dove, butterfly and rabbit. Trees that are associated with Chamuel are cherry and apple.

Use pink candles and orchids or pink roses to attract a quick response; if you write a letter to attract his attention, use pink paper and allow 28 days to pass, then burn the letter.

Elephant energy is associated with longevity, wisdom and overcoming obstacles on your spiritual path.

Spiritual healing Archangel Zadkiel is the archangel of divine joy. Zadkiel's name means the 'Righteousness of God'. He is the guardian of the Violet Flame of spiritual transformation and healing. Zadkiel is the archangel of mercy, who teaches trust in God and the benevolence of God. He brings comfort in our hour of need.

The essential oil Benzoin is used to contact Archangel Zadkiel to gain spiritual wisdom, understanding, detachment and the letting-go of painful emotions. Zadkiel's element is fire and his domain is the Crown Chakra; his crystals are Amethyst and Amatrine. He is regent of Jupiter and his day of the week is Thursday. Lilac or lavender flowers are associated with Zadkiel; his trees are oak, ash or cedar; his animals are elephants, whales, swans or ducks.

Violet, lavender or amethyst-coloured candles should be used to contact him. Expect results within days or weeks.

Education Ask Archangel Jophiel and the angels of illumination to help you study and pass exams. They can also help you absorb new skills and offer illumination and wisdom to fuel your creativity. Jophiel is the archangel of wisdom. His name means 'Beauty of God'. He connects you to your higher self. Invoke Archangel Jophiel when you feel blocked or your creativity needs a boost. If you ask him, he will heal, cleanse, activate, balance and align your mental body, which stops feelings of low self-esteem and mental fog.

Lemon essential oil is used to contact Archangel Jophiel; it is very energizing, bringing clarity of mind, it refreshes the spirit and it breaks apathy and inertia. Yellow foods, such as corn on the cob, yellow peppers, bananas, lemons and grapefruits, honey and hazelnuts are his foods; his animals are the salmon and kestrel.

Jophiel's ray is yellow so burn yellow candles and use yellow flowers such as sunflowers. Expect results very quickly – write to him on yellow paper and burn it after seven days.

Romance See Archangel Chamuel (see page 122). He specializes in relationships as well as emotional healing. If you ask for his help, he will also seek out your soulmate for you. He directs the angels of love – the angels who specialize in making your daily life more harmonious. There is no task too small or too large for them; they will help in any situation that requires heartfelt communication.

Passing exams and gaining wisdom are rites of passage and initiation.

Marriage See Archangel Chamuel (see page 122) and the angels of love who work for the harmonious unfolding of love throughout the entire cosmos.

Protection Archangel Michael is the protector of humanity. Call on him for strength and empowerment. Michael's name means 'Who is like God'. His main colour is yellow; the fire of the solar plexus is his first domain, but because he carries a sword made of a blue flame he is often associated with the Throat Chakra, the colour blue and the element of ether. Michael is commander-in-chief of the archangels and he leads the heavenly forces against demons. The Blue Ray represents the power and will of God, as well as faith, protection and truth.

Frankincense and Myrrh are the essential oils used to contact Archangel Michael. Frankincense is used for purification, protection, courage, consecration, meditation and helps in overcoming fears and negative feelings. Myrrh is considered one of the holiest essential oils. It is used for purification, dispelling harmful or negative energy, protection and letting-go of sorrow or grief. Michael's metal is gold, his animals all cats from lions and tigers to domestic tabbies, stoats and all black birds. His planet is the Sun and a good day to invoke his help is Sunday. His tree is the laurel.

Use white paper and gold pen to write to Michael. Keep your letter of petition from Sunday to Sunday, then burn it.

Childbirth Archangel Gabriel guides all midwives and everything to do with childbirth. His assisting angels are Armisael (angel of the womb) and Temeluch (protector of children at birth and infancy). Gabriel is the awakening archangel, the soul's guardian. Gabriel's name means 'God is my strength'. He helps you to interpret dreams and visions. Gabriel is also the angel of the Annunciation, resurrection, mercy and revelation. He guides the soul on its journey back to paradise. He carries a trumpet to awaken your inner angel and bring good news.

Essential oils of Jasmine and Camphor are used to contact Archangel Gabriel.

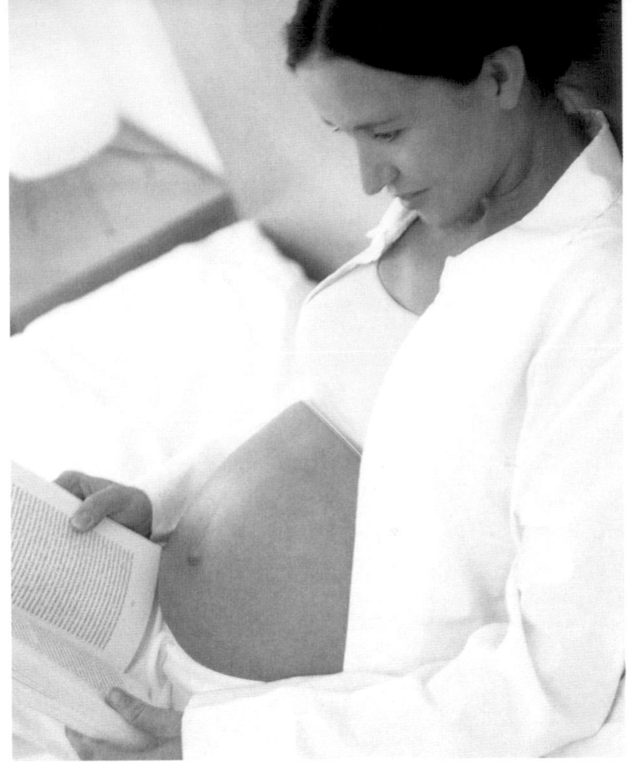

Summon Archangel Gabriel to guide the midwives at the time of birth.

Jasmine induces optimism, lifts sadness and opens us to the angelic realms. Camphor dispels negative energy, brings purification and can be used to cleanse crystals. This angel messenger's planet is the Moon, his day is Monday and his metal is silver. He is associated with white lilies, wolves, owls, pear trees and weeping willows.

To aid at the birth, light a bright green candle to Armisael as labour begins. It also says in the Talmud to recite Psalm 20 nine times. Alternatively, write a letter of petition to Armisael before labour begins. Psalm 20 can also be recited on behalf of the mother. If further assistance is required, summon Archangel Gabriel to assist you.

Choosing the gender of a child Archangel Sandalphon, the angel of prayer, is said to decide the gender of a child as it is conceived. Angel Lailah is the angel of conception (petition her if you are having trouble conceiving and do not mind what gender the child is).

Light a white candle and invoke the help of Sandalphon to assist in conceiving a child.

Sandalwood essential oil and incense is used to contact Archangel Sandalphon; it brings spiritual awareness, inner peace, alignment with higher energies and spiritual purpose.

It is important to focus on why you desire a child of a particular gender. Write a letter to Sandalphon on a Friday night (energies of Venus and love) stating your reason(s) for the gender choice of the hoped-for child. On the night of conception light a new white candle, burn some Sandalwood incense, take a relaxing bath and put on a clean white nightdress.

Transition Archangel Gabriel is the angel of death; he guides the soul on its journey back to paradise. There are other 'shepherding' angels who can assist on this journey. If death has been sudden, owing to manmade or natural disasters such as earthquakes or bombings, and many souls are involved, you should still summon Archangel Gabriel and request the help of other shepherd angels such as Suriel, Cassiel, Azrael, Kafziel, Metatron, Yehudiah and Michael. For the death of an animal, summon Meshabber.

The burning of incense as part of ritual is found in the traditions of many different cultures.

If you are attending a dying person, stay calm, radiate peace and reassurance and comfort. Imagine a ladder of golden light and see the angels descending to receive the person and guide them back up to Heaven.

Bereavement The angel of bereavement is Yehudiah according to the *Zohar*. When someone is about to die, Yehudiah descends with thousands of attending angels to carry the soul to Heaven. So Yehudiah is known as the beneficial angel of death. The death of a loved one, close friend or relative is frequently a very difficult experience. Often we feel an overwhelming sense of grief, loss or abandonment that can test our faith in God, especially if the death was sudden or we feel the person died before their 'allotted time'. We may feel life is meaningless or pointless, and it may seem hard for us to carry on with the aching emptiness inside.

Different religions have different allotted periods of traditional mourning. Invoke Yehudiah and say prayers to God for as many days as you feel is required. You may also like to pray each year on the person's birthday and on the day of transition. Place a photograph of your loved one on your angel altar (or create a special one); you can then light a white candle and burn incense in front of that particular photograph.

GLOSSARY

Glossary

AGE OF AQUARIUS

In astrological terms, the transition is being made from the Age of Pisces, a time of paternal influence when people handed responsibility for their behaviour and spiritual growth to others, into the Age of Aquarius, in which this responsibility will be taken personally. New Agers believe that a new golden age will develop in which all forms of discrimination will end.

THE AKASHA

An archive existing beyond time and space that contains information on all that was, is, or will be (the Akashic records). These are stored as 'codes of light' and can be accessed with the help of higher-level beings or by raising our personal vibrational rate.

ANAMCHARA

A Celtic angel or soul-friend.

ANGEL

The word is derived from the ancient Greek *angelos,* meaning 'messenger'. Angels, obedient to cosmic law, act as a channel between God and the physical world and are a focus of God's love towards us, and are pure spirit. They come in all forms – some are complex and powerful – others bring comfort, inspiration or joy and some never leave our side.

ANGELOLOGY

The study of angels. Over the centuries many manuscripts have been written on angels and angelic hierarchies and these provide the sources of angel lore.

ANGELS OF THE RAYS

Each archangel is associated with a specific colour ray of spiritual enlightenment. The coloured rays affect both the physical and emotional body and can assist with healing and overall harmony and well-being.

ARCHANGELS

There are seven archangels, named by the Book of Enoch as Uriel, Raguel, Gabriel, Michael, Seraquel, Haniel and Raphael. They control and harmonize everything in God's creation.

AURA

Also known as the biomagnetic energy field. The subtle-energy field found surrounding the human body. It consists of seven levels that correlate to the seven master chakras. The word aura comes from the Greek word *avra* meaning breeze.

BOOKS OF ENOCH

The three Books of Enoch are extracanonical writings, attributed to the great-grandfather of Noah and written down by various authors between 200 BCE and 100 CE. The Book of Enoch refers to 1 Enoch, which survives completely only in the Ethiopic language. Further fragments from 1 Enoch have been discovered among the Dead Sea Scrolls. There are two further books that have survived: 2 Enoch or the Testament of Levi in old Slavonic and 3 Enoch in Hebrew.

CELESTIAL HIERARCHY

There have been many different rankings of the angelic beings, including the Old and New Testaments, the *Celestial Hierarchy* by Dionysus and work by St Thomas Aquinas. The first sphere contains the three highest orders to God: the Seraphim, the Cherubim and Thrones. The second sphere contains the Dominions, Virtues and Powers, and the third the Principalities, Archangels and Angels (including guardian angels).

CHAKRAS

Centres of subtle energy in the body, chakras are important to physical and emotional well-being and spiritual growth. There are seven master chakras associated with specific organs that process subtle energy, all positioned on the centre line of the body. The word Chakra comes from the Sanskrit word *Chakram*, which means wheel.

CHANNELLING

Channelling is a more direct route than dreams to inspiration and contact with the angelic realm. It is necessary to raise your vibrational rate to unite with your guardian angel, who can open a harmonious channel so that you can write down what is given to you.

DHARMA

To gain enlightenment by releasing illusion.

ELEMENTALS

These are nature spirits who create abundance and balance on Earth. Elementals include fairies (earth spirits), mermaids (water spirits), salamanders (fire spirits), sylphs (spirits of the air) and Devas – Devas often work with humans and are more evolved than the elementals. They are also found dwelling in Clear Quartz crystals, and can teach about healing.

GEM ESSENCE

Distilled water that has been subtly energized by crystals.

GUARDIAN ANGEL

Each person has a guardian angel, appointed to them when they first incarnate, who never leaves them. Its task is to protect, guide and strengthen against the forces of evil. Guardian angels channel angelic light towards people, comforting and assisting throughout life.

THE KABALA

A Jewish mystical tradition and a rich source of angelic lore. *Kabala,* meaning 'to receive inner wisdom', is passed on as an oral tradition. Two original texts exist – *Zohar,* the 'Book of Splendour', and the *Sepher Yetzirah,* the 'Book of Formation'. The core element to the Kabala is the Tree of Life, a visual map that attempts to represent the return pathway to God, via the ten sephiroth, which are formed from divine energy descending from above.

LIFE-FORCE (*QI*)

Vital energy that is distributed around the physical body via the chakra centres. It can also be called '*chi*' or *ki*. *Qi* permeates everything and therapists can focus and direct it to induce healing.

LIGHTWORKER

Someone who is aware that they have a higher spiritual purpose. Lightworkers seek to heal themselves and others, as well as the environment.

MIASM

A subtle-energy imprint that lodges in any of the chakras, causing emotional or physical illness. There are four types: karmic, acquired, inherited and planetary.

SPIRITUAL HIERARCHY

This hierarchy is made up of ascended souls such as the Ascended Masters, saints and Bodhisattvas who oversee the spiritual evolution of humanity.

STARGATE

An opening to another dimension or reality.

SUBTLE ENERGY

Life is influenced by different energies, some of which – subtle energy – cannot be seen or sensed by most people. The human body is surrounded by a subtle-energy field (the aura) and subtle energy resides in each of the chakras.

TEMPLE OF LIGHT

Each archangel has a temple 'anchored' in the etheric realm (the physical world). They are normally situated over 'power' vortexes – where ley lines cross or over remote mountain ranges, for example. They can also be found over sacred sites on Earth, such as the Egyptian temple at Luxor. Temples of Light were established by the Spiritual Hierarchy under the guidance of archangels. Each one has a different purpose and focus – when spiritual seekers visit a temple during meditation or through dreams they are inspired by the cosmic virtue of that particular temple.

VIBRATIONAL RATE

Also known as vibrational frequency or state of consciousness. This is the frequency of brain activity in the cerebral cortex. A higher vibrational rate, where the two hemispheres of the brain are completely balanced, brings on states of bliss. By raising the vibrational rate the aim is to achieve finer states of brain activity (spirituality) and greater unity with God.

INDEX & ACKNOWLEDGEMENTS

Index

Figures in *italics* indicate pictures.

Acknowledgements

AUTHOR ACKNOWLEDGEMENTS

I would like to thank the angelic realm for all their help and guidance when I was writing and researching this book and my other angel books. I would like to thank all my angelic friends especially Glennyce Eckersley and Diana Cooper. A special thank you to the thousands of people who have attended my angel seminars over the last 16 years and freely shared their experiences, stories and ways of looking at angels. Finally, I would like to thank my family for their unconditional love and support.

Executive Editor Sandra Rigby
Editor Jessica Cowie
Executive Art Editor Sally Bond
Designer Annika Skoog for Cobalt Id
Illustrators Kuo Kang Chen, Stephen Angel
Picture Researcher Jennifer Veall
Production Controller Simone Nauerth

PICTURE CREDITS

Andrew Alden, geology.about.com 330. **AKG, London**/British Library 68. **Alamy**/Eddie Gerald 83, 377. **BananaStock** 217. **Bridgeman Art Library**/British Library, London, UK 175, 198; /Collegiale Saint-Bonnet-le-Chateau, France, 356; /The De Morgan Centre, London 100; /The Detroit Institute of Arts, USA, Bequest of Eleanor Clay 148; /Galleria degli Uffizi, Florence, Italy, Alinari 196; /Galleria dell' Accademia, Venice, Italy 370; /Louvre, Paris, France, Peter Willi 15, 193; /MAK, Vienna, Austria 71; /Musee des Beaux-Arts, Rennes, France, Giraudon 61; /Musee du Petit Palais, Avignon, France 91; /Museo del Castelvecchio, Verona, Italy 59; /Art Gallery of New South Wales, Sydney, Australia 11; /Padua Baptistery, Padua, Italy, Alinari 181; /Palazzo Ducale, Urbino, Italy 177; /Private Collection, by courtesy of Julian Hartnoll 212; /Private Collection, Dinodia 183; /San Marco, Venice, Italy, Cameraphoto Arte Venezia 55; /Sanctuary of Santa Maria delle

Grazie, Saronno, Italy 53; /Sanctuary of the Blessed Virgin of Miracles, Saronno, Italy 334; /Trustees of the Royal Watercolour Society, London, UK 57. **Corbis UK Ltd** 352 bottom right, 355 top; /Archivo Iconografico, S.A. 199; /The Dead Sea Scrolls Foundation, Inc. 12; /Digital Vision 362 bottom centre left; /Emely 214; /LWA-Stephen Welstead 42; /Ron Watts 191. **Getty Images** 202; /Amanda Hall 82; /Gavin Hellier 41; /Jasper James 96; /LaCoppola-Meier 345; /LWA 375; /Manchan 268; /Ralph Mercer 156; /Sasha 189; /Jean-Marc Scialom 211; /Elizabeth Simpson 103; /Siri Stafford 247; /Peter Teller 206; /Vega 161; /Simon Watson 39; /Toyohiro Yamada 162; /Mel Yates 248. **ImageSource** 21, 94, 215, 264, 379. **Octopus Publishing Group Limited** 18, 144, 146, 220, 281 top right, 286, 288, 290, 292, 294, 296, 298 top, 298 bottom, 300 top, 300 bottom, 304 top, 304 bottom, 306 top, 306 Bottom, 308, 310, 312, 314, 316 top, 316 bottom, 318 top, 318 bottom, 320, 322 top, 322 bottom, 324 top, 324 bottom, 326 top, 326 bottom, 328, 332 top, 332 bottom, 342, 347 top left, 348 top left, 348 top right, 349 centre, 350, 350 centre, 351 bottom left, 353 top left, 353 top right; /Frazer Cuningham 27, 31, 221, 228, 231, 285; /W. F. Davidson 352 bottom left; /Walter Gardiner Photography 241; /Janeanne Gilchrist 270; /Marcus Harpur 354 bottom left; /Mike Hemsley 368; /Ruth Jenkinson 340, 347 top right; /Andy Komorowski 255, 302; /Andrew Lawson 349 bottom; /William Lingwood 355 bottom; /David Loftus 147; /John Miller 179; /Peter Myers 232, 237, 238; /Sean Myers 351 bottom right; /Ian Parsons 378; /Mike Prior 234, 256, 336, 339; /Peter Pugh-Cook 38; /William Reavell 337; /Russell Sadur 16–17, 24, 25, 28, 29, 33, 34, 36, 99, 153, 194, 258, 266, 272, 341; /Gareth Sambidge 86, 354 bottom right; /Unit Photographic 19, 224, 283, 365; /Ian Wallace 35, 145, 343, 346; /Mark Winwood 26, 246

Lo Scarabeo 261. **Photolibrary Group**/Botanica 23; /Francois De Heel 373; /Meyer Richard 254; /Bibikow Walter 165. **PhotoDisc** 9, 22, 49, 50, 62, 64, 118, 136, 140, 141, 155, 158, 164, 168, 170, 242, 358, 359, 374. **The Picture Desk Ltd./The Art Archive**/Dagli Orti 46; /Turkish and Islamic Art Museum Istanbul/Harper Collins Publishers 184; /Turkish and Islamic Art Museum, Istanbul/Dagli Orti 172; /Eileen Tweedy 200. **Scala Art Resource**/Smithsonian American Art Museum, Washington DC, USA 278. **Werner Forman Archive** 280